D1446254

FARIDA

Amal Ibrahim

Copyright © 2022 Amal Ibrahim

All rights reserved

The characters and events portrayed in this book are fictitious. Any
similarity to real persons, living or dead, is coincidental and not intended
by the author.

No part of this book may be reproduced, or stored in a retrieval system,
or transmitted in any form or by any means, electronic, mechanical,
photocopying, recording, or otherwise, without express written
permission of the publisher.

ISBN-13: 9798422928477

Cover design by: M & Co Design & Print/Michelle Ordev
Printed in Australia

To my beautiful mother,
Your voice is heard.

FARIDA

PROLOGUE

I still remember the day I died.

I remember the Godawful stench; something akin to rotting flesh, vomit, and faeces. There was a smell and a taste to that day. A texture that could be felt without the sense of touch. I remember the smell of the air and the dark, brooding sky as it loomed large, the salt that hit my tongue as I sank to the bottom of the ocean and drowned.

I struggled.

I pushed my feet against the water as I tried to surge upward but found myself instead sinking further down.

I fought and struggled against the tidal wave that smacked against my head, lurching me forward through the air.

I drowned in fear more than any body of water.

Anyone that tells you a child doesn't know fear is lying.

That was the day I died.

It was also the day I was born.

PART 1

THE BOOK OF FARIDA

CHAPTER 1: AAIDA 2016

I sit to my mother's right. That's where I've always been. To her right. During conversations. During dinner. Always at her side; on the right side. It's an unspoken rule in our home, amongst our family. Still now, as I fumble through my forties, I had never noticed this until my 18 year old daughter verbalised this fact by saying "mum, do you realise you've always sat at tayta's right side?" My mind scrambles through its lens to find a time when I was not at my mother's right side. I can't find it. Can't seem to find a single event where I was not right there by my mother's right hand.

I squeeze her hand in mine, a soft squeeze across her broad, now wrinkled fingers, urging her on as she purges her secrets to me. All the things I didn't know. All the things left unsaid. All the secrets she tried so hard to keep while at the same time trying to protect me by moulding and shaping me into the kind of person that would inevitably rise above the constraints of culture and society and not allow history to repeat itself.

"When would you like to go?" I ask my mother, squeezing her hand gently. She sits quietly with a far away look in her eyes. She is with me, I know she is, barely holding on because she has something to say. No, not something. Some *things*.

"The spring would be lovely," mother tells me. "Remember the years we visited there, and how you would love the springtime? The sun would caress your face as you sat on your balcony and read endlessly. We all loved spring there."

"Then spring it is," I tell her, pulling out my phone and messaging Nada to book the flights.

I'm already packed. I've been packed for almost 40 years. I'm only 42 years old. But my first memory is of me at 3, throwing a tantrum because I didn't want to leave my beloved Lebanon. I didn't want to go away from "teta" and "jeddo" and the cornfields we roamed during the day. I didn't want to leave them. So, subconsciously, I never really unpacked when I got to Australia. Mentally, I was always back there in Lebanon, amongst my brethren, mixing with the townfolk and living a simple life off the land.

"Pack light," my mother says. "No heels. Make sure no heels. You know they still have not fixed the roads to a standard worthy of heels."

I laugh and look down at my feet encased in a pair of beautiful Jimmy Choos. Mother was always complaining about my heels. "You'll fall over and break your neck.....how do you walk in those skyscrapers?.....You'll end up with scoliosis..." And my personal favourite-"Backs simply weren't meant to carry heels, they were meant to carry children." On and on she went, and all us girls sitting around would crack up laughing, rolling over each other at her wit, her tongue sharpening with something so unbelievably random every time.

"I'll leave the heels behind, mum. What about books, can I take some books?"

"No. You'll be too busy."

I squint and look at her carefully.

"Busy doing what?"

"Writing your own story. You've read every damn story you could possibly get your hands on. Twice over. Isn't it time you wrote *your* story?"

CHAPTER 2: THE FIRST FARIDA

Farida: Arabic name assigned to a female, meaning "unique".

My parents named me Farida.

Not for any uniqueness I held even before I was born.

They named me Farida for the Legend of Farida.

It was said, in our village, Tul Ghosn, about a hundred years ago, there lived a woman with mesmerising dark eyes and black hair like the blackest night. She went by the name of Farida. She was a beautiful, stalwart girl whom men lusted after and women envied. The young girls of the village all idolised her, accepting the wayfarer into their village after she broke from a Syrian Bedouin tribe and exiled herself in Lebanon.

Not much was known about the beautiful stranger, except that she lived in a tent on land owned by a farmer who had sought a better life for his family in Sweden, thus leaving the land vacant and unoccupied. She must have been in her late 20's when she came into the town and set up her tent, and when asked, had exclaimed that she was merely passing by on her way to see her grandmother in Beirut.

Although many of the town folk thought it strange that a female would be travelling on her own through the countryside of North Lebanon, most realised, and indeed, exhaled a sigh of relief that she was not their problem to deal with. However, it was soon apparent that the village children, and majority of the women took to Farida and welcomed her into their midst.

It was said that Farida was able to predict the future and forewarn of calamitous events, preventing massive disasters. She was also able to predict the weather and successful crops, as well as who would marry whom.

To many, Farida's visions and predictions were a Godsend and helped the townspeople avoid certain disaster. But of course, there were those, struck by one chaotic event after another, who accused her of using magic and sorcery to create mischief on the land, and called for her to be hung by the neck until she died and the evil spirits were expelled from her body.

On one such night, all those many years ago, as the women of the village gathered for the send off celebration of a local bride, a handful of men banded together and conspired to do a dastardly deed. They kidnapped Farida, placing a hood over her face, but not before she could see who they were, and took her to a deserted plot in a neighbouring grove where they set up a makeshift gallows and proceeded to string her up. Her voice rose in protestations as she fought and clawed at the noose at her neck, to no avail.

"I bet you didn't see this one coming, did you witch!" one of the men cried.

Another screamed at her (perhaps in a momentary lapse of guilt) that he was trying to protect his wife and daughters and all the womenfolk of the village from her vile magic which was threatening to infect all their homes. Perhaps this had been him justifying his actions to himself and to his Lord.

"Any last words?" one screamed at her, his hand steadying the chair on which Farida's legs were standing.

"You don't know what you're doing! Let me down," she pleaded.

"Tonight you die here, witch!" another screamed. "Tomorrow, you will be gone and the women will be none the wiser. Our village will be safe. Our women and daughters and sisters will be safe from your corrupt magic."

"Last words, witch. Do you have any last words?" The man holding the chair asked again, his hand shaking as it hovered near Farida's feet. Another man looked at him and could see the fear and remorse in the man's eyes as he started to have regrets about what he was doing.

And just as Farida cried out "I curse all your houses for generations to come," the second man kicked the chair from under Farida and she shot upwards into the dark. Her body spasmed and her feet twitched for several minutes as the life seeped out of her and Farida met her end. The man who'd been holding the chair looked away in despair, conflicted about whether or not they had done the right thing. The man who kicked the chair looked at him in disgust then turned away and spat on the grass nearby. Several more minutes passed before Farida was lowered to the ground and loaded onto the back of a pickup truck and the men started on part two of their journey towards a life without Farida.

To further compound the crime, they denied her a proper burial in the town, and her body was thrown into the sea, where some say, her spirit still lingers exacting all manner of revenge on the descendants of those who murdered her. Her things were bundled in an old cloth bag and also found their resting place at the bottom of the ocean.

The men believed that the women would be none the wiser; Farida had merely packed her things and left the village, they would explain; a true Bedouin at heart who sought to travel from village to village, wreaking havoc on the common people with her mischiev-

ous ways.

The day after Farida was martyred, a heavy storm blew into the village. The winds sounded almost as though they were howling in mourning as they travelled at extremely high speeds and reaped destruction throughout the land. The village lost every crop for the season as winds and floods worked in tandem to leave as much damage as possible. Some of the livestock succumbed to drowning, and even a young child was pulled into the deluge and swept away to his death.

The irony was that Farida had already forewarned them of the storm days before her death and advised them to herd their livestock to safety and pick as much of the crop as they possibly could prior to the storm hitting. She had given them explicit instructions, right down to almost the hour on what should be done to minimise the damage to the land and had even warned that every village person, young or old, be safely ensconced in their home by Maghreb prayer time to ensure their safety.

For the women, the fact that Farida had left had somehow rendered her future premonitions obsolete and they ignored her warning. While the men, glad to be rid of the mischievous dark eyed girl with the raven hair had totally overlooked this prediction and thus lost everything.

The child who was sadly and innocently dragged through the deluge was the grandson of one of the men who had conspired the extermination of Farida from the earth.

It was Abu Nader, the man who held the chair at Farida's hanging, that finally broke. The weight of what they had done and the burden of guilt that weighed on his shoulders ensured he was never the same again. The storm that swept in and ravaged the town,

ensuring he lost a whole season's crop, agitated him even more and promoted in him a fear to even step outside his own home. His wife, already suspicious about the changes in him since the disappearance of Farida, urged him to cleanse his soul and unburden himself to her by telling her what it was that caused him such restless nights.

Finally, he broke down and told her the whole story, his version coming out in sobs and hiccups as he recalled bits and pieces of the event he had tried so hard to shove into the deepest recesses of his brain.

"And she cursed us all as she took her last breath?" Em Nader asked for the fourth time, wide eyed.

"She cursed every last one of us and our descendants. And now Moin has lost his grandson. We have all lost our livelihood. We don't know what is yet to come."

"Well, there is nothing much that can be done now, Abu Nader. The girl is gone. She's dead. At the bottom of the sea."

Abu Nader winced as each one of his wife's descriptions of Farida's final resting place burst forth from her mouth. She spoke with clenched teeth, her anger surging through her and blotching her skin as she loomed over him in disgust.

"You tossed that poor girl into the sea and made shark meat out of her. For the first time in our married life, I am ashamed to call you my husband, Abu Nader! That girl did no harm. She looked after our children and gave the village guidance on what was to come and how to deal with calamity!"

"She was a sorcerer!" Abu Nader defended.

"Are you so blind that you can't see the way of the world? The girl spent her life wandering the land and sleeping in a tent-of course she would have learnt to read weather patterns and best conditions for crop!" Em Nader threw up an exasperated hand and looked to the sky for salvation. "I tried to tell you over and over again-she was not a soothsayer. She learnt to predict the weather. She was a keen observer and could tell who would marry who by the furtive glances the children would throw one another. She estimated when a woman would give birth depending on how low a woman's pregnant belly fell. I told you all this!"she hissed. "And yet, you still managed to ignore what I said, shutting me up every time I opened my mouth to speak, and followed a bunch of stupid uneducated spineless and cowardly men to commit MURDER! You stupid, foolish man!"

Abu Nader sat dumbfounded, looking at his wife as she continued to rant and berate him. She had never spoken to him this way. He never would have allowed it. He was the man of the house. But now, sitting and listening to everything she had to say, he knew she was absolutely and undoubtedly right. If he had just listened to her and ignored the vicious whispers of the other men, he would not have become involved in this drama and would not now be living in a constant state of crippling fear or carrying the guilt of a hundred men.

"Tell me what I can do," he begged, his voice a raspy whisper.

"There's nothing you can do, Abu Nader" the woman hissed. "The girl is gone and I hope this teaches you a valuable lesson. My advice to you, make sincere istighfar and pray as much as you can that Allah forgives you. Pray for that poor girl's soul and make penance...give charity in her name and give plenty, because if I were Farida, I sure as hell wouldn't forgive you."

Em Nader was adamant that the village elders, especially the women, knew what became of Farida. If only for the fact that she was afraid of Farida's curse and wanted to warn everybody. It started with one whisper, from Em Nader to Bushra, whose husband also took part in the killing, until all the women whose husbands had had a hand in Farida's demise came together to meet *and discuss the repercussions of their husbands' wayward behaviour.*

"The rest of the village must know," one stated.

"Why must they know?" enquired another. "This could become bigger than you or I and end up in the hands of the police. Then, where would we be?"

"You can't carry a curse and not know who cursed you and why," a third woman responded. "Everyone should know so that they can protect themselves."

"It was an evil deed that these men perpetrated," Em Nader reminded them. "We are all responsible, men and women alike, those who did participate and those that did not. We are all responsible to right this terrible wrong."

They planted a tree in Farida's honour. Right when she had piked her tent into the ground, on the abandoned land of the man who had left the village for greener pastures on the other side of the world.

They paid alms and built a second well for the sake of Farida's memory.

They named their daughters Farida in the hope that this would quell the legend of the curse of Farida.

And the legend was passed on from generation to generation, as each in turn tried to do enough to reverse the curse of the tormented girl who had been thrown into the ocean.

CHAPTER 3:
FARIDA 1970

The day I left…the day I was taken…four men with *khafiyehs* wrapped around their lower faces to hide their identities drove up close to me and Aujene as we were about to exit the mouth of the olive grove and commence our journey home on foot. I walked ahead, Aujene always lagging behind as she stopped to inspect the stumps of the trees and other vegetation to make sure no illness had befallen them. It would take us some fifteen minutes to get over the hill and walk down the winding road into the village, another seven minutes to reach our house, but with Aujene dragging her feet, we could so easily add another five minutes to our trip.

Two men jumped out of the back of the pickup truck, startling us both, grabbing me by the arms and dragging me to the car. I understood immediately what was happening and started to struggle, kicking and screaming as one of the men clamped his hand down on my mouth. I bit him, and he yelped in pain as he jumped back, never letting go of my hand. I could feel the sting of his slap as his hand crashed down on my cheek, forcing my head back in shock. I gasped and looked to Aujene, who stood frozen in her place, staring at a man who was now approaching her.

"Aujene! Run!" I screamed, my fearful face giving her all the incentive she needed to spring into action. If anything, Aujene was nimble on her feet and could outrun the best of men. "Run fast!" I screamed again, as I watched her disappear into the grove with the man hot on her heels.

"Grab her!" one of the men screamed after Aujene's assailants, as they both faded from our line of sight.

I continued to struggle against the two men who held me, one now putting a hood over my face as the other held my hands behind my back trying to tie them with something my struggling hands were rejecting.

"Let go of me!" I hissed. "What do you want?"

"Shhhh…" one of the men said, pulling at my arms to be quiet.

"Let me go," I repeated, stomping my feet until I connected with someone's foot. I stomped harder, then heard a deep grunt, and was lifted and thrown into the back of the pickup truck. They tried to tie my feet together as I floundered like a fish out of water. I knew I was not going home today-that was one thing that was for sure-and I determined that I would not be taken without a fight. I would make as much noise and wreak as much havoc as possible. That would be my only salvation and my only chance of escape.

Shortly, as I continued to struggle on the flatbed, I heard the men as they were having a discussion amongst themselves. It looked like the man who had run after Aujene had returned, and I stopped my movements so I could hear the conversation.

"Where's the girl?" one asked.

"I lost her," was the reply.

"What do you mean, you lost her?"

I recognised a third voice speaking up. "It doesn't matter. She can't identify us and she only would have been a hindrance."

"You don't know that she can't identify us," the second man countered.

"I know that we have our faces covered and we're not from these areas. How could she ever identify us?"

"The only thing that's going to identify us," began a fourth voice "is if we continue to stand here and waste time and the girl comes back with help. Get in the truck and let us move. Now!" he bellowed.

I heard the slamming of the truck doors and we began to move. I could tell they drove through the grove, instead of driving back the way they had come. The grove was littered with rocks and debris. We drove for well over an hour, or maybe, in my desperation, a few minutes seemed like an hour.

Two of the men sat in the flatbed with me, their idle chatter a sprinkle of words in an otherwise uneventful drive.

"I can't believe you couldn't catch up with her," one man spoke.

I recognised the voice of the man who had been following Aujene after she ran. "I think she fell into a ravine," he whispered. "I lost her at a drop on the side of the grove. I couldn't get close enough because it was too steep, but it's a sheer drop. No way she'd survive that." I could her him exhaling. "But I don't want to believe that's what happened – I'm not in the business of murdering little girls."

"Look around you," the other man hissed. "You do whatever needs to be done to preserve yourself. You'll soon realise you've entered a world where it's either kill or be killed. And don't make a mistake like that again."

There was silence as the men went quiet and I breathed stead-ily. I knew the ravine the man was talking about, but there was no way Aujene went into that ravine. She knew the land better than she knew the back of her hand and would know exactly which trees to weave through in order to lose her assailant. She knew where every ravine and valley and nook was and would know exactly what to do to avoid capture. She was also smart, my little sister, smart enough to avoid detection, yet maintain the illusion that she had gone into the ravine and met her untimely demise. A soft smile played at my lips as I thought of Aujene. My wayward sister was fine. She had to be. Even now, I knew without doubt that she would already be at home, spurting out the story rapidly, driving my parents crazy with the actions she'd be making with her hands as she spoke.

I wondered if I would ever see her again. Wondered if there'd ever be occasion for our paths to cross again and I would sit and twirl my fingers in her curls, watching as they bounced back up after I pulled them. The chances of my parents catching up to this convoy before it left the village were zero. There was no way they'd find me before we left. And with a shaky breath I didn't know I'd been holding, I exhaled in resignation and sent a silent prayer that I was strong enough to deal with whatever lay ahead for me.

CHAPTER 4:
AUJENE 1970

I ran and ran and ran.

As fast as my legs would carry me.

I didn't want to.

I didn't want to leave Farida, but I would never disobey her instructions.

Never.

Farida was the smartest person I knew.

And Farida knew best.

So when she told me to run, I collected every ounce of my strength and sprinted into the grove, the sound of gravel digging up behind me along with the dust that rose like a bad omen then settled back down as though it was exhaling in relief.

I weaved through the olive trees, twisting and twining in an effort to lose my pursuer. I knew this land well, and it had never let me down. I ran past bracken and a low rising fence covered in the vines of hanging berries, heading for the caves that littered the side of the mountain. Known as the fastest runner in the village, I could even outrun grown men who boasted long legs and heights of six feet, but I met my match in this race as my assailant gained ground on me. I could hear his boots as they shuddered on the ground, louder and more violent than any hoofbeats as he closed in on me, my heart thumping unbearably as the fear enveloped my heart.

Just as I rounded the corner to avoid the slippery slope of the slide into the deepest pits of the land, he reached out and grabbed me by the back collar of my dress, pulling me back so aggressively that my whole body lurched and I was wrestled to the ground. He placed one knee on my back and pressed me into the ground until my mouth was spitting out dust and leaves.

"Not a word," he whispered, close to my ear.

There was a pregnant pause and I listened, waiting for what would come next. But all I heard was his deep breathing and I could swear, the heavy thumping gallop of a heartbeat as he rose and turned me over so that I looked up at him. I could see only his eyes and the soft blush of dirty blond hair emerging from beneath his khafiyeh.

I could feel the overwhelming hopelessness of fear as it encompassed me, and he aimed his rifle at my stomach, his chest rising rapidly in heavy breaths. He watched me, his brows folding in consternation as he stood looking over me, saying nothing. I willed him to speak, to say anything, give me any clue as to his intentions, but there was only a swirl of intense confusion in his dark blue eyes as his brows continued to knit together and he said nothing.

I shifted slightly, making a move to remove myself from under the butt of his rifle, but he just dug it deeper until I winced, then yielded a little when he saw me retreat from my ill thought out plan to escape.

"Listen carefully," he rasped.

19

I continued to look at his eyes, for fear that I would blink and miss the second that decisiveness hit him and he proceeded to pull the trigger.

"I'm going to remove my gun. When I do, you get up, and you run. Run as fast as you can. You don't have much time."

I opened my mouth to say something, stunned, but no words emerged. I felt the butt of his gun move away and he stepped backward, waiting for me to stand. When I made no move to get up, he nodded his head once, an approval that I should do as I was told. Slowly, I stood up and stood before him, lifting my eyes to meet his. I could hear hoofbeats again, thumping away like a human heartbeat.

"Do a turn and go back the way you came. Don't travel any path that a truck can pass through," he continued to advise.

"My sister," I breathed.

"Your sister is lost to you. Go! You don't have much time."

I looked at him, my eyes and unspoken words asking him why he was helping me. But I dared not stay any longer, for fear there would be more men coming. I also had a paranoid fear that he would shoot me in the back as I ran away, but for some reason, that didn't seem likely. I turned away from him, then looked back once, before I took flight and headed for the caves, but not before I heard him whisper "run, little one, run."

CHAPTER 5:
TALA 1970

There came to pass many days and many months. It could even have been years. I lost all track of time, all semblance of normalcy. Day became night and night became my prison. I came to be known in the village as 'the lost one'.

That's when the hand wringing began. I would walk through the village streets, wringing my hands and muttering. Muttering what, I do not recall. I only know that I mumbled and cursed and sighed as I wandered listlessly through the streets in search of my beautiful Farida.

My lost daughter. No one knew anything. She was just gone. Lost to everyone. Farouk, her fiancé, would come by every few days, looking devastated and feeling sorry for himself. He was beside himself with grief, but he was useless. While we scaled the earth, from village to village in search of our beautiful Lost Farida, he went about his life as he had when living it previously. Working. Sleeping. Eating. Crying over things he didn't deserve in the first place. I realised that, no matter what had befallen Farida, it could not have been a fate worse than marrying Farouk. Farida embodied everything beautiful and pure and light in the world-she deserved, at the very least, a man who would make her the centre of his universe. A man who would love her to such an extent that he would search high and low to find his missing love. But Farouk, if anything, proved to be a spineless wretch, not worthy of a token lock of Farida's hair.

So I continued to search, as the days spilled into weeks and the weeks rolled into months...walking barefoot from village to village, asking if anyone had seen my beautiful Farida with the long black hair and equally mesmerising black eyes.

I remember at times I would be so exhausted, I would lay by the side of the road to rest my weary eyes, and wake many hours later to the dark of night, with no way to know what time it was, except that I was the only person out in the dead of night.

It was the same questions, over and over, on auto repeat:

"Have you see my girl?"

"Do you know where she is?"

"Do you have any information; do you know where I can look?"

Until I finally came across a street vendor named Emad. A shepherd from a nearby village pointed me in his direction and said "if anyone can find your daughter, it will be Emad, the street vendor on First Street-go and see him. But it will come at a price."

The shepherd had turned away from me and started on his way even before I could ask him what the price would be. We weren't a family of considerable means. With a family comprising 8 mouths to feed, we lived within, if not just below, the poverty line. We both worked the land, Amjad and me, to put food on the table. Each time I was with child, we went through even tighter times because I wasn't able to contribute to our livelihood. Amjad would constantly harangue me about this fact-like the fact that I was with child was my fault and mine alone. Even after giving birth, there would be no rest. I would swaddle the newborn within a week of giving birth and attach her to my chest in a makeshift pouch as I joined Amjad on the land and recommenced work.

I carried on toward the street vendor and finally came to be standing in front of him. He was an imposing man, with a cigar dangling from his mouth, slouched in a chair by the side of the road like he was anticipating his next article of prey. He had small beady black eyes that shifted left right left any time there was movement on the road. When he opened his mouth in greeting, his lips curled to the side in a leering manner derelict of any consciousness of soul. A burst of heavy cigar fumes rushed forward from his mouth as he let out a breath and waited for me to instigate a conversation. When I did not, he steered the conversation in his own way.

"I know who you are," he said, pointing toward my chest matter-of-factly. "Why you're here. What took you so long?"

I remained silent. Of course he knew who I was . The man made a living out of other peoples' misfortune - it was his job to know what was happening to whom at all times and to anticipate a visit from a needy stranger.

His manner gave me pause to consider my decision to seek him out. I was not an educated woman. I did not mingle and mix with many people...in our village, and even though it was small and everyone knew their neighbours, we all kept to ourselves. I had not travelled and could not claim to be worldly or well versed in the art of human behaviour, but I did possess that one human trait inherent in all women-instinct. The man instilled in me an odd feeling I had never encountered before. I felt as though something was crawling under my skin, dying to burst forward.

"Can you help me?" I asked.

The street vendor looked me up and down, his mouth permanently set in a leering smirk. I could almost see the wheels turning in his brain as he considered his next words.

"What can you offer me?" he asked.

"I don't have much. For the sake of God, can you help me find my daughter?"

I stood watching him uncomfortably as he continued to leer, his eyes stripping me naked as he peeled back layer upon layer of my clothing. I needed the help, was desperate for some guidance to find my daughter, but the longer I stood there, the more I felt like I was selling my soul to the devil. I realised what he was proposing when his hand slid down his front to his throbbing member and he turned to indicate a dark alcove behind his cart. At that, my deepest instincts took root and I took flight without a second thought as he continued to cackle and indicate his desire to have his way with me. I removed myself from the situation as fast as I could and continued on my way in my tireless search for my missing daughter, not once looking back.

CHAPTER 6:
AUJENE 1970

Our father gave up on us. That's all I know. He blamed our mother for Farida's disappearance. He blamed our mother for everything, and nothing was ever the same between my parents after Farida was gone. At night I heard my mother whimpering, followed shortly after by two heavy slaps, whereby she would emit a sharp gasp, her voice trembling as she continued to cry and my father slammed the door on his way out of the house. She wore the soles of her shoes thin walking from village to village asking about Farida's whereabouts. She shut the whole world out, overlooked her other children, neglected her home, and drove herself slowly insane with grief.

CHAPTER 7: FARIDA 1970

An underground bunker was my home for the next 42 days. I know it was 42 days because I used the stick tally method of counting that my illiterate mother had taught me. I took a stick I found lying in the cell and scraped a faint line into the wall after every breakfast was served. A stick for every 4 days, then on the fifth day, a line running through the sticks from top right to bottom left to signal a unit of 5. I counted 42. 42 days away from my home. Living underground. No sun, no sky, no sea...just the arid, musty air that breezed through the cell and made the days and nights interminable.

The floor of the cell was one of dirt, and in the corner lay a mattress stripped of sheets, on which I lay my head most hours of the day.

I thought of my family, and wondered why they hadn't come for me. Farouk crossed my mind, but in the way that you would feel as though that person was one you knew from a long time ago. To be honest, I didn't know what I felt for Farouk. Obviously I didn't love him with a jaw clenching urgency or bone weary thirst that clutched at me and threatened to strangle me. No. Indifference. I was indifferent toward him. Really, I couldn't care less.

I ran my fingers gingerly over the tally etchings and wondered who had been here before me, if anyone had. Had they sat in this very spot and wondered the same thing about who came before them, who came after? I scoffed to myself; mother always said I was a curious day dreamer.

There was the sound of boots thudding down the stairs as someone entered the huge cavern and came to stand before me. I held my breath every time someone came in, never knowing what to expect. I exhaled in relief when I realized it was only Jihad.

"Any news?" I asked him, my fingers curling around the bars of the cell.

"The Shaikh will come to see you soon," he whispered, looking over his shoulder. "Farida, do you need anything? Have you eaten?" he asked eagerly. "I can't stay long."

"I just want to go home, Jihad. Why won't they let me go?"

He bit his lip and looked down at his boots, caked with mud. I surmised we must have had a particularly bad rainfall.

"Things will appear clearer once the Shaikh comes to see you. Then we will know what will happen."

"I have a bad feeling, Jihad," I said worriedly. "Girls aren't usually stolen just to be held in underground bunkers."

He looked over his shoulder again, agitated and concerned, before turning back to me.

"Whatever happens, know that I have your best interests at heart," he informed me.

"But can't you send word to my family?"

"Farida, this is not the sort of clan you want your family to go up against. They are the most ruthless in the region. Only another equally powerful tribe can go up against them. I have to go now. I will come and check up on you again soon."

CHAPTER 8:
FARIDA 1970

No one really knew whether or not the story of the first Farida was myth or legend, or a mix of both. But then...didn't every story come from a grain of truth? Someone could be listening to a rerun of my history one day and wonder if it were a true story or merely something concocted by someone's vivid imagination.

But I guessed the first Farida's story had to have come from somewhere. And there had to be some truth to her story, otherwise why would the town folk, year after year, and birth after birth, insist on naming their daughters Farida, if not out of superstition that if they did not do so, then the ghost of Farida would haunt and curse them til the end of time?

My mother had told me the story of the first Farida, and her mother, my grandmother, had told her the story before that. My father also spoke often of the first Farida, recounting bits and pieces as he'd heard from his parents and grandparents over the years. By the time I was 12, I had pieced together the first Farida's life simply by listening to stories from everyone around me, from the village elders to my own family and the various shopkeepers who had also been handed down their own stories. I didn't consider a story authentic unless it was reinforced by a second source, and sometimes a third similar yet independent account of events. Once all the stories were told and retold, a picture emerged of a sad and tragic life that had been cut too short by the evil hands of a few ignorant fools.

Farida had been a beautiful traveller. A wanderer who happened across our little village one day and set her tent upon unused land to rest her weary head. No one knew exactly why she had broken from her clan, but a popular theory that kept emerging was that she had been heartbroken when her one true love had chosen to marry her sister instead of her. Farida, with her snow white skin, flaming black hair and dark brooding eyes, had been welcomed into the bosom of the village and taken under the wing of the women, who loved her carefree spirit and appreciated her interaction with their children. She played with them and told them stories, even held lessons for them, teaching them to read and write basic Arabic. No one knew how or why she was literate, especially as girls attending lessons was not commonplace in the day.

She was helpful and warm, concerned when any woman got sick and rushing to her aid to help cook and clean for the family to give the mother much needed rest. She was smart and funny and articulate, wise beyond her years, and possessed an intelligence not found even amongst most men. She refused the advances of many a man who tried to entice her, and gave selflessly of her time and patience to those in need.

All the stories I heard about Farida, which I had committed to memory, told the story of a young girl who had an uncanny intuition to deduce things before they happened. She was able to predict weather patterns and relay communication as to how these would affect various crops. She was able to determine if a woman would give birth to a boy or a girl. During her time in the village, she had made many judgements that had come to fruition.

Farida's predictions were what eventually got her killed, her body weighted down at the bottom of the ocean for the fish to feed on. Her murder, by all accounts, was at the hands of a group of councilmen who accused her of witchery. Over the years, there had been many rumours as to which families had participated in the death sentence, but too many conflicting names had led me to believe no-one really knew who was responsible. The poor Farida was hung up by the neck until it snapped then thrown into the mercy of the sea, where she ceased to be.

The women of the village, when they finally found out what had happened to Farida, had been devastated. The children were inconsolable. The men believed they had rid the village of a sorceress, while the women screamed and raved that they had killed an innocent girl for doing what most educated people do – guess the gender of a child by the mother's cravings and the way her stomach is formed, look to the stars and the moon and sky for confirmation of incoming weather conditions, foresee success of crops according to weather patterns. Each and every one of her "divinations" could have been explained by science, yet the men had gotten it into their heads that the village would be safer without the local magician and taken matters into their own hands. And there began the curse of Farida.

There were stories of children inexplicably dying without reason. Women miscarrying their unborn babies. Crops failing year after year. The temporary flourish of wealth that the village experienced suddenly ceased to be upon Farida's demise. The women surmised that was due to a curse placed upon the village, for the great injustice that had befallen a guest, the senseless murder purging the village of any remaining good.

The women banded together and built a well in Farida's memory...which quickly dried up. They started to name their daughters Farida, in tribute to the martyred girl. They made endless dua and supplications for forgiveness, willing the banishment of the torment they felt to vanish. They banished their husbands from their beds, blaming them for the catastrophe that had befallen them, and the women rose as one voice, blaming all of the village's misgivings on male stupidity.

Now I wondered what people would think of my story. Of my imprisonment. Would they believe that a girl was stolen and held captive underground for a number of weeks, or months, possibly even years? Would they find my bones and bury them, lay a marker where the townspeople would visit and say a little prayer, and condemn the evil that had grabbed me from the safety of my family to see out my last days in a bunker no bigger than a closet?

I could see now the truth in the first Farida's story. Sometimes, no matter how hard you tried to deny the facts, even the most unbelievable stories held some truth. They held a morsel of a lesson for all to learn and live by. I wondered if I would meet the same fate as Farida. She had died for nothing. Simply for being Farida. Simply for being there. Simply for being an intelligent young girl who could lead a village to prosperity, something no man had been prepared to bear witness to.

I was merely a girl. Who happened to be at the wrong place at the wrong time, doing the right thing. Yet here I was now, sitting on the dirt with my legs tucked under me, making dua and drawing on the first Farida's strength to guide me through my darkest hour.

What would become of me? Would I be immortalised? Written about in books? Etched on the rocky ledge of the caves that were scattered in our village the way the original Farida's name and face had been etched many many years ago? Would I still be remembered in a hundred years? Would I be mourned by my family? Nieces and nephews I would never meet? How would my story be narrated

I had all the time in the world and no where to go. My mind wandered, playing games with me, enticing stories out of the hidden recesses of my brain that I would turn over in my mind's eye, then play over and over again as the days swept by to pass the time.

I envisioned myself going home, engulfed in the arms of my mother. My father's face would be a well of sadness deep in the pits of grief. My younger siblings, all grown, would not remember me. Aujene would be married, and she'd have a girl named Farida and possibly a boy named Farid. I smiled at that. Aujene was known as the tomboy of the village – to imagine her married and shackled to a man who would control her every move was near hilarious. For although she resembled me a lot in her colouring and features, and she turned many a head as we walked through the village to tend to the olive grove, Aujene had never really reconciled with herself just how beautiful she was. She was stunning by all accounts, and this was evident in the way that people looked at her, but all she could think about was climbing trees and toiling in the land. The earth was her soul. The dirt was her salt. She lived and breathed the land the same way most people lived and breathed life. I missed her. I missed her with a zest reserved only for those closest to one's heart. I imagined conversations with her, and at times, Jihad would emerge from the darkness of the tunnel leading into the bunker frowning, asking me who I was talking to. I would simply smile and tell him "My sister Aujene -she keeps me company while I wait for the day to be free of this prison." Jihad's eyes would soften in sadness, and I would feel sad that I had made him join in my misery, but at the end of the day, I was on the wrong side of the bars, so I was allowed that concession.

I no longer thought about Farouk. By now, he seemed like a distant memory, and if I focussed hard enough, I could even make the thought of him vanish just by clearing my mind of all the chaos and clutter that lurked there. Eventually, he would marry, I realised, thankful that one good thing had come of my imprisonment. I would not be forced to marry Farouk, who my father had pronounced was the family's saviour. A young man who had lived his life between the village and the city, commuting back and forth to further his education, and had eventually ensured his future by winning a government job, which promised a bright future and a secure lifetime pension after retirement. My father seemed to think Farouk's good fortune would rub off on our family, or that his wealth would somehow end up in his own pocket. A thought that didn't make sense in the least, especially as for the time we'd known Farouk, he had never once visited carrying so much as a loaf of bread, which was against the age old custom of a visitor bringing a gift when entering another's home. I recalled that when we'd visited with his family, my mother and father had argued over what sweets to take the family. Another time, it was a watermelon. A third time, a kilo of freshly ground coffee beans. And even though Farouk's empty hands had confounded my father, he never ever would have backed down from an agreement or brought up the fact that Farouk was not playing by the cultural norms everyone else around us adhered to religiously. I saw this trait in Farouk as one worthy of kicking him to the curb, and said as much to my mother, who looked to me with an exasperated sigh, agreeing silently but telling me with her silence that her hands were tied and my father would not recall his agreement to give my hand in marriage to Farouk, who pushed incessantly for a closer wedding date.

CHAPTER 9:
FARIDA 1970

On the 43rd day, I felt, before I saw, a shift in the air of the prison cell. Shortly thereafter, a scuffle of excited activity as a flurry of men entered the space beyond the cell and milled about a man I had not seen before. An imposing man in a heavy, embroidered robe, a smattering of delicate hair sprinkled across his chin, masquerading as a beard. I assumed this was the Shaikh of the tribesmen who had kidnapped me but said nothing as he approached my cell door.

The newcomer regarded me carefully, then furrowed his eyebrows and squinted, looking toward me for something I could not comprehend, but something that became apparent a mere few seconds later.

"You fools," he muttered. "While I applaud you on capturing such a fine beauty, this is not the girl you were tasked with obtaining."

He berated and belittled the men milling behind him, assuring them that they had "captured" the wrong girl.

"But shaikhna," one of the guards started, lowering his gaze in respect as he spoke to the newcomer. "This girl is Farida, who you asked for, grabbed from the Boden olive grove, at the precise day and time that you indicated she would be there."

The newcomer turned to the speaker and raised an eyebrow

before speaking. It seemed like he was measuring his words carefully.

"You may have obtained her from the place I indicated, and her name may indeed be Farida, but she is not my Farida. Did you even stop to ask her and confirm her identity?"

"Why yes sire, several girls at the site indicated her name is Farida."

"And did it not occur to you that there may be more than one girl working the olive grove who was named Farida? You seem to forget, the legend of that village's history was named Farida and half of the girls in that village carry the name of Farida!"

The guard looked at me dumbfounded and shook his head in confusion, then turned back to his master, perhaps not fully comprehending the immense magnitude of his actions. And there, in that instance, holding my breath, I thought everything was right with the world and I would be sent back home.

A shuffling sound behind the newcomer diverted my eyes from one man to another, and I felt the moment that a shadow of fear crossed my mind. Jihad, standing behind the Shaikh, had moved slightly, and I could sense this was in agitation of the unfolding conversation. Something had him worried.

"Return her and bring me the real Farida!" demanded the Shaikh.

"But shaikhna, we cannot do that. The local cultural laws are designed to protect the honour of the clans and their families. If a girl is removed from her home then returned, she is tainted. She will be killed, along with each one of us, strung up by the neck in the town square if the local villagers get a hold of us."

"Then you know what you must do," the newcomer said, turning away with a flourish of his robe.

And in that instant, with the eyes of half a dozen men cemented on me, my fate was sealed as I realised there would be no going home.

CHAPTER 10: FARIDA 1970

Jihad came to see me the next day while making his rounds. He looked at me as he approached, a look of consternation on his face. For as long as I had known him, from that first time he came into the bunker after I had been there for two days, I had known that if there was any hope for me at all, it lay with Jihad. I had recognised him as the guard who had followed Aujene into the grove on the day that I was taken and everything changed. He was the one that had gone running into the grove after my sister.

He had produced a chocolate bar and passed it through the bars, telling me it was all he had. He kept looking over his shoulders, maybe a little worried that he would be caught in the bunker when he wasn't supposed to be there.

"I'm not supposed to be here," Jihad said.

"What happened to my sister?" I asked, hurriedly. "Where is she?"

"She's safe. She got away."

"Who are you? Why are you doing this to me? When can I go home?"

"So many questions," he tsked.

"I just want to go home to my family."

"Well, that's not up to me."

Jihad went on to tell me his name, and I could see that he was only slightly older than me. He informed me that I'd been kidnapped at the behest of a very powerful local shaikh, and he didn't know what would happen next, but advised me to keep my head down and not get feisty with the guards when they turned up.

"Have they been coming?" he asked.

"Someone brings breakfast in the morning. Sometimes a late dinner. They give me water. But I don't see them much."

"I'll come to see you again when I can," he murmured, before turning to leave.

"Wait!" I urged. "Why are you doing this?" and I held up the chocolate bar in silent thanks.

"I have a sister. I don't know what I'd do if something like this happened to her. Maybe the good I put out there will be the karma I get back."

CHAPTER 11: FARIDA 1970

Every few days, Jihad would come to visit, usually in the afternoon. He would tell me stories about his life, and his family, with whom he had broken ties because of an incident that had happened in their village back in Syria. I would sit by the bars, listening intently, a lilt in his voice as he relayed to me stories of the outside world.

"So how did you end up here with this clan?" I asked him, taking a sip of water from the fresh bottle he had provided me.

"Self-imposed exile, I guess. After what happened in the village, I had to leave, so I travelled across the border and ended up on the side of a road. One of the guards picked me up and invited me to join the security board for the shaikh of a local clan. I had no idea who he was when I committed to the job, and eventually when I did find out, well…it's not the sort of situation where you just get up and leave."

"Why not?" I asked him.

"He's a very powerful man, with long reaching arms. He can basically reach anyone anywhere, or so I've been told. Once I have enough resources to head off to another country, maybe I'll take my chances, but not now."

"That's no way to live a life," I whispered.

Jihad shrugged as if to say it is what it is and that was it.

"I wonder what life has in store for me," I muttered softly.

"Just keep your head down like you've been doing, don't say anything and don't agitate them. These are very dangerous men playing a very dangerous game."

"And you're playing with them," I reminded him.

"With any luck, this will all be over soon," he whispered, getting up to leave.

"Promise me something," I urged him, my fingers wrapping around the bars of my cell in desperation. Jihad looked at me sadly. I knew if there was a way, he would have broken me out of the cell and helped me escape. I knew that with everything in me, especially after he had told me the story of how he had let Aujene go that day in the grove. If not for Jihad, I feared the same fate-maybe worse-would have befallen my younger sister.

"Anything," Jihad whispered, reinforcing my conviction that he was a good man.

"If they..." I paused and took a deep breath, not knowing how to go on with my request without breaking down. My eyes fluttered with moisture and I looked at the ceiling in an attempt to stem the flow of tears before it began. I knew all the tell-tale signs that told me I was on the brink of a break down. "If they do come for me...If I should end up dead..."

"Don't say that," he interrupted me.

"You said it yourself, these are dangerous men. And dangerous men will do anything to save themselves. There's no way they're taking me back to the village."

"It's not over yet," Jihad reminded me.

"If I don't make it," I implored him "please let my family know. They will need some sort of closure."

Jihad looked down at his feet sadly and said nothing. I could see the anguish on his face, his pain mirroring my own. Jihad cared for me, not in a romantic way, but in a brotherly, protective way. The same way he would care for his own sister. I realised that in here, in my prison, he was the closest thing I had to family. And I knew, should my worst fear become a reality and I should cease to exist, that Jihad would do the right thing and send word to my parents about my demise. No matter how long it took him, he would grant me my last dying wish.

CHAPTER 12: HASSAN 1970

"Shu badhu?" I asked. *What does he want?*

"I'm not sure, shaikhna, all I know is he's come from the Waqas tribe and asked to meet you personally."

"He's not on our radar?"

"No, but apparently he hasn't been with them long."

I stared out the window and watched the field workers as they tended to the crop and carried baskets on their shoulders, transporting produce back to the village. I marvelled at the simplicity of the act of waking up, going to the land, seeking refuge amongst the vegetables, and having that sole responsibility to deal with. How simple and easy that would be-laborious, maybe, but sometimes I envied the *fellaheen* their position of simply having to take orders, rather than having to make hard decisions and choices you questioned at every turn.

"Bring him in," I told him.

"But shaikhna..." the guard started to protest. I turned and looked at him sharply, and he went quiet, looking down at his feet solemnly and knowing that in debating my decision to meet with the stranger, he had overstepped his authority.

"Tell me what you're thinking," I asked, walking slowly toward him. Letting him know that he had a voice and I would allow him to share it.

"What if he's been sent here to spy? Or to hurt you?" the guard argued.

"Would you allow him to hurt me, Sajed?" I asked.

"Never, shaikhna," he said, bowing his head in respect.

"Then you bring him in and you stay. Watch him carefully."

Momentarily, the man was shown into my den, and we sat down on the pillows that created a semi-circle in the room, meant for the gathering of men during important meetings. If nothing else, we respected any and all who entered our homes and treated them with courtesy. Sajed stood by the window watching carefully as we sipped our tea, whilst another guard stood by the door, his rifle flung against his chest, daring any-one to get past him.

I looked at the man as he sipped his tea, his hand shaking as he raised the cup to his mouth. He winced when he realised it was too hot and set the cup down. He couldn't have been more than a boy, maybe 20 years old, with fair hair and dark blue eyes, like the night sky at midnight. It was rare to find a Bedouin with eyes that were such a mesmerising colour. I urged him to speak after several minutes had passed and he hadn't said a word.

"I need to know that I'll be protected from the Waqas tribe for being the traitor that brings you this news," he said, seeking my protection.

"You are in my house, and you are protected."

"What about when I leave?" he asked, his face earnest, yet a frown was crested in his brow.

"What sort of news could you give me that would warrant

protection?" I asked. "I don't know that I would want to be involved in what you have to give me."

He looked down at the rug before him and seemed to watch the swirls of the ornate design before letting out a deep breath. He lifted the tea cup to his lips and took another sip, his hand still shaking. I waited patiently for him to deliver the news that he so obviously believed he had risked his life to bring me.

"I didn't know what they were doing." He shook his head and looked at me, his face a defeated mask of regret. "I had to flee Syria due to family circumstances and found myself entwined with the Waqas tribe. I didn't know anything about them, and I had no-where to go. The day after I joined them, some of the men told me they were going on a trip to harvest some olives in Tul Ghosn and I was to go along."

The man stopped talking long enough for me to ask him his name.

"Jihad," he replied. "My name is Jihad."

"Go on," I urged.

"That day, they took a girl from the olive grove. They stole her," he clarified. "I was helpless to stop it, but I ran after her sister and scared her off to safety without them knowing."

"They took a girl? Why?"

Jihad shook his head helplessly and pursed his quivering lips, the regret eating at him from the inside out.

"I didn't know why until yesterday. The Waqas shaikh went to see her and made his intentions clear. He had asked the men to extract a particular girl from the village, but it appeared they had taken the wrong girl." There were a multitude of questions in my head, but I allowed him to continue on.

"The men realised they couldn't return her to the village, or they'd be strung up alongside her. They decided the best thing to do would be to kill her and try again to extract the girl they were originally supposed to."

I shook my head and put my cup down. "They've killed her?"

Jihad shook his head in response and went on. "They're planning to do it, but they haven't got the nerve yet to do it. The guards, they're brutish and can be violent, but they don't just kill innocents, and never unless specifically ordered by the shaikh."

"Where is the girl now?"

"In an underground bunker on deserted land a fair drive from here."

"And you know where this bunker is?"

"Na'am, shaikhna, I visit with her often when I know the guard is not there."

"Aah...," I mumbled, my face contorting in understanding like I had discovered a long hidden secret. "You have taken a liking to the girl," I mused.

"Not in the way you may think, shaikhna. I felt sorry for her, an innocent plucked from her family's arms and destined for slaughter for no reason but that she was in the wrong place at the wrong time."

"So what would you have me do?" I asked him.

Jihad shook his head in confusion, telling me he wasn't sure what I'd be able to do, but he remembered his father telling him, at a very young age, that the only way to defeat a powerful man was to form an allegiance with another more powerful man.

"I don't know what I thought you could do, I am just trying to save the girl. The men have mentioned on many an occasion that you are the only shaikh more powerful than Shaikh Waqas. I just felt an urge to come and tell you what has happened."

"And they plan to take another girl?"

"Yes, shaikhna. As soon as they have disposed of this girl and made room in the cell for another, they will bring the other girl."

"Has anyone touched her?"

He shook his head adamantly.

"So what will you do, if I tell you I can be of no help to you. What will you do?"

"Go back and try to find a way to break her out of her dungeon."

"And then?"

"Send her home."

I asked him if he knew the customs of the local tribes and the etiquette on a girl returning home after an unaccompanied absence. He shook his hand and listened as I told him. "She can't go back home. If she does, she will be killed."

Jihad gasped and looked up at me sharply, a strand of his hair falling over his right eye.

"Then I will send her away," Jihad proclaimed, somewhat naively.

"Where would you send a young, broken girl without getting her into more trouble, Jihad? Life is not as abstract as you may think. The girl's fate if she returns home, or gets set on the streets, will be exactly the same as if she were to meet her death in the confines of her prison. And if they know you set her free, surely they will kill you too."

"I'm not afraid to die for what I believe in," Jihad proclaimed, his right hand beating against his chest. "What is wrong is wrong, and I will not stand by and let them kill an innocent girl."

I felt myself smirk. No matter how hard I tried to stop it, my mouth, of its own volition, curled up at the corner into a lop-sided grin as I studied the young boy.

"You're fighting mightily hard for a girl you say you have no feelings for," I pointed out.

"I'm just trying to do the right thing here."

"And what's that, Jihad?"

"Not bear witness to a senseless murder that will take an innocent girl's life and make me lose my mind with guilt and regret."

CHAPTER 13: FARIDA 1970

On the 46th day of my capture, everything changed. Jihad approached my cell, looking over his shoulder quickly as he came to stand before me. I recognised the pained look on his face and sadly, with my eyes, silently let him know that he was not responsible for my fate. He had done all he could, short of letting me go. He lowered his head and looked at his feet before looking back up at me and sighing.

"I don't know what to do, Farida. I came to this tribe for protection, but I find myself involved in something bigger than myself."

"You've involved yourself in a very dirty game, Jihad," I spoke softly. "This is no way to live."

"I can't protect you anymore."

"Then just let me go," I insisted.

"There is no way you can go back to your family without getting yourself killed and sparking a raging war between the clans. Your family will be wiped out, you know this Farida."

I looked at him sadly and realised the truth of what he said. My family, even if they did accept me back into the fold, even if the village elders did grant me clemency, which was so unlikely I dared not even think it, did not have the resources or capability to go up against the clan that had kidnapped me. They would try. But they would fail. Of this, I was certain.

"There is another neighbouring clan," he started to explain. "A local one. One that presides over the affairs of the clans in the region. I have been to see their Shaikh and bring with me one final salvation."

I scoffed. "What salvation could there possibly be if my death is imminent?"

Jihad moved to answer, but didn't have a chance to do so, as he was cut off by the thud of heavy boots tramping through the bunker. A man I'd not seen before came to stand beside him. Jihad shook his head in disbelief as he looked at the man, then looked at me with a fearful look in his eyes.

"That is all, Jihad, I will take it from here," the newcomer said. I jutted my chin and prepared to do battle again in defence of my life.

"I don't think you quite understand your predicament," the man started.

"I understand that I'm here against my will and you have no right to hold me."

He mulled my words. "This is true. And true again. But I am not the one holding you prisoner here."

"So I can go?" I asked him, quite naively.

"Not quite."

I watched him as he shuffled around the space in front of the cell, then moved to wipe his brow before speaking again, measuring his words delicately.

"The Shaikh of the Waqas tribe sought the extraction of a girl named Farida from your village," he began, by way of explanation. "Obviously, not you. The fact that you were taken in error is a serious one. Local custom dictates that when a girl leaves her family home for an extended period of time, regardless of circumstances, she is to return to her home only in a coffin. You will be considered tainted and hung up by your neck until you meet your death. Regardless of whether or not you are guilty of anything. You know this."

My face paled as I realised what he was saying and understood the magnitude of going home.

He was right, word for word; that was exactly what would happen. For no matter how hard I desired to go home, I knew, without a doubt, that my return would not be looked upon favourably. I'd have a lot to explain but even moreover, a lot of convincing to do to persuade the village elders that I was still intact. The elders still held on to outdated customs and traditions, along with even more invalid practises such as "kill now, ask later".

"I know that you going back would result in your unjust death. There will be no one to protect you – the word of the tribe elders is law."

"And yet, I should be given a death penalty?" I whispered in disbelief. "For someone else's mistake? Is this what a girl's life is worth?"

I tasted the salt as my tears rolled down my cheeks and blended with my words as I made my case.

"The general consensus amongst the men of the tribe is that you should be killed."

I gasped. Knowing it and hearing it uttered were two different things.

"Here. Killed and disposed of and they can wash their hands of this fiasco and move on. They just need this problem to go away."

"So I'm damned if I stay and damned if I'm returned. All this for having the same name as another girl?" I looked at the man incredulously and shook my head in disbelief. "What sort of a life is this when a girl is plucked from the bosom of her family, caged like a wild animal, then slaughtered because someone made a mistake."

The man sighed heavily and let out a long breath.

"I have sisters. Believe me, I know."

"Then just let me go,"I whimpered. "Please, I won't tell a soul."

"You're not mine to let go. I don't belong to this tribe, nor do I subscribe to their practises."

"Then who are you? What are you doing here? If you don't hold the same beliefs as they do, you could just open this door and let me go," I argued, with a determined yet frustrated clenching of my teeth.

"And where would you go, hmm? Where would a young girl, on her own, with no money, go if she can't go back home be-cause she'll be killed if she does? Give me a relevant answer."

I had no answer. I looked at the stranger helplessly and knew, with everything in me, that the laws of the tribe would be up-held and I'd be sent to my death. Yet staying here, I was also guaranteed certain death. At least, going home, there may be a chance, no matter how slim, that I may be excused from a death penalty...

"They're going to kill me anyway. You said so yourself. I may as well take my chances back home."

"You'd only be delaying the inevitable. You can't go back there."

"What are you going to do?" I asked, my voice a mere whisper.

"There is one other option, although you might not like it."

"I'm facing a death penalty either way; what could be worse than that?"

Jihad returned to the bunker after the visit from the clan member and spoke to me at length about the options the visitor had given me.

"I can't believe you would do that," I whispered, as Jihad looked at me with anguished eyes.

"Believe me, Farida, it was the only option. You don't know how these things work."

"I know that I've been stolen from my family, deprived of a normal existence, and tossed back and forth between two tribes while they figure out what to do with me. This is what I know," I hissed.

"Your best bet at survival is with the Damour clan. Hassan is a just and honest man. He is the only one that can protect you-from the clan that took you and from your village elders."

"What will happen now?" I asked.

"Hassan will meet with the Waqas Shaikh and broker a deal with him. They will hopefully reach some sort of civil agreement where the Damours will take on responsibility for you."

"You say "hopefully". Does that mean there's a chance I could still stay here and die?" I asked him, incredulous.

"Shaikh Waqas is not known to be a diplomatic man. If anything, he is a tyrant and a master manipulator. He will make this as hard as possible on the Damours, squeezing every last drop out of the arrangement to his advantage. I'm amazed you're actually still in one piece. The man is known for the violence he likes to inflict on others, especially women I hear."

"And the shaikh that came here today, is he any better? He's practically buying me from this prison to send me to another."

"Farida, make no mistake. Shaikh Hassan Damour didn't have to come here. He didn't have to offer you a reasonable way out of this situation. And he definitely didn't have to sully his hands with this situation. The fact that he even came here is a big deal in itself. That he's made you this offer is not one to be trifled with."

"You're asking me to be grateful that someone I've never met has offered to marry me."

"To save your life," Jihad clarified. "He can have his pick of wives, and yet he's chosen to sacrifice his own desires to help you."

CHAPTER 14: HASSAN 1970

I heard the soft strains of a female voice answering back as Jihad tried to talk sense into the girl. The mellow lilt of her tongue betrayed her anger and she became more determined in her conversation with the man as he tried to break down the situation for her.

I went down the stairs, deliberately thumping my feet heavily so they would know an intruder was in their midst.

If her voice was like a melody of delicate petals falling on sand, her face was something to behold.

I took a quick look and noticed her chin go up, her defence mechanisms in place. I hadn't expected such a beauty. But I could see why Jihad had been drawn to her...her presence was like a magnet, pulling me in to her orb.

I dismissed Jihad and told the young girl how much trouble she was in. She accused me of holding her prisoner and asked me to let her leave. Her naivety was doing things to my chest I couldn't explain, her beauty causing me to turn away and wipe at a bead of sweat that had gathered above my brow. I tried not to look at the raven hair peeking out from under the front of her scarf and falling in a sheet down her back. Her eyes, the blackest black of the night, were shining, and I couldn't tell if that was their natural state or the blemish of tears as they formed under her long lashes.

I explained to her the implications of going home a "returned but tainted girl", which was what she would be labelled, regardless of whether or not anyone had touched her. The elders would seek to make an example of her and would put honour above the exaltation of her return. I made it clear to her, in the simplest of terms, that she was going to die; be it at the hands of the village elders or by the hands of the Waqas tribe, her destiny had the same outcome.

I could see the moment she understood the ramifications of what I was telling her, and she stumbled lightly, holding on to one of the bars for support. And in that moment, I understood that the sheen in her eyes I'd seen earlier had been a natural shine, like a beacon to her beauty, and now the strength of real tears emerged from her eyes and rolled in thick heavy drops down her cheek.

She tried so hard to argue with me, that it wasn't anyone's right to make a martyr of her, as though I held the keys to the cell and could make the decision to let her go. She understood fully that her fate had been signed and sealed, and that she was now merely living on borrowed time.

She gasped for breath, hyperventilating, understanding the enormity of her situation.

I couldn't erase her pain as she stood there looking defeated, knowing her days were numbered. I couldn't offer her clemency or closure, or any of the things she sought to find in the mayhem of her short life. She was barely a child. Maybe just a year or two younger than Jihad. And I could see why he had probably taken such a keen interest in her-the age gap ensured he looked at her like a baby sister that he had to save at all costs.

Still standing at the door to the cell, I removed my hands from my pockets and looked at her carefully, trying to hide the effect that emotions ravaging through her were having on me. I hadn't quite made up my mind what I would do when I met the young girl, but now as I looked at her, assessing the situation and the tormented conflict shadowing her eyes, I realised there was only one thing I could do.

I made her an offer. One I knew she probably wouldn't want to take. But her only option, and the only one I could possibly put on the table.

"There is one other option, although you might not like it."

"I'm facing a death penalty either way; what could be worse than that?"

CHAPTER 15: HASSAN 1970

Of all the things I could have envisioned, a beautiful young girl with dark, almond shaped eyes and hair the black of the darkest night was not one of them. Farida had been a surprise. And I had wondered what sheer madness Shaikh Waqas suffered from, to have taken the girl then discarded her without so much as touching a hair on her head. And now he wanted to be rid of her. Because she was not the girl he had asked for. Sheer lunacy.

I had gone to the bunker with the intention of seeing the girl and consoling her, perhaps finding out who her parents were and sending word to them of the situation and seeing if they expressed an interest in saving her. But when I had seen her, and listened to the soft humming of her voice, something in me clenched at my chest, squeezing my heart for every last shred of compassion. Knowing her parents would take her back only to make a martyr of her. The only other option was that she would die at the hand of Shaikh Waqas, who had been a thorn in the side of all the local clans for years. His father had been a just ruler, revered by all his tribesmen and respected by all other shaikhs in the region. But upon his untimely death, his eldest son Ahmad had inherited his title, throwing the whole region into disarray with his foolish, ill thought out actions.

And now, it seemed, he had taken to stealing girls from

their families for his own deviant purposes. When those girls no longer served a purpose, they were simply discarded. The worst of it was that he had inherited his father's loyal soldiers, who, although never having done any of the dastardly deeds for the deceased shaikh, were now being put in the unlikely position of having to hurt and dispose of innocents at the Sahikh's command.

And now, as I paced back and forth on the ground floor balcony, watching the sun disappear behind the horizon, I wondered at the unlikely turn of events that had brought Jihad to me and Farida into my line of sight. I had gone to the bunker more out of curiosity than anything else, and perhaps a misguided sense of offering Jihad a morsel of hope, but upon meeting Farida, everything had changed, and I had opened my mouth and delivered her the only alternative which I knew-almost certainly-would allow her a chance to live.

I had offered to marry her, even as the voice of reason deep inside me asked what I was doing. I had offered to marry her, knowing she would probably resist. I had offered to marry her, not knowing anything about her or her family, nor even having the slightest inclination to be married before I stepped into that bunker. I offered to marry her, knowing the situation wasn't as simple as it appeared to be, and there would need to be some negotiating with Shaikh Waqas to ensure her safety and her migration from one cell to another. Because essentially, marrying me, a man that she didn't even know, that's what she would be getting.

"What will you do?" Waleed asked, coming to stand behind me.

I shook my head in response, indicating that I had no idea. After meeting Farida, I had sent Jihad back to his own village, willing him to stay quiet and let me deal with the situation. He had tried to argue with me, telling me he had to know my plans for Farida, otherwise he would have to find another way to save her. I envied him his commitment but respected it, urging him once again to go back to the village, and no matter what happened, no-one was to know that he had met with me. I told him I would protect him from any conversation that would arise with Shaikh Waqas about Farida, and I was a man of my word.

"You can't let them kill her," Waleed responded. "It's wrong. Further, Shaikh Waqas' behaviour is going to open the eyes of the police and bring them to our doorstep. He's become a liability for the clans."

My brother and I agreed on this, along with various other members of the neighbouring clans. However, having him deposed of his duties was no easy task, and with no-one to step in and lead the clan, we faced a turf war the likes of which we had never seen and only ever heard about from our forefathers.

"I don't intend to let them kill her," I told my brother.

"Do you think she'll take you up on your offer of marriage?"

"I don't see that she has much choice, brother," I replied, squeezing his shoulder as I walked past him.

"Even if she does, how will you do it without starting an all out war with Waqas? Besides, you know that only his men know about the bunker-he'll know someone has sold him out."

"Set up a meeting with him tonight," I said, looking out over the land thoughtfully. "I have a plan."

CHAPTER 16:
HASSAN 1970

Shaikh Waqas was a pretentious man, if nothing else. At every opportunity, he sought to show off and flaunt his wealth, conveniently forgetting that the riches he squandered were a product of his father's tireless work and efforts to bring stability to the region by opening trade with the outside world.

We entered what Waleed termed "the harem", so called for all the beautiful women floating around, all of them Waqas' wives or mistresses. I realised, with a lurch in the pit of my stomach, that this would have been Farida's fate had she been the girl he had requested. But for some reason, even with all her youth and beauty, Shaikh Waqas had not been taken with the girl and remained focused on obtaining the girl he originally sought.

Surprisingly, it was Jihad who collected us from the company of the guards and escorted Waleed and I, along with two of our own guards, down the long, narrow hallway to a huge room scattered with throw rugs, cushions and pillows, on which we were to sit. He had looked at me in surprise, a momentary flash of fear crossing his face, before he regained his composure, straightened his back, and asked us to follow him. A true soldier, not allowing his emotions to betray him. Willing to lose his life for a just cause. Capable of facing the consequences of his actions if it came to that.

Shaikh Waqas was not waiting for us in the room when we

entered. In true hubristic fashion, he sought to make an entrance, entering a few minutes after us, his back heavy with a thick robe heavily embroidered with spun gold. He welcomed us and waited for one of the women to catch his robe as he shrugged it off his shoulders. Once we were alone, with a feast of nuts and berries and enough exotic fruits to feed an army, Shaikh Waqas told us what a pleasure it was for him that we would honour him with a visit. Which was a polite way of asking us why we were there and what we wanted.

"We've been meaning to come a while," Waleed stated, getting to the point "But we do have some pressing business to discuss."

Shaikh Waqas looked up at us both, stopping mid-chew after he had popped a berry into his mouth.

"Business. We've not had the pleasure to work alongside one another before. But of course, I always welcome new opportunity." Always the opportunist, Shaikh Waqas displayed his greed and played straight into our hands.

I grabbed some nuts in my hand as I tried to buy time and slowed my rapid breathing in an attempt to appear calm and collected. This proposal could go either one of two ways, but I knew I had to keep a level head as the discussion unfolded. I couldn't appear too invested or concerned by his answer if it was not favourable to us.

"I was approached by a broker from another village not too far from here seeking a girl…"

And arrogant as he was, he cut me off before I could even finish off my sentence. "Well, if it's a girl you're after, you can take your pick," he said, smiling as he clapped his hands together twice.

An array of young girls walked into the room, parading before us in a flurry of colourful garments. Pinks and yellows and blues and greens, each more beautiful than the other. Waleed and I watched as the girls shuffled past us, feigning interest out of politeness, but having no urge to share in Shaikh Waqas' hobbies.

"I wouldn't know the girl in question, but it is important that I locate her. I thought she may have been brought or even offered to you," and the air lingered with my unspoken accusation that he was the man to see when it came to locating lost girls.

"Why don't you tell me more and let's see if I can help you. Why is this girl significant? And why are you involved?"

"The girl's father has been searching for her. She was taken from the Boden olive grove a few months ago." I saw a tiny flicker in Shaikh Waqas' eyes before he was able to mask it by popping another berry in his mouth.

"And her significance to you? I wouldn't imagine this is the kind of work you've built your fortune on."

"Most of our olive oil consumption here in the lowlands derives from that olive grove. They offer the finest oil in the quantities we require."

Shaikh Waqas nodded his head in agreement "They do offer the best oil."

"Our purchasing power means they sell solely to us, and we on sell to the neighbouring villages and the South of Lebanon, and further afar to other countries in the Middle East. As you know, this is a lucrative business. Not only financially; we all benefit from the best raw, undiluted olive oil in the country."

He shook his head again and shrugged in agreement, waiting for the punchline.

"The parents have spent the past few months looking for their daughter, with no success."

"I still don't see what this has to do with you," Shaikh Waqas said, and if it wasn't for me having to respect him in his own home, I would have held up my hand to wordlessly tell him that I was coming to that.

"The shaikh has asked me to intervene to see if I can find the girl and return her to her home."

"You and I both know the ways of the clans, Hassan. No girl is accepted back into the fold after leaving the family home."

"She didn't leave, Shaikhna, she was taken," Waleed interrupted. "The parents may have sought clemency and been granted it."

"I still don't understand why you were approached. And what this has to do with me."

"The olive oil deal is a long standing agreement between myself and the village broker. They're considering voiding the contract if the girl is not returned. Once we lose the contract, it's gone for good."

Shaikh Waqas sat up straight and lifted his chin in defiance. I knew he understood the severity of the situation once I mentioned losing the contract. A contract that brought in several hundred thousand dollars in revenue annually. A contract which was not only profitable for all the clans in the region, but it also provided countless jobs for men and women who worked in the plant bottling the oil for export and the truck drivers who transported the oil across borders to various locations. The loss of this one contract could prove to be a devastating economic blow to the clans.

He also understood, like a lightbulb coming on in his head, that if he was found to be the one who took the girl, that all the other tribes would turn on him and he would most definitely become an outcast, denounced and discarded like he had never existed.

"Again, what does this have to do with me?" he asked, playing coy.

"No-one mentioned your name, Shaikh Ahmad. I have merely come to you hoping that you are able to give me information regarding who may have the girl so I can return her to her family and uphold the integrity of the contract."

For a long time, he did not say anything. He looked down at the table, then grabbed another berry and put it in his mouth. If nothing, I would have learnt tonight that the shaikh is fond of berries.

"I may have been offered a girl who was taken from that olive grove. Give me some more identifiers and let me see if I can find something for you."

"Do you think he bought it?" Waleed asked me as we drove away into the night.

"He bought it. Didn't you see him? He all but pissed himself when I mentioned we might lose the contract."

"Do you think he'll come through? The way I read him, he's the type that would kill her just to cover up his misdeeds."

I clucked my tongue and shook my head. "He won't kill her. But he will lie through his teeth and say he had nothing to do with it when he hands her over. He'll make himself out to be the hero, having recovered her from a band of robbers. When we all know, this is what he's spent his life doing-taking what is not his for his own amusement."

◆ ◆ ◆

Shaikh Waqas sent word to the village the next morning that he had found the girl and knew her whereabouts. The only condition, he said, was that he could not reveal who took her or where she'd been held for the duration of her capture, and the girl's captor demanded a promise that this would not be delved into in order for the girl to be released. That in itself told me she had been held under his instruction. I sent word back to him that she was to be delivered to my village at the earliest possible time so we could organise for her to be returned to her family.

At the same time, I met with Jihad secretly and secured Farida's positive response to my proposal. He informed me that Shaikh Waqas was planning to move Farida tomorrow, and an envoy would be depositing her to the village so the exchange could take place.

"Won't he be suspicious when the girl ends up married to you?" Jihad asked, like he had every right to do so.

"He won't care. As long as the girl is out of his hair and he doesn't have to sully his hands with her. He may be curious, but he won't do anything about it. Especially not after I float the rumour of how the girl was not accepted back into the village so I had to marry her."

"You need to tell mother," Waleed reminded me.

"Well, now I've got my answer from Farida, I think it's safe to do so," I commented.

Needless to say, my mother did not take the news well. Traditionally, clans did not marry outside of their jurisdiction. This was to strengthen ties within communities and to enforce the integrity of clan bonds and traditions. Very very rarely did a clan member marry outside their village, but there had been exceptions over the years, albeit few of them.

That was her main concern. Her second concern was that she had never met the girl nor her family, so how was she to know if the girl was acceptable marriage material? And for a shaikh, no less! To which I replied that Farida was the girl I would be marrying, regardless of her pedigree, and they had to start preparing for the wedding, which would take place the next day.

Which brought us to her last concern. Preparation for a wedding that no-one had anticipated. Usually, such matters took weeks, if not months to prepare, my mother reminded me.

"There's nothing to worry about, mother. Lita and the girls can do the cooking. Find Farida a white dress and the girls can do her makeup. Keep it simple."

"You mean, she doesn't even have a dress?" my mother asked, aghast at the thought.

"She only found out yesterday that she'll be getting married, mother. Please get her a dress. I think she's Amar's size."

My mother shook her head in disbelief and asked "who is this girl? Why don't you know her size? Where did you meet her? *Hasbi Allah wa ne'emal wakeel.*"

I laughed as I walked away and went in search of my sisters Zelekha and Amar, knowing they would be more help than my mother, who would probably be in shock until well after the wedding.

CHAPTER 17:
FARIDA 1970

62 days after my incarceration, I left my prison. I was taken out of the bunker and walked out into the sun, where my eyes slammed shut as they attempted to adjust to the light. The gatekeeper had a car waiting and drove me the short distance to a nearby village, where I was secreted in a house I assumed would be my marital home.

Hassan came in a short while later and found me sitting on the bed looking out at the cornfields. I rose as soon as he came in and looked down at my feet, too shy to even make eye contact with him. I heard the door click as he closed it but made no move toward me.

"I trust that you'll be comfortable here," he said, by way of greeting. I merely nodded. "This will be your new home."

I looked around the sparsely furnished room. There was a huge bed, a dressing table with a bench, and a single chair pulled to one side by the window in an otherwise huge space, then turned to look at Hassan, the leader of the Damour tribe. I wondered what his motivation was for marrying me. Until a few days ago, he had never even met me and did not know my name, and although I had been referred to in our village as "the most beautiful Farida" – there were four of us – I did understand that he could in fact have his pick of women. Why would he settle for someone he had just met?

"What will become of me?" I asked.

Hassan looked at me for the longest time and was careful to measure his words before he spoke again.

"You will live here as my wife. You will be safe under my protection and the protection of the Damour name. I have reached an agreement with the Waqas tribe and they will not have any rights over you."

"They never had rights over me," I clarified. "Taking me was one thing, but having rights over me was something entirely different."

"That is true in theory," he agreed. "But they had you first-in their unenlightened way of thinking, you belonged to them."

I shook my head in disbelief and told him I couldn't believe that there were still functioning tribes with this mindset.

"The thing with bedouin tribes is they find it very hard to let go of centuries old habits and traditions."

"You belong to a Bedouin tribe," I reminded him.

"But I don't act the way they do. We have discarded many of the old traditions that don't align with modern day standards. Many traditions we've retained, but we've also let go of many that are no longer relevant to today's societal norms."

"So why have others clans clung to outdated cultural practises?" I asked, confused.

Hassan shrugged. "It's the norm. Some of these outdated traditions allow them a certain sense of power or privilege that they need to exert over others."

There was a long silence between us as I mulled over his

words. I walked to the window and looked out, viewing beautiful tracts of land planted with all manner of vegetables for as far as the eye could see. I felt Hassan standing, staring at me, and turned to face him, realising that for some reason, I wasn't afraid of him, nor was I nervous in his presence. I took in his height (he was slightly taller than me), his wavy light brown hair and the sprinkle of soft hair that caressed his cheeks and chin. His eyes were a golden hazel colour, dancing like two lanterns against his skin.

"My sisters Zelekha and Amar are outside. They'd like to come in and help you get ready for the ceremony."

"Today? Already?" I asked, taken by surprise at his announcement.

"It wouldn't be right for us to stay in the same house without a marriage contract," he advised. "This is just a formality."

I nodded again and lifted my eyes as he opened the door and beckoned two giggling girls into the room. They couldn't have been much older than me, looking very much alike and very beautiful, with waves of brown hair peeking out from beneath their scarves.

"Hassan, *shu helwe!*" one exclaimed, as the other came closer and took a strand of my curly hair in her hand. Out of the corner of my eye, I saw Hassan smile quietly, then turn to leave us as the girls started to fuss about me and prepare me for my wedding.

"*Metl el le3bi,*" the other sister commented as they sat me down in the chair at the dressing table and peeled back my scarf.

"Could I perhaps shower first?" I asked, looking at the girls, who stopped fussing around me and looked to Hassan. He nodded and they showed me to the adjoining bathroom, brought me a towel and robe and told me they'd wait outside the room until I was ready to have them back inside.

The shower was a much needed one. I stayed in there for what may have been an hour, shampooing my hair over and over again to get the grime out of it, and scrubbing my skin raw to get the feel of the cell off me. When I finally saw the water run clear as it cascaded off my body, I turned the tap off and wrapped myself in the luxury of the towel, drying off then slipping into the robe. It was strange, I felt, that simple things I had previously taken for granted now felt like a luxury after having been without them for so long.

I sat dumbfounded, looking into the mirror as Amar and Zelekha proceeded to prep and primp my face and hair in preparation for the night. The girls continued to give me compliments on how beautiful I was and how my face looked like a doll's face all done up. I sat rigidly, nervously picking at my nails as I considered the events ahead.

When Hassan had initially proposed his solution to my problem, I had been aghast that he would suggest such a thing. Firstly, technically, I was still engaged to Farouk, who I knew without a doubt I had no feelings for. Wouldn't I have at least missed him a little bit if I did love him? Secondly, the thought of me marrying a stranger I had met a mere few minutes ago seemed like the most bizarre thing to consider. And finally, the fact that I didn't know him, or anything about him or his family, had me pressing all my panic buttons. These people could be anyone, I thought to myself.

"Suit yourself," Hassan had shrugged nonchalantly. "Sleep on it. Think about it. You have only a few days before the clan decide to take matters into their own hands." Meaning, they would kill me and dispose of me and no-one would ever know what had become of Farida.

Hassan was a good man. Of that, I was sure. No man brought himself grief by taking on someone else's problem and went head to head with a neighbouring tribe over what to do with a woman after her use had been expended. He was a good man doing the right thing at the right time.

I couldn't say the same about his mother, who came into the room while the girls were working on me and sniffed at me like I was a stray wet dog that had been dragged in off the road.

"So you're the one," she intimated, eyeing me carefully.

"Isn't she just like a doll, mother?" one of the girls asked, her hand on my shoulder. I still couldn't tell the girls apart; their fussing and fixing had kept me overwhelmed enough without memorising who was who.

"Doll? No," she said forcefully. "She is just like all the others that came before her. All the ones that came to challenge us and make us change our ways, believing theirs was a better way of life. Let's just get one thing straight, little girl..." the older lady said, taking hold of my face ferociously as one of the girls argued that she'd ruin my makeup "...I do things my way here, and you will follow our way of life to the letter. Is that clear?" I could merely blink my response from the crushing hold she had on my face.

"Don't mind mother," one of the girls said after the matriarch left and tears formed in my eyes. "She likes tradition and isn't open to change; she thinks every outsider that comes into our village is here to reform our way of life. And maybe they are. That's why we tend to marry from within our village-to keep our customs alive. She's just worried you'll want to instil your own ways upon us and the men will gladly follow."

Every village in the north had its own customs and traditions. They varied depending on the distance between the villages, but usually neighbouring villages shared some commonality in their ways. I looked down sadly and wondered what I was getting myself into. I yearned for my family and my home and the familiarity of my village. I yearned for the customs we had, but not as a way to override the traditions of my current situation, but in the sense that I knew what our customs were and knew how to abide by them. Here, it felt like I was walking blindly into the unknown.

"Come," one of the girls beckoned."Hassan will be waiting. We must get you into your dress before the ceremony begins."

CHAPTER 18:
FARIDA 1970

"Why did you marry me?" I asked, as Hassan turned to leave the room after the ceremony.

I had been sitting on eggshells throughout the wedding ceremony, nervous about what I was doing and what would come later that evening. Although I had been engaged to Farouk for many months, neither he nor any other man had ever so much as more than held my hand in his own. It was the custom still for a girl to be a virgin on her wedding night, and having never been with a man myself, I had only vague references as to what went on in the marital bed. I did, however, understand that once I was married, I would be sharing my bed with a man and could no longer hoard all the pillows for myself.

Hassan turned back to face me. "What do you mean?"

"Why did you marry me if we're going to sleep in separate rooms?" I clarified.

"I married you because it was the right thing to do. I don't expect anything of you."

"But your mother does," I reminded him, pointing my chin in the direction of the door, where I knew his mother was waiting for us to consummate the marriage. Again, tradition dictated that the groom's mother would view the blood stained bedsheets proving a bride's virginity, then wash and hang them from a line to confirm to the village that the marriage had been consummated successfully. This tradition dated back hundreds of years, and although losing traction in some parts of the country, was still a significant custom in most parts of the North. Amongst the Bedouins, it was an extremely important part of the marital ceremony.

"My mother will understand that you're tired."

"And tomorrow? What will you tell her then?"

Hassan regarded me with a thoughtful look; I knew he could see I would match him with a debate at every turn. I was a planner and always thought ahead. My life had always been structured and organised, but my two month incarceration may have lent credence to my fight or flight instinct. I had come this far; I would do anything to stay alive.

"Let me take care of my mother," Hassan said, as he walked away.

"I married you to save myself," I blurted before he could leave. "I knew what I was signing up for and that this marriage would be long term. I know it won't be feasible for us to conduct a "fake marriage.""

"It's been a long day - you rest. Let me take care of my mother," he repeated, before turning to leave the room.

CHAPTER 19:
HASSAN 1970

I had not anticipated feeling this way. When I offered to marry the girl, it had been a spur of the moment decision. Wallahi, I had merely gone to the bunker out of curiosity and to verify Jihad's story. Perhaps I could intervene and save a life somehow? I had sisters…suppose it was one of my sisters imprisoned in a bunker-wouldn't I want someone to reach out a hand and help her? Why would I turn my back without at the very least trying to find a solution for the young girl? For what sort of a man would I be, to have all this influence and power, yet not use it when it was required most of me? What sort of a man was I to allow an innocent girl to be sent to her certain death?

Yet, I had not expected everything that followed. For starters, the girl was stunning. She possessed a beauty that was altogether otherworldly. The sort of beauty that drew you in and threatened to stomp on your heart if you allowed it free reign. Her eyes were mesmerising; slivers of almond the colour of the darkest night, and her thick black hair fell in waves over her shoulders and past her tiny waist. Even in the state she'd been in, living underground without proper food, no bathing, no change of clothing, she was a sight to behold. It was actually a surprise that Shaikh Waqas had not been taken with her.

My sisters had done an amazing job of preparing her for our wedding. Where she was a natural born beauty as is, after they had primed her, she was breathtaking. I watched as the villagers looked at her, mesmerised, watching her every move. Everyone in the crowd was drawn to her, and I felt a little territorial as I noticed several men's glances linger on her too long. A lot of the women watched her in awe, then whispered amongst themselves, no wonder wondering where she had come from and why none of her family was present. I felt it was prudent that people knew as little as possible about Farida, if only to protect her from the fury of her own village people. The less they knew about her, the less likely it would be that she would be found until I was ready to let her be found. For found, she would eventually be. What I hadn't told Farida was that I had every intention of reuniting her with her family. But this would be on my terms, when I was sure she would be safe from repercussions and accepted back into the family fold.

I closed the door after I left the bedroom, telling Farida that I would see her in the morning. The poor girl was worried about me and how I would explain to my mother why we weren't sleeping in the same room. That was the least of my concerns. I was more concerned with the fact that I couldn't erase the image of Farida in her wedding dress from my mind. She was legally my wife, and I was free to do with her as I wished, but one thing I was not was heartless. I was true to my word – I had offered her a way out of her predicament and nothing more. There had been no talk of consummating the marriage, or living together as a couple under one roof for an indefinite amount of time. I had offered her the only viable way out, and she had taken it. But the fact that she had taken it did not mean I was inclined to take advantage of her. She had been through an ordeal, taken from her family without warning and hidden underground for months without the hope of salvation. I didn't want to compound that by mistreating her or heaping more abuse on her. That just was not my way.

But as I walked away from the room, my heart doing a steady

gallop in my chest, the thought of Farida lingered in my mind, and her face remained etched in my mind as I sought to control my breathing and move as far away from her room as possible. God help me, I thought, wondering how I would get through the next few days in her presence.

CHAPTER 20: FARIDA 1970

The morning after I was married, Hassan woke me with a tall glass of *Ayran* on the bedside table. He drew the curtains back and allowed the sunlight to stream into my room, causing me to sit up in bed dramatically at the sudden unexpected change in lighting.

He took the only armchair in the room, which sat facing the bed, and watched me as I stretched and put a hand to my hair. Even though I was wearing pyjamas, I lifted the blankets to my chest self-consciously, fluttering my eyelashes shyly as I looked around the room, anywhere but at him.

"You should drink your ayran before it gets warm."

"*Sabah el kheir* to you too."

He chuckled and crossed a leg over his knee as he watched me drink the thick yoghurt. Which I had to admit, was better than any I'd had before. As though he could read my thoughts, Hassan said "fresh goat yoghurt." I stopped drinking and looked at him for further explanation. "We herd our own goats. In fact, all the neighbouring villages in this region are renowned for their supply of goat yoghurt. It's some of the best in the whole Middle East."

"Definitely the best I've ever had."

"We grow our own vegetables. We have orchards for as far as the eye can see. Grains, seeds...we subsist off the land."

"I don't understand. I know you're Bedouins. How do you have your own land? Your own home?"

"We descended from Bedouins and remain under the umbrella of the Bedouin society. However, some of us have opted for a more settled, urbanised lifestyle. We buy land, we grow the land and build infrastructure and homes, while maintaining our values and traditions. The land we bought here," Hassan continued, making a sweep with his hand in a semi-circle around him "is land no-one would have thought to buy. It was low lying, eroded, clumpy earth...swampy in some sections. We bought it for mere cents per metre because no-one else wanted it. And we've made it into something that will remain for generations to come."

Hassan spoke quite proudly of the communitie's achievements. I could see he had a deep seated fondness for the tribe as a whole and their way of life. Yet I could see also that they had retained a lot of their tradition and continued to practise their culture at every possible opportunity.

"The house-what I've seen of it, is beautiful," I told him, taking another sip of the yoghurt.

"I'll show you the remainder of the house today. Yesterday was a busy day; there was no time."

"You don't have to work?" I asked him.

He scoffed. "A new groom has the right to take a few days off to spend them with his bride."

I regarded him carefully. I knew so little about him, but I had a sudden itch to know anything and everything about him. For even though I missed my home and my family terribly, no-one had ever treated me with such kindness. I couldn't even recall a time when Farouk and I had conversed in more than one word sentences.

"Where did you go?" Hassan asked, after I had been quietly entranced in my own world for several minutes. I snapped out of my reverie and looked up at him, a soft smile playing on his lips.

"I'm happy to be alive, Hassan," I whispered. "I would never wish on any girl to go through what I went through and live in fear that she would be killed."

"You're my wife now. You're protected as long as you carry my name and live in my home."

"Wasn't there someone else?"

"What do you mean?" he asked.

"You married me. But wasn't there someone else in your life you would have rather married?"

"No. Maybe. A long time ago. When I was 17," he laughed. "About your age now. But obviously, I was too young. She's married with eight kids now, I think." I laughed along with him as he made a ridiculous face at the number eight.

"And how old are you now?" I asked.

"27 years," he replied, his eyes questioning me on something, although I don't think it was my age, as that was quite apparent from the paperwork we filled in for the Shaikh yesterday, but was maybe a concern as to what I thought about the age gap between us. I had just turned 18, so there was little under ten years between us.

"I just realised this is the longest conversation I've held with anyone in two months."

"Who was the last person you had a conversation with before you were taken?" he asked.

"My sister Aujene," I replied wistfully. "She's a few years younger than me, but she's my best friend." I turned to look at him, a hopeful look in my eyes. "Do you think I'll ever be able to see her again?"

"In time, perhaps. For now, let's concentrate on cementing your place here in our village. We also need to furnish our home-the bedroom was all I had time to prepare, but we can change it if you don't like it. Shall we have breakfast then I can show you around the house?"

CHAPTER 21: FARIDA 1970

The house was bigger than the house I shared with my parents and five siblings on one single level. It had been designed in a way where the living rooms and kitchen were on the ground floor, with pillars curtaining the outside of the house to maintain the boundary of a wrap around balcony. The first floor had four bedrooms, two bathrooms and a sitting area. The master suite, where I had slept last night, while sparsely furnished, was the biggest of the rooms and Hassan suggested a full couch and rest area so it was more like a suite. I wasn't used to such extravagance and all these new ideas designs, in an era where houses were one storey and more compact, overwhelmed me as he finally showed me to the kitchen.

Zelekha was busy at the stove and Amar was chopping away at the bench. They both smiled brightly as they saw me and cooed *"Kif el 3arous?"*, to which I blushed. How long could this charade go on before people actually found out that we hadn't consummated the marriage and tongues started wagging, I wondered.

"Breakfast is almost ready," Zelekha announced, setting down a plate of fried eggs and labne, while Amar set down the chopped sides and olives.

"Won't you stay for breakfast with us," I asked, as the girls made to leave.

"Oh no, we just came by to check up on you. It's customary for the bride and groom to get spoilt for a few days ," Amar answered with a wink. "We'll check in on you a little later."

And with that, the two girls left in a flurry of fabric as their dresses sashayed around them.

"We'll have to eat here," Hassan said, as we stood at the kitchen bench. "Remind me to order the dining table when we meet with the carpenter later."

"You know, I've heard in some villages, people still eat on the floor," I reminded him, by way of telling him that I didn't mind the dining conditions at all.

"That's an idea," he smirked. "Would you like me to get the *Haseeri* which we haven't bought yet?"

Together we laughed at the situation we found ourselves in as we started to eat the food his sisters had prepared for us. We ate in comfortable silence and I mused at how easy it had been to fall into the role of his wife. It amazed me still that he had married me just to save me and had not asked anything of me in return.

"I have a wedding gift for you," Hassan said, smoothing his hands down the front of his jeans in what I would later identify as a nervous tic. We had literally polished off our plates, then placed them in the sink where Hassan refused to let me do the dishes, advising his mother's housekeeper Lita would be around later to do them and complete for us some basic household chores.

"You've already done enough for me. I don't need any gifts, Hassan."

"This is a special gift. I want you to have it."

He led me to the back porch, where we stood looking out towards the fields. We were fortunate enough to have a beautiful open view of the land from the rear of our home. The front faced other homes that were all scattered in a semi-circular fashion with a huge open yard in the middle where the children often played.

Hassan folded his tongue in his mouth a gave a low whistle. Soon enough, there was a flutter of wings, and he held his right arm up as a beautiful blue bird came to rest on it. He turned to face me and held his arm up so I could get a better look at the marvellous creature which had spirited itself onto our porch.

"This is Port, he's a Sapphire-bellied Hummingbird."

I rubbed softly under his beak and my finger caressed its feathers softly as I took in the vibrant hues of blues and greens and greys that made up his armour. It was the most colourfully exotic thing I'd ever seen, a bird so out of place in this so ordinary place. It stood spectacularly on Hassan's arm, folding its neck to the side as I tickled it on one side and laughed as it stretched lazily against my fingers.

"It's the most spectacular creature I've ever seen."

"Careful, he'll get upset if you refer to him as a creature," Hassan explained, and the bird perked when I used the word. "Port, sing for me."

There was a soft pause, then Port began to buzz and chirp. There followed a whistling tune, soft but mellow, and more chirps, like he was singing a beautiful orchestral tune.

"This Hummingbird is an endangered species native to Columbia. Don't ask me how, but it ended up on our side of the world somehow. Found him on the port on our way back from a fishing trip. His wing was badly damaged and he was limping on gravelly rocks, at death's door. I brought him home, thinking for sure he wouldn't make it, but somehow, miraculously, he did. He's been here ever since and has never left my side."

"He truly is the most beautiful thing I've ever seen," I murmured, as Hassan transported the bird to my arm.

"Port, make sure you look after this little woman," Hassan said, stroking the bird's feathers.

"I'll take good care of him," I promised Hassan. "Does he have a cage?"

"No, he's free to fly around. Never goes far."

"Hear that, little one," I quipped. "You're free as a bird! Freer than I was a few days ago." Hassan laughed at my reference to my incarceration and reminded me that we had to get going if we were to make it to the carpenter before he closed.

I sent my arm flying in the air, and Port shot off like a rocket and zoomed into the sky, doing a sort of happy dance as he looped around in circles and flew through the wind, his feathers a blazing cacophony of hues in the sky.

"You see that?" Hassan asked. "He's just as happy to have met you as I am."

CHAPTER 22:
TALA 1970

The day the world ended could be measured by the disappearance of the sun, the stunted growth of the leaves in spring, the murky grey green water that lashed at the creek bed running through the valley. Time seemed to catapult to a stop, its frenzied seconds like an ache in the bosoms of mothers and the souls of fathers.

The one thing that tethered the community together was that familial bond we all shared. Everyone related to someone. Everyone related to someone who related to someone who related back to the village. We were a family. We were comfort. And then all of a sudden, there was a yawning chasm where laughter and love and solidarity used to be.

Odd, that...that something so terrible could cause such anguish, divide a valley, and cause a once peaceful and loving community to turn on one another, for fear that one family's misfortune would taint another's.

89 days after my Farida went missing, the second Farida disappeared. She, too, was taken while working the olive grove, snatched from within the grove when she went to relieve a full bladder. Never in a million years had anyone anticipated a second disappearance-what was that saying "lightning doesn't strike in the same place twice". The same could be said about girls going missing. It was not a common occurrence, but now

the village had lost two girls, and life would never be the same again.

Everyone thought it odd that both girls had the same name. They also had many other similarities, and indeed, had been friends in passing on many an occasion. They shared many commonalities-small, petite frames, luminous black eyes that dazzled with light, shiny black hair that fell in a straight sheet to their waists. Both girls were young and beautiful, though not educated. In those days, girls receiving an education was not a priority-a girl's place was to marry and bear children, creating a happy sanctuary for her spouse. The similarities between the two girls, when you thought about it, were eerie; they could have easily passed for sisters.

Immediately, the rumours started...

This Farida had used the first Farida's disappearance to run away and gain her independence.

It must be a villager taking our girls-how else would an outsider be able to infiltrate our close knit community whilst evading detection?

And the most ridiculous of all the theories-the curse of the original Farida, her ghost brought to life to avenge her murder by ridding the village of all those who had been named after her.

The rumours just kept coming, the ladies of the village with their wagging tongues sending the local menfolk on ridiculous search expeditions with each story they concocted and swore was "verified". So while the men banded together to search for the missing Faridas, acknowledging a serious problem that required urgent attention, the women of the village banded together to unwittingly deter, rather than enable, a speedy resolution to the matter at hand.

All but a few. A handful of women grouped together to support Rabiaa in her grief over her missing daughter and assist, where they could, in the maintenance and upkeep of her family home until the woman was on her feet again. As the men searched the countryside, the small group of women surrounded the grief stricken mother of the second Farida and urged her to remain strong.

It was on one such morning, as a neighbour brought Rabiaa a glass of warm milk and dates, urging the woman to drink and eat something, that Rabiaa's head snapped up decisively and she sat up and straightened her back, then cleared her throat. Surrounded by a bevy of neighbours, Rabiaa scanned each and every face before she spoke.

"I must go to see Tala. She will know what to do"

The women all looked at each other quizzically, obviously realising the same thing all at once, with no one courageous enough to voice the unspeakable-that the first Farida still had not been found, and probably would never be.

"Sister, what good will that do you? It will only compound your grief. Tala was here yesterday and she passed on her thoughts and prayers to you"

"I cannot be alone in this grief," Rabiaa merely whispered. "No one can possibly know what this feels like unless they have lived it."

The women stared at their feet awkwardly, acknowledging her words whilst also secretly praising God that their daughters were fine. And they would remain fine, as not one girl in the village had been allowed to leave her home since the second Farida's disappearance.

"I hope and I pray to the Almighty that none of you will ever have to succumb to this deep wound that is lacerating my heart. I thank you all, and appreciate what you have done for me, but I cannot just sit here feeling sorry for myself when I could be doing so much more. And you, all of you, it is time for you to return to your homes and guard your daughters. Guard them well. We know not what evil lurks in our midst."

Most of the women dispersed at that, having been discharged of their duties, whilst a handful accompanied Rabiaa to Tala's home, where they rapped on the heavy metal door and awaited entry. Shortly, there was a shuffling behind the door, which was answered by Tala's youngest daughter, Nazma. She pointed to the rear of the breezeway, where they could see Tala sitting in the grove beyond her home. She sat with her back to the door, hunched over and poking at a burning fire underneath a large washing cauldron. After removing their shoes, the women entered the home and tentatively made their way to the rear of the house.

"Em El Banaat" Rabiaa breathed, by way of greeting, suddenly realising she had come empty handed. It was customary in their little part of the world, when visiting another, especially for the first time, to bring a little gift. Some home made sweets, or a tub of yoghurt, anything that would show the homeowner the visitor's token of appreciation for accepting them into their home. Rabiaa realised, too late, that she had never visited Tala before, and commiserated the fact that they were socialising under such miserable circumstances.

A rumble of murmurs and greetings followed as Tala rose to meet the women, welcoming them into her home. Nazma brought stools woven from straw, on which the women sat in a circle around the cauldron of fire, sipping cinnamon tea. Rabiaa looked at Tala and wondered if her own face would mirror Tala's grief after months of not having seen her daughter.

"We are united in grief, *ya Em El Banaat*," Rabiaa started. "We barely know each other but in passing, but I feel we share a unique grief that no one else can touch. Whilst these beautiful women have been my saviours throughout this ordeal, I come to commiserate with you, as only you and I can measure the magnitude of this loss."

"Akkkh ya ekhti," sighed Tala. "I wish I could give you the answers you seek. I have searched high and low, followed every single lead I was fed, no matter how ludicrous and far fetched it seemed. The only constant for me was my unwavering belief that God has a plan. For me. For you. For Farida. For both our daughters. I have put my faith in the Almighty, and hope that one day our daughters return to us. This is the only thing that allows me to sleep at night. The firm belief that they will return."

"But how, Em El Banaat. How do you go on with your life "not knowing". Is she alive? Is she warm? Has she eaten? What happened to her? What has become of her? Does it not eat you alive not knowing?"

"My dear sister Rabiaa, the "not knowing" is what led me down a deep and dark path. I almost lost myself. In my quest to find out what happened to my Farida, I almost lost myself and my family. At some point, you must evaluate the balance between knowing and dying inside and not knowing yet surviving. Not knowing gives me hope - that one day, I will know, and I will have closure. I will have her back again. I couldn't go on the way I was at the expense of my family, my other children. They still need me. Farida still needs me."

Tala looked down sadly at the fire as she stirred. A heavy silence followed, and the women sat mesmerised as she sat stirring the stick inside the cauldron over and over again. Rabiaa, as entrenched as the others in this most ordinary of tasks as Tala continued to stir, thought how she absolutely had needed this visit to highlight the ordinariness of life going on. Tala looked up and caught Rabiaa's eyes fixated on the stirring of the cauldron.

"So you see" she began again, continuing to stir "Farida may be lost to you now. But she will be found again one day. Let the men do what they are meant to do. Go home and look after your home and it's inhabitants. Feel your grief. Own your pain. But know this, there are others that need you and depend on you. You can't lose yourself to your sorrow and let it destroy you. Farida will be back one day."

The women started to walk away solemnly as Rabiaa delivered one last hug to Tala and thanked her for her hospitality.

"You come back and see me when you need to share your grief. I will be waiting. And don't forget-your grief is only as heavy as you allow it to be."

CHAPTER 23: FARIDA 1970

I quickly realised my husband's importance in the way that people dealt with him. The carpenter just about bowed when he entered the house and deferred to Hassan as *"amirna"*, "our prince." He advised a crew of men would work around the clock to have our furniture installed by the end of the week, which I found was a miraculous feat in itself.

"I'll have Em Nemaat come past and speak with your wife about soft furnishings and the kitchen," the carpenter said, for which I was immensely grateful that I wouldn't have to go through the process myself, as I had no idea where to start.

After the carpenter took his leave, Hassan suggested we go for a drive. I hadn't had a chance yet to take in my surrounds or appreciate the beauty of the land here. Now as we walked to the car, I lagged behind Hassan as I took in the long wide drive-way that led to where we were. There were houses on either side of the drive, which led in a flourish as the land circled at the end of the drive and ended with our home. Our house was literally the one at the end of the "street", directly opposite the mouth of the drive. It was also the grandest and I gasped as I looked up at the soaring peaks of the magnificent house made of stone.

"My mother lives in that house," Hassan said, pointing to the right of our house, and as though he had conjured her merely by uttering her name, she appeared at her front door then hurried down towards us. I could see several other people were also at their doors...women sweeping imaginary dust off their stairs, and a scattering of children running around. Two men sat at the front of a nearby house smoking and drinking *ahwi*, regarding us curiously. All eyes turned to us as my mother in law reached us.

"Shu, ya ebni, la wayn rayeh?" my mother in law asked, her voice sharp and blunt with reproach.

"We're going for a drive, *emi*," Hassan replied.

"Ya ebni, 3ayb. 3ayb alaykon tutlaou hayk kum yawm ba3ed el3res."

"Mashi emi. You go inside and you won't see anything."

"Bas, ya ebni," she implored, looking at her son sharply.

"Rouki emi, it's just a drive. I want to show my new bride our area. We'll have some sweets and return before nightfall. As for the villagers and their wagging tongues, let them talk. This is one tradition I don't agree with."

And with that, Hassan herded me into the car and we drove down the long driveway covered with the shade of pine trees and left the village, admiring the seaside as we drove along the main road that led to Syria.

At a local ice cream parlour, the owner again deferred to Hassan with utmost respect, congratulating him on his marriage and offering us anything we wanted free of charge. We grabbed our cones and crossed the road to sit on the low brick fence that divided the road from the sea and stared out at the ocean.

"Everyone knows you," I commented, looking over at Hassan as he watched the fishermen below.

"We're all tribesmen here. Even though we may belong to different clans, everyone pretty much knows everyone else."

"No," I tsked, shaking my head. "Everyone I've met reveres you. It's almost awe-like."

Hassan said nothing, retrieving a bottle of water from the car that he tipped at an angle so we could wash our hands.

"We have one more stop to make," he said, as we climbed back into the car and headed in the opposite direction of where we'd come. I turned in my seat to face Hassan, admiring the soft chisel of his cheekbones in private. I silently breathed a sigh of relief that I got lucky and married a man that was easy on the eyes. Hassan was good looking, respectful, what people in the village called an *"abadoi"*, literally translated to mean "strong hero." There was no denying that Hassan was the spokesperson for his clan, revered amongst other neighbouring clans, his word final whilst also just. The fact that we had met under such unusual circumstances which resulted in our marriage was a bizarre concept even I couldn't grasp.

"Did you ever think you would meet the woman you would marry the way you met me?" I asked him.

"Always so curious, aren't you, little one," Hassan commented.

"We're going to live together-probably forever-shouldn't we know about each other?"

"If I answer all your all questions today, what will we talk about tomorrow?"

A smile spread across my face as his words infused my soul. The mere thought of him wanting to have a conversation with me tomorrow warmed my heart.

"We'll always have something to talk about," I told him. "And when we run out of things to discuss, I will create more things for us to talk about."

CHAPTER 24: FARIDA 1970

Our final destination for the day happened to be a jewellery store. The sun was almost setting as we arrived. The owner came rushing out to stand by the driver's door so he could greet Hassan. He seemed excited to see him, and the two men slapped each other's backs in a friendly manner as they walked toward the store.

Hassan turned back when he realised I was still sitting in the car.

"Farida, *yallah*. Come down," he called, holding the store door open for me as I approached.

"This is Maher, my oldest friend," Hassan introduced us.

Maher smiled and nodded in greeting, apologising that he and his wife had not been able to attend our wedding because his wife had gone into labour that day.

"*Shu ya 3arees*," Maher joked "How is married life treating you?"

Hassan clapped Maher on the back and asked him how father-hood was treating him in response. I realised that Hassan had a steady, subtle way of detracting from a conversation rather than answering in half-truths. I watched him carefully, eager to learn every facet of this intriguing man who had done me an enormous service and treated me as an equal.

It was ironic, the way I had grown up and been surrounded my whole life in an environment dominated by males who treated their female counterparts as maids, rather than life long partners. This had always been the norm in Tul Ghosn. Women didn't have a voice, were told what to do, their life choices dictated either by their father, husband or brother. My father used to say *"Elmara bi rebe3 akl"*, or "a female has a quarter of a brain", another way to describe a woman's mind in a derogatory way. Granted, it was a condescending phrase jokingly passed around through the generations to describe women, but my father, like many others, took it to heart and interpreted the phrase literally.

"Farida, *waynik???*" I heard Hassan's voice calling me as I snapped out of my reverie and focused on my husband. "That's my Farida," he said, turning to Maher with a wink "always daydreaming."

"May God bless and protect you both," Maher stated. "I'm glad to see you happy."

Maher brought out a few trays of gold and placed them on the glass countertop. I looked on silently as he placed one after the other in a neat row in front of us, their gold winking and glimmering in beckoning welcome.

"I have more in the safe if none of these are suitable," Maher explained. "I am showing you here the latest arrivals."

Hassan picked up a necklace and balanced in in his hands, turning it over and smoothing his hands over the distressed metal that formed part of the design. "What do you think, Farida...do you like this one?"

I stood mute and shrugged, watching him as he continued to

collect and inspect a series of necklaces and bracelets. I wasn't sure what we were doing here and what was required of me, so I just stood waiting for further instruction.

"You don't like any of them?" Hassan asked. I shrugged again and was at a loss for words.

"Let me get you a few pieces from the safe," Maher suggested, leaving us alone to retrieve more gold from a back room.

"What's wrong?" Hassan asked, lifting my chin so my eyes and his were level.

"What are we doing here?" I asked him.

I could see there were a million thoughts and questions swirling in Hassan's mind as he regarded me with soft eyes. "I didn't have a chance to buy you a wedding gift," he explained.

I looked at him quizzically, not fully comprehending what he was trying to tell me. Finally, he spoke, explaining that he had brought me here so that I could choose my own wedding gift.

"But you've already given me Port."

"No," he laughed. "Port was a gift. This is your wedding gift. It's customary among our clan that the groom buy his bride some jewellery when they marry."

"You don't need to buy me anything, Hassan. You've already done enough."

"I know that a lot of what's happening…and what's going to happen, is probably not what you're used to. You need to know that you are safe and things are done maybe a little differently here."

"I have this exquisite piece here that I was going to give my wife to celebrate the birth of Ruzaina," Maher said, coming back into the room inspecting an amazing wide gold cuff bangle with an intricate weaving of knots.

"Something that is meant for someone must not be given to anyone else," Hassan admonished his friend.

"This is from a set of three that were made explicitly for a customer who later decided she did not want them after all and asked me to sell them for her. Only three of a kind...if you like this one, I can obtain one of the others for my wife."

"It *is* beautiful," Hassan mused, turning the cuff over in his hand, before lifting my hand in his to snap the cuff around my wrist. He held my hand out and admired the bangle, which seemed to sit perfectly against my skin, like it had been commissioned specifically for my hand.

"It's beautiful," I agreed, when Hassan asked me what I thought about the bangle.

"*Tayeb*," Hassan said, turning to his friend. "That's settled. Create a matching set for it and let me know when it's ready to be picked up."

I stood aside admiring the bangle as the two men exchanged salutations before we got into the car and made our way home.

"Thank you," I whispered, still admiring the gold, twisting it around my wrist so every side grazed my skin "it's beautiful."

"The one who wears it is beautiful," Hassan murmured, and I blushed as I looked up at him.

CHAPTER 25:
FARIDA 1970

Hassan and I settled into a comfortable routine in our married life. At daybreak, Hassan would wake me and we would kneel together in prayer, supplicating for God to grant us strength in our steadfastness and mercy in our weaknesses.

I would make Hassan a breakfast, usually of eggs and sujuk and labne, which he would devour with the zest of a man going to war.

We still slept in separate rooms, creating the perfect illusion of a happy couple, with no one the wiser as to what happened in our home behind closed doors.

He always started his day early, tending to the fields to oversee the management, doing the rounds to make sure everything in the village and neighbouring regions was running smoothly and without issue, and meeting with other clan members to touch base on any issues that may have arisen overnight or problems that required urgent attention. He would put in a day's work and be home, usually by 3pm, just in time for *Asr* prayer.

About six weeks into our marriage, when the clock had struck three thirty and there was still no sign of Hassan, I fidgeted and fretted, suddenly missing his loud entry into the home every afternoon at 3pm. At four thirty, with my anxiety levels peaking, I made my way next door to my mother in law's home.

"*Mart 3ami,*" I breathed, coming to sit beside her on the couch. She still had not warmed up to me, but the saving grace was that we stayed out of each other's paths, and when an occasion called for us to be in each other's company, we were nothing if not civil. "*Mart 3ami,* Hassan hasn't come home yet," I told her, and I could see, by the way she looked at my concerned face, that where she wasn't immediately concerned, she was after she saw the terrified look on my face.

"*Ma3laysh...bikoun et3khar bil shegel,*" she told me, trying to allay my fears. He must have been delayed at work.

"*La3, mart 3ami,*" I argued. "He always sends someone to let me know if he's going to be late."

My mother in law rose slowly from her seat, suddenly alert to my misgivings, and asked Lita to fetch her husband from the garden. When Lita's husband emerged in the doorway, my mother in law directed him to take the car and drive out into the fields to see if he could locate the whereabouts of either Hassan or Waleed, who she believed to be together.

I sunk into the couch after the man had left in a hurry, my heart palpitating quickly at the thought of something happening to my husband. For even though our marriage had come about in the most unlikeliest of ways, and though we still kept separate sleeping quarters, I considered him my best friend and the rock behind which I felt the safest.

My mother in law, in a seamless act of mercy, came to stand by the couch and looked down at me. I could see that she not only pitied me, but she now held concerns for the safety of her two sons. I remained seated on the couch, joined by Amar and Zelekha, who by now also held the same fears as I did, the thought of going home to an empty house the last thing on my mind. I moved from my place only to pray and make supplications that the men would return home to us safely.

At five o'clock, we sat tethered to our fear, which had grown out of control since Lita's husband had gone out and not returned. We were alerted to the sound of the outside world by a sharp thud and a rush of men's voices as car doors were being opened and quickly slammed shut. We all rushed to the door, where we saw men being carried out of cars, heading towards my house. I ran out, not noticing that I had left my shoes behind, entering the house right behind the village doctor, who it seemed had already been alerted to an incident and had sat outside waiting for the cars to arrive.

Lita's husband and another man acted as crutches, supporting Hassan as they entered the house. Waleed was held on either side, by his hands and feet, by two villagers who grunted and tried their hardest not to drop the man. All the women of the house gathered into my home as the doctor started to work on Hassan, who was conscious, but seriously delirious. I could see a patch of blood where it seeped out of his right hip and cascaded down his leg.

I stood stock still, not daring to move, holding my breath out of an unconscious fear that if I let it out, something in Hassan's condition would change. I could only look on in horror as the doctor cut open Hassan's shirt to reveal the deep gash that had lacerated my husband's side. I felt my mother in law move as she hurried into the kitchen, where Waleed had been set down on the kitchen table.

"Hot water, towels, the wound needs cleaning," the doctor screamed, and I could see that Zelekha and Amar had already jumped into action and were preparing the doctors instructions as he ran to tend to Waleed.

Hassan fell in and out of consciousness, but not before he

called my name and beckoned me over, grabbing my left hand with this and clinging to it as I sat by his head. The doctor alternated between Hassan and Waleed, ensuring both got the care they needed, his wife at his side, obviously having been trained to aid him.

"Farida," Hassan whispered, in between his many bouts of unconsciousness.

"Shhh, I'm here," I told him, smoothing his hair back gently.

"Bandage will need to be changed daily," the doctor said, as he wrapped the last of the muslin around Hassan's torso and injected him with antibiotics.

He went in to check on Waleed and came back momentarily, satisfied that his work was done and both men would recover nicely.

I saw my mother in law standing in a corner of the room with four men, deep in thought as they relayed the events of the afternoon which had resulted in Hassan and Waleed almost losing their lives. I could see her as her face gave way to her fury and her voice rose, cursing the perpetrators who dared lay a finger on her sons.

CHAPTER 26:
FARIDA 1970

For the next ten days and nights, Hassan lay in my bed, where I tended to his every need and nursed him back to health. He drifted in and out of consciousness, the doctor explaining that the loss of blood would render him helpless for a few days until he got his strength back. I made him hot chicken soup which he didn't eat because he was never conscious enough to take in a meal, put a wet cloth on his forehead when his temperature would spike, and summoned the doctor for fear of infection.

"He'll need another round of antibiotics," the doctor advised, preparing his needle.

"We should take him to the hospital," my mother in law decided.

"That is your choice," the doctor started "but there is nothing they can do for him that I can't do for him here. Plus, there will be questions."

"I have faith in God that my sons will heal no matter where they are," the old woman surmised, then dropped the matter and allowed the doctor to administer the injection. She visited Hassan daily, sometimes twice, commiserating with me that his condition wasn't getting any better, but steadfast in her firm belief that things would turn around soon. Waleed, too, who had been moved to his mother's home after that first night, came in to see Hassan daily. His condition had seemed more dire than Hassan's, but he was now visiting his brother and willing him back to good health.

On the twelfth day of his road to recovery, Hassan woke and found me not near him. I stood at the kitchen sink looking out at the fields, a deep crater sitting in the pit of my stomach as I wondered what would become of us. Amar, who I had entrusted to watch over Hassan while I took a few minutes to myself to decompress, came running into the kitchen screeching that Hassan was awake and was asking for me.

Afterward, I couldn't even recall how I came to be standing by Hassan's bedside, only that I somehow flew, floating magically on air, like I had teleported myself into his presence. This was the speed with which I reached him. Amar left us alone as I closed in on him, sitting in the chair adjacent to his chest and taking his hand in both of mine when he held his out. I wrapped my hands around his and held it to my mouth, breathing him in and exhaling, my gaze matching his in intensity as a thousand unspoken words passed between us.

"Where did you go?" he rasped.

"Shhh, rest. I was just downstairs resting."

Hassan shook his head slowly back and forth, then looked up at the ceiling, almost helplessly.

"Do you want something to eat?"

He moved his head to the left as if to say no and continued to look at the ceiling.

"Hassan," I spoke, guiding his gaze back down to me. "What can I do for you?" I asked.

"Stay," he croaked.

I had never seen him so vulnerable. I left the chair and climbed into the bed with him, careful not to come in contact with his bandaged side. I lay on my side and wrapped my arm across his chest, cradling my head in the crook of his arm. He turned his head and sniffed my hair, inhaling deeply as he breathed in my scent, as though that would somehow breath him back to life.

"All I could think about, when it was happening, was…"

I shushed him again and told him that we would talk later, when he got his strength back. But Hassan merely ignored me, starting to speak again, like there was something sitting heavily on his chest and he needed to confide his worries.

"All I could think about was you, and what would become of you if something happened to me," he said, in between heavy breaths.

"I'm just glad you're okay and you came back to me."

He brought his head closer to mine until the edge of his forehead tipped and touched my own, holding it there in reverence.

"Help me up," he stated.

"You can't Hassan. You need to rest."

"I'm not going to get better laying in bed. I need movement."

"Hassan, please, let me help you sit up, but you need to stay in bed until you're better."

"Make me some tea, please, while I shower." He was forceful and I could see there would be no swaying him. The *abadoi* needed to get up and move around and control everything around him so that things ran efficiently.

"You can't shower alone. I'll fill the tub and bathe you," I offered.

Hassan shook his head and defended his efforts to shower himself.

"Whether you shower or bathe," I announced "I will be in there with you. I will not leave you in there alone. So make it easy on me and let me bathe you."

"That would involve you seeing me naked," he tried to smirk and failed miserably.

"You're my husband. I'm allowed to see you naked. And it's about time that you stopped playing coy and let me be your wife," I said, injecting some humour into the conversation. I was glad he couldn't see my face, still hidden under his arm, otherwise he would have seen the nervous blush that covered my face.

"Run the bath then," he decided, after several seconds of silence had passed.

I rose gingerly, avoiding his injury at all costs, and moved to the bathroom, where I ran the bath, adding some healing salt to the water.

Hassan was sitting on the side of the bed when I emerged from the bathroom.

"You should have waited for me," I admonished, helping him stand up and heaving his arm over my shoulder so he could lean on me and support himself.

"You don't have to do this. I can get one of the men to come and help me up."

"I'm your wife," I repeated. "I'm just as responsible for you as you are for me."

It took me a while to get him undressed and take off his bandage. I layered plastic wrap around his torso and secured it with a pin to minimise water getting in to the wound.

"You ready to come out?" I asked him, after he'd been in the bath for thirty minutes and the water had grown tepid.

He nodded once and moved to rise from the water. I gave him my shoulder to lean on and grabbed a towel for him so I could dry him off before we entered the bedroom.

After I had put a new bandage around his wound and we were dressed, Hassan sat up in bed and watched me as I brushed my hair loose of any knots.

"Have you ever cut your hair?" he asked me.

I shook my head in reply.

"Don't ever cut it," he warned me.

I watched him watching me in the dressing table mirror as I continued to brush my hair. He looked like he was in pain as his eyes covered every inch of my face and body. He had never been so blatant about his desire for me, and I realised I liked the attention he gave me and the power I held over him in this strangely fascinating life we'd built for ourselves.

"How about some tea?" I offered, rising from the bench.

CHAPTER 27: FARIDA 1970

"Are you going to tell me what happened?" I asked Hassan, as we sat on the balcony looking out at the fields, enjoying a rare day of sunshine in an otherwise gloomy world.

"You haven't heard yet?"

"I want to hear it from you. In your words. We share everything every evening when you get home. How my day went. What you got up to...In this instance, you've been out of commission for a few days, but I'd like to hear it from you."

Hassan sighed and adjusted himself in his seat. I offered him another pillow and set it behind his back so he was comfortable.

"The day started like any other," he told me, and I watched him intensely as he relayed the story to me. "I checked on the crop, met with a few other clan members to discuss issues that had arisen, then picked up Waleed and we went to a meeting with a neighbouring shaikh. We were on the way home via the road that cuts past the port. There's a little vagabond setup right there on the beach-I'm not sure if you've ever seen it. Refugees passing through. They stay a while, then pack up and move along. Then another group of Bedouins will set up residence there, and so the cycle continues. Every few months, its' a different tribe. They don't stay here long enough to put down roots, and the clans rotate so often, it's hard to ever know exactly who's staying there unless you go in and meet them."

"We've lived side by side with them for decades, there has never been a problem, but on this particular day, as we were driving along the road, I noticed that the camp had been infiltrated by a couple of horsemen. They wore *kaffiyehs* around half their faces to protect their identity, and rode around the camp, brandishing swords that they slashed through the vinyl of the tents, tearing the campers' homes to shreds. The women were screaming, the children huddled in a corner, fearful and frightened. A few men had stood up to them, but they were helpless against the horsemen; one older man received a boot to his face and was knocked over." He looked down at his hands and took a deep breath before continuing.

"Waleed made a quick detour and we entered the camp, hoping to scare the men off, but they still stayed and couldn't be convinced to leave. I asked them what they wanted and they told me the clan knew what they wanted and for us to stay out of it."

"But you wouldn't do that," I whispered, so sure about what my husband would not let pass. He shook his head and smiled at me.

"You know me so well, better than I know myself," he told me. "In these areas, no one looks the other way when someone is being terrorised. What sort of a shaikh would I be if I didn't offer my help, regardless whether or not they are my people."

"Go on."

"I jumped out of the car and tried to reason with them, but they were very particular about removing themselves from any responsibility towards their actions. Even when one of the clansmen referred to me as "shaikhna", they would not be swayed. They didn't care who became collateral damage, so long as they inflicted as much damage as possible. When I ordered them off the land, they brandished their swords my way. I ducked out of their way, but not fast enough, and the blade nipped me in the side. Waleed was thrown metres in the air when one of the horsemen charged him and knocked him unconscious. That's when they left. After they delivered their message."

"And what message would that be?" I asked him, concerned.

"Waleed has since met with some of the tribesmen from that clan. There's an investor that's just purchased the plot of land opposite the shanty town. He plans to repurpose the land into a mall, with a high rise hotel and several restaurants, in the hopes that the development will attract international tourists. The vagabond village obscures the beach and doesn't provide the development with a great view."

"So he's sending in troublemakers to try to get the vagabonds to leave," I surmised.

Hassan smiled. "You're more than just a beautiful face," he told me, proud that I had caught on quickly.

"What will you do? The beach belongs to no-one and it's out of your region."

"That's true on both counts, but we won't allow people to terrorise our neighbours. It's an unequal fight. These are helpless men and women with nowhere else to go."

"I don't know what I would've done if something had happened to you."

"Would you really have missed me?" he asked.

"You know I would."

CHAPTER 28: FARIDA 1970

After a few more days of recovery, Hassan was able to get up and move around on his own, albeit slowly. He had requested the presence of a few men to come to the house so they could discuss some business that required immediate attention. Waleed, by now feeling a lot better, sat in on the meeting and I could hear the men as they finished up their meeting and told a few jokes on their way out of the house.

"Are you happy here, Farida?" Hassan asked me, as we sat sipping tea at the dining table after dinner.

The question was so far out of left field, that I didn't know how to respond, so I laughed it off.

"What a way to change the subject."

"Answer the question," Hassan said, narrowing his eyes at me.

"Where is this coming from?" I asked, setting my teacup on the table and turning to face him.

Hassan sighed and his head fell forward onto his chest as he realised how his words must have come out harsher than he meant them to.

"The whole time I lay there bleeding out, all I could think about was you, wondering what would become of you if something happened to me. I sat there wondering what my punishment would be for taking you from one prison and placing you in another. That was my reckoning, I guess."

I said nothing, merely listened attentively as his words poured out. I dissected every morsel of every word he threw at me. These were the moments I lived for, when Hassan would come home and regale me with stories and jokes and his thoughts. If anything, he had become a best friend to me more than anything else. The chemistry of lovers was there, sure, but we hadn't crossed that bridge, and as much as I was excited for the next chapter in our story, I was also apprehensive with fear that crossing that line from friends to lovers may alter the fabric of our relationship somehow.

"And now?" I asked.

"I still worry about you, Farida. And I'm willing to take that leap with you into the wild to see what we can become. But I need to know what you want."

"You thought about sending me home?" I asked, finally realising what he was getting at. If he wasn't here to protect me, the only others he could entrust with that protection would be my parents.

"I did," he admitted. "I need to know if you're happy here. I can find a way to get you back home and guarantee your safety."

"You can do that now but you couldn't do it then?" I asked incredulously, turning away from him.

"At the time in question, what was required was some quick action. Your neck was on the proverbial chopping board. What is required now, as an afterthought, is some preparation, some reconciliation, and a few good men on my side to bring the elders around. But it can be done."

I looked at Hassan with something akin to disappointment, a

mixture of hurt and confusion burning in my soul.

"So...what...? It's as easy as that? You just give me back to my parents? That's what you want?"

I was sure Hassan could hear the hurt in my voice but chose to ignore it as he continued to try to prove a point to me.

"I'm only thinking of what's best for you."

"And how do you know what's best for me, Hassan?"

Hassan looked at me with confused eyes and measured his words carefully before he spoke again.

"I thought this is what you wanted."

"At the time in question," I started, throwing his words back at him "that's what I wanted. What I want now is not the same thing I wanted then."

"Tell me what you want," he breathed.

"If there was ever any inclination in your heart to let me go home, you shouldn't have brought me here. You shouldn't have lied and married me," I accused.

"I did not lie to you, Farida," Hassan justified.

"You did or you didn't. It doesn't matter either way," I snapped. "Do you know what you'd be doing, sending me home after you've married me?"

"The marriage was never consummated," he reminded me.

"Who in their right mind would believe that, Hassan? And why would you even think it's okay for people to know that the marriage wasn't consummated? Is there something wrong with me? Is there something wrong with you? That's all that people will be asking!"

"You shouldn't care what people think."

"That's ok for you to say, Hassan. You're a man. It's easy for you to get past something like this to go on and get married. It's not so easy for a divorced girl to remarry! Once again, I am the sacrificial lamb here."

"Tell me what you want, Farida," Hassan repeated.

"You know what. Nothing!" I spat the words out at him. "I want nothing from you!"

Despite the fuming rage boiling within me, I rose and started packing the table, the plates clattering in the sink where I threw them angrily. I stood there, my hands grasping the lip of the sink as I looked out the window towards the fields, willing my tears to remain where they dwelled in the recesses of my mind. I couldn't turn back to the table where he sat, knowing as soon as I saw him, my tears would escape and roll down my face.

"Farida." It was one word. A summons. In his soft, caressing voice that commanded people to do things which they wouldn't otherwise. "Farida," he called again. I shook my head where I stood, silently telling him that I wouldn't turn around. I couldn't understand why all of a sudden he had had a change of heart and was now challenging my stay with him and suggesting I return to my parents.

"Farida!" he called, and in the next instant, he was grabbing my arm and spinning me away from the window to face him. He held his face close to mine, his eyes darting across my face trying to find something. I tried to pull away from him, but his fingers dug into my skin as he held me tighter.

"Tell me that you want to be here," he whispered, his eyes

searching mine.

I shook my head again, my pain too deep and raw and my throat constricted with a choking sob that threatened to erupt at any moment.

Hassan let go of my arm and lifted his hands to my face, cradling it, kissing my tears away gently before touching his forehead to mine. I held on to his wrists, willing him to stay that way forever, rather than forsaking my happiness with him.

"Why won't you tell me what you want?" he asked, his thumb tracing my lips.

When I shook my head again, although not as aggressively, he lowered his mouth to mine and touched my lips for the first time since we'd married eight weeks ago. My hand stroked down his arm as his hand lifted my hair from around my face and he smoothed it back as though it were silk.

Without warning, he lifted me into his arms and carried me upstairs, his lips still glued to mine as he headed to the bedroom.

"Tell me where you want to be and with who," he whispered, and I knew that this would be the last time that he would pose this question to me.

"Here. With you."

CHAPTER 29: FARIDA 1970

Hassan started coming home at two o'clock in the afternoon. Sometimes earlier, for lunch, before he would go out for a meeting with some of the neighbouring clan heads, then come back home shortly thereafter. There was a persistent smile on my face as I saw a whole other side of him – as my best friend, he had been courteous, respectful, interested in anything and everything I had to say, and even a little playful. As my lover, he was loving and attentive, and at times, as we sat in the evening discussing things, he would sit looking at me as though mesmerised by some unseen power.

"So you've finally done the deed," my mother in law smirked as she entered my home one morning after Hassan had left for work. Even though she was trying to insult me, I couldn't help but smile at her words and ignore the malice in her tone. I knew she was secretly happy that we had finally consummated the marriage, but there was no way she would ever admit to that.

"Next comes a child," she announced.

"God willing," I replied, the only way to appease her.

"*Yallah,* get ready and come to the house, the girls want to have tea with you."

I raised my eyebrows in disbelief that first, she herself had come to summon me for tea, and second that she would use her daughters as an excuse to invite me to her house. She had never so much as willingly invited me into her own home.

"I'll be there in a few minutes, *mart 3ami.* I just want to leave a note for Hassan in case he comes home."

"*Ma fi daei,*" she started "he already knows where you'll be."

Hassan asked me about the tea party later that afternoon when he came home from work. I looked at him and smiled conspiratorially.

"It was strange that your mother would invite me," I told him.

"Long overdue, I think." And with that, he pulled me down onto his knee and wrapped his hand around my waist, squeezing softly but firmly, his way of reminding me I belonged to him.

"What would you like for dinner?" I asked.

"You," and we both broke out in laughter as he tipped me backward playfully, then brought me back up to touch his lips.

"Don't cook today. Let's go out for dinner," he suggested, and I nodded, agreeing with him.

CHAPTER 30: FARIDA 1970

The day I found out I was pregnant with my first child was the day I got up midway through breakfast and bolted for the bathroom. As I ran out of the room, I could see Hassan with his hand in mid air, his mouth open in preparation to take another morsel. I heard the scrape of his chair as he rose and followed me, his face stunned as he saw me bending over the toilet seat.

After I had finished, I sat back and breathed heavily, my stomach turning at the thought of the food sitting on the dining table.

"I'll get the doctor," Hassan said, more as a way of asking if that's what I wanted, rather than telling me that's what he was doing.

"I'm fine, I must've eaten something bad," I said, as he helped me up off the floor.

No sooner had I entered the kitchen, the smell of food hitting my nostrils in full force, than I was headed back to the toilet again, bending over myself as I dry heaved, the nausea overtaking me.

"Sit down and rest," he said. "I'll be right back with the doctor."

When Hassan returned with the doctor, his mother was also

on his heels, a look of concern on her face. But once she saw me, my pale complexion and my hair matted to the side of my face, her face suddenly perked up and she was beaming at me.

"I'll draw some blood and run some tests," the doctor said, bringing his kit out.

"No need," my mother in law said, her eyes dancing with the secret she knew that no-one else was privy too. "She's pregnant," she announced.

"Mother, we don't know that for sure," Hassan admonished, looking back at me.

"I know what I know," his mother replied, matter of factly. "I've seen many a pregnant woman, and this is exactly what they look like when they're suffering from morning sickness. Run your tests, doctor," she commanded, her voice excited "while I go next door and get Lita to make Farida some freshly squeezed juice."

"*Hasbi Allah wa nemaal wakeel,*" Hassan breathed, throwing his hands in the air in mock defeat. "The whole village will know about this before sundown.

CHAPTER 31: FARIDA 1970

No one was as excited about the pregnancy as Hassan, fussing around me day and night, ensuring I had a stack of pillows behind my back at all times. Every day he came home with all manner of exotic fruit and ice cream and nuts, urging me to eat so the baby could grow strong and healthy.

"A fat baby is what I'll be having if you keep this up," I complained.

Hassan laughed dismissively and rubbed my belly, even though there wasn't even so much as a bump yet.

"A healthy baby," he amended.

"A fat baby," I argued. "Would you like a boy or a girl?" I asked.

"Taking orders now, are we?" he joked.

"No. But when you envision yourself, do you see yourself holding a boy or a girl?"

Hassan gave me a non-committed shrug and advised me he'd be happy with either, as long as the baby was beautiful like me.

"What about names?" I asked.

"Well, that's an easy one. Khaled for my father, *Allah Yerhamou*, if it's a boy. Farida if it's a girl," he smiled "after my one and only true love." He entwined his fingers with mine and kissed my lips as one hand went back to my belly, as though willing the unborn child to life.

CHAPTER 32:
FARIDA 1971

Many months after my marriage, when my belly was heavy with child, the unthinkable happened.

Zelekha did not join us for breakfast one morning, and when Lita checked her room, the young girl's bed was neatly made up as though it hadn't been slept in. My mother in law ranted and raved and sent her sons out scouring the countryside for her. Pretty soon, the whole tribe knew that Zelekha had disappeared and whispers started to surge through the people like breaths on the wind. No one was courageous enough to speak out, but many had noticed the inordinate amount of time that Zelekha had spent at her bedroom window looking out at the foreign builders working on the house. Many also had noticed Zelekha's long day walks through the meadow and her dishevelled state when she emerged from the fields carrying corn or eggplant, or whatever was planted as a means of explaining her absence. Many, that is, except her own family.

At one point, my mother in law turned to me, her eyes fierce radiants of fire as she lashed out at me, proclaiming me to be the curse upon their home that fractured their structured lives.

"If not for you, Zelekha never would have considered leaving this house!" she screamed, subconsciously already aware that Zelekha had left of her own free will. "Look at you!" she bellowed "living in the lap of luxury. You left your family and look where you are now! All she's seen is that girls who behave this was are rewarded!"

Very early on, no matter what she said or did, I had learnt to hold my tongue. Out of respect for Hassan and out of respect for the family, who all rallied behind me at every turn and did not allow me to be treated unfairly. Now, too, I allowed her to rave like a madwoman, her voice undoubtedly reaching the ears of the whole tribe. She went so far as to lunge at me in an attempt to assault me, held back only by Amar and Lita and their begging voices urging her to leave me be. Truth be told, I would have let her hit me. Anything to extinguish the anguish in her heart, even if that made me a martyr.

It was mere seconds before Hassan arrived with his brother Waleed on his heels. He looked from me to his mother, then back at me, his eyes scouring me from head to toe to see if I was hurt.

"Mother," he whispered, in his calm stoic voice. Always level headed and patient, he measured his words carefully, and had a way of bringing his mother around to his way of thinking, no matter how angry she was. "Not a soul in the courtyard didn't hear you speak ill of Farida. We've spoken before about you raising your voice to my wife."

"She's the cause of all our problems," she hissed.

Waleed scoffed and moved toward his mother to deliver a few choice words, but Hassan held up a hand and Waleed stopped. No matter that he was older than Hassan, he had always been the hot-headed one, quick to temper and quick to jump into a raging fire wherever there was one. He had also always been my biggest fan, supporting me no matter what, even though everyone else in the village had looked upon me as an un-wanted outsider and viewed me with suspicion.

"Mother, you know quite well how Farida came to be here with us. It was not by choice. And she has been nothing but a Godsend to this family since she joined it. Do not treat her unjustly."

"You bringing her here has made the local girls think it's okay for a girl to leave her family home!" my mother argued. "They think it's acceptable to marry outside our tribe." She continued to grasp at straws. Anything to lay blame anywhere but at her own doorstep.

I looked down at my feet, ashamed, but unsure of what. If anything, I loved Zelekha like my own sister and I was devastated that she was gone, hoping as the minutes ticked by that she would miraculously reappear again.

"Mother. You know, and I know, and this *whole damned village knows*," Hassan started, and for once, I could see him losing his composure as he raised his voice the loudest I'd ever heard it. Even Waleed gasped and turned to Hassan to ensure he had heard right. "We *all* know," he reiterated, "that Farida was taken from her family against her will. I don't know what's floating around in your head, and where you're coming up with this nonsense, but..."

I moved closer to him and put my hand on Hassan's forearm, tugging lightly and urging him to look at me. He turned to look at me, his furrowed brows questioning me. "Now is not the time," I whispered. "We have to find Zelekha."

On this, we all agreed.

Hassan took a deep breath and let it out in one exasperated blow, looking thoughtfully at his mother. "A lesser woman would constantly complain about the way she's treated by you. Look how she grounds me and says things to diffuse the situation and divert my anger away from you," he pointed out to his mother. "I don't know how she can be so forgiving."

Later in the afternoon, as the call to *Asr* prayer reverberated through the village from the one little mosque housed at the entry to the village, Waleed came into the house in the company of the construction foreman, who removed his shoes at the door and held his wide brimmed hat in his hands.

I sat with my mother in law and Amar, waiting for some news on Zelekha, steadfast in our hopes and prayers that she would soon be returned to us.

"Forgive me, madam," he said, addressing my mother in law "I would have come sooner but only now did I receive word." Waleed indicated to me to beckon Hassan, who had left for our quarters to make ablution in preparation for prayer.

"Nizar oversees the construction here in Dhar Khamra and Aysha Yesr. He has something interesting to tell us," he explained as Hassan came bursting through the door.

"I split my crew between the two construction sites," Nizar said, and we all detected the heavy lilt of a Syrian accent. "They work on a rotational basis according to where they're needed. I'm missing one of my men. He didn't stay in the bunkhouse last night and didn't turn up for work this morning. Some of my men in the village have seen him on occasion speaking with your daughter. I wondered if the two disappearances might be connected and that's why I came to you."

"The men don't know anything?" Waleed asked.

"He had a friend on the site who he confided to. Apparently, he was very taken with your girl and could think or speak of nothing but her."

I moved to prop my mother in law up when it looked like she would drop to the ground upon hearing this news. Lita squeaked and ran to get the old woman's blood pressure pills as I navigated her to the nearest couch.

"We'll find her, mother," Waleed proclaimed.

"And what if you do," my mother in law wailed "you know well the customs and traditions of our tribe. She comes back either in a coffin or a veil," she reminded him.

The days and nights and weeks and months bled into one as life moved on and there was no sign of Zelekha. Hassan, Waleed and their cousin Musab, to whom Zelekha's hand had been promised in marriage from the moment she was born, made several trips to Syria in search of their sister.

They had been able to verify, through initial enquiries along the way and confirmation from several witnesses on the Lebanese/Syrian border that Zelekha had indeed left, of her own accord, with the construction worker in Dhar Khamra who had infiltrated their lives and dared to take that which was not his to take. Yet, many months later, as the search continued, it seemed like she and the construction worker had simply vanished off the face of the earth.

Hassan, stoic Hassan, enraged that such a thing had happened, applied to the elders for a sanction against any outsiders doing any further work in their village, stating any and all work should be carried out by the men of the village to maintain and uphold the age-old traditions of their culture. Needless to say, his application was met with nods of approval and it was deemed that any person not belonging to the Badu

tribe not be allowed access to the village under any circumstances. The tribe closed ranks and shut out trade with all outsiders, imprisoning themselves behind a fortress of stone, the
townfolk becoming extremely vigilant about who was allowed
into their midst.

CHAPTER 33: FARIDA 1971

Hassan was by my side for the duration of my pregnancy with Khaled, leaving only on the rare trips to Syria when it was believed they had received credible information regarding Zelekha's whereabouts or to conduct trade with another clan to whom they were related.

"You won't hurt her, will you?" I asked him before he left on the third trip. The information they had received was credible, Hassan was sure they would find Zelekha on this latest journey.

"By God, if I find her, I will string her up by her neck myself!" Hassan declared, in a show of anger that was becoming more frequent lately whenever his sister's name was mentioned. "She has brought nothing but shame upon our family name," he added. "This will not go unpunished."

"Do you think it's right that you-or a bunch of tribal elders-be judge and jury of your sister's sin? How can you even *think* to hurt your own flesh and blood."

"I denounce Zelekha, Farida. I have nothing if not my honour. This is the way of our land."

"But..." I faltered as I looked at Hassan helplessly. "I understand very well the ways of the land, Hassan. But how can you allow your culture to cloud your religion? Your traditions dictate what you must do, but your religion tells you not to take a life."

"Don't fight me on this, Farida," Hassan said, lifting my chin to meet my eyes. "I have a few hours before I leave; let's not waste it fighting," he prompted, sliding his hand down my arm until our hands touch, our fingers entwined.

That was the last trip that Hassan took to Syria in search of his sister. When he came back, he commanded that Zelekha's name never again be uttered in the house. The matter was settled, and that was that, he reported, without further explanation. It would be many many years before I would finally learn what happened to Zelekha.

CHAPTER 34:
FARIDA 1971

The birth of Khaled was a joyous event. And as promised, I bore Hassan a fat, yet healthy baby, with a fluff of light hair atop his head, and mesmerising grey eyes that enchanted us. Khaled had taken the best of me and the best of his father, the tiny bundle piercing my heart from his first wail.

"The hair I can understand," Hassan remarked, running his hair through his light brown waves as he looked at his new-born son. "But the eyes...," he scrunched up his face in confusion and continued to stare at the child.

"Don't get too excited," my mother in law laughed. "All babies are born with coloured eyes. This is no indication of their natural eye colour. It will change in a few months."

"I kind of like the grey," Hassan complained, cooing to his son.

"And I would have loved to hold on to the blue eyes I was born with," my mother in law joked, as she let out one long *za-lghouta* after another to announce the birth of Khaled.

Khaled became the centre of my universe. Everything that came before him ceased to exist. His every breath, his heart-beat, his tiny fingers and toes; I obsessed over every inch of him and was overwhelmed by the amount of doting those around us heaped on him.

Hassan was surprisingly adept at adjusting his life to accommodate a crying baby and lavished love upon him. He quickly assumed the role of protector and I would catch him cooing to the baby whenever he thought no-one was watching.

The only cloud that hung above the birth of our miracle was the fate of Zelekha. It had been months since she'd fled the village, and although I missed her terribly, I hoped that she was far enough away that she would not be found and held accountable for her actions.

I marvelled also at the fact that my first born would probably never know my own family. He'd never know my mother and father, and he would not grow up amongst my family in Tul Ghosn. Nor would he be in the presence of my beloved sister Aujene's own kids – who would teach him the ins and outs of life if not Aujene? I asked myself that question often, yearning for my sister with a deep sadness that settled in the very depths of my soul.

PART 2

THE BOOK OF AUJENE

CHAPTER 35: AUJENE 1970

My mother's grief was palpable. It consumed everything in its path, ensuring nothing would ever be the same again. At night, on the nights that she was not out scouring the countryside for Farida, I heard my father berating her in his chiding, demeaning way. He spat words at her, his cruelty knowing no bounds, accusing her of being less than a woman because her grief hadn't allowed him into her orbit in weeks. I guess eventually he started taking what he wanted by force, because all I could hear through the thin walls was my mother's whimpering and her muffled sobs. At the time maybe I was too young to understand or articulate what was happening, but hindsight is such a beautiful thing.

In the mornings following such episodes, I would find my mother standing at the kitchen sink, a far away look in her eyes as she soaked the same plate over and over again. Where once she was happy and smiling, laughter oozing out of her soul, she was suddenly struck with a terrible sadness that infected everyone around her. Her grief poisoned our lives. It contaminated our family, our blood, our lives as they were, and as it was, rendered our futures obsolete and allowed things to happen which, at any other time, would not have been allowed to happen.

It was my mother's grief, and my father's fear, that ensured that I was cast out from the family and sent to live with a local land baron and his family. My father believed there I would be safe. My mother, too consumed with her grief over Farida, did not realise what was happening until all was said and done and there was no reneging on a gentlemen's agreement on the sale. Because ultimately, that's what this was. Me being sold to a local merchant for dollars and cents. It was me being sold into slavery and servitude.

CHAPTER 36:
AAIDA 2016

My mother never learnt to drive. I never understood this.

My mind flits to me as a child. Sitting in the back of dad's prized possession... his caramel coloured Datsun 240b. I still see it in my mind's eye. The car starts, dad driving, mum in the passenger seat, and me ensconced in the back seat. We're going on an adventure. Actually, we're not. Our trips were few and far between. It was probably *Eid* and we were going to my aunty's house-a twice yearly trek that was a treat for me, a chore for dad, and a nightmare for mum.

As the car starts to move, mother turns in her seat, toward the back seat, facing me. Only, she's not looking at me. She's looking through the back windshield, at something far off in the distance, her brows furrowed. She would remain that way until we exited our street and made the first turn, usually a left.

She spent each and every "adventure" sitting ram rod straight in the passenger seat, her fists clutched at her sides and her teeth clenched so tight I could actually hear their stifled grind.There was never a conversation, never a joke, never any verbal commentary unless she turned, teeth gritted, to check if I was still awake.

Lack of noise seemed to agitate her. I don't remember much of dad during these adventures, only that he was always in the drivers's seat, his right hand hanging out of the window with a cigarette in between his long fingers, and Mother never learnt to steer a car.

CHAPTER 37:
AUJENE 1970

The day they came for me, my parents fought endlessly. My mother screamed and ranted and cried, telling my father there was nothing to gain by sending me away. He, in turn, tried to tell her that it would be safer for me with a well-to-do family far from here who could keep me out of harm's way and it was best that I not bear witness to any information regarding Farida's demise. From the way he spoke, I could tell my father had already given up on Farida. He thought she was dead and lost to us forever. And now that a second girl had gone missing, he was even more determined to extract me from the family home and deposit me with a family who lived well away from Tul Ghosn.

"But my name is not Farida!" I argued, as though that would be enough to sway him. My 15 year old mind was convinced that only girls named Farida were being stolen, and this conviction went right over my father's head.

The Nawfels came to collect me in a shiny white Mercedes. After collecting me from my home, and assuring my father that I would be in safe hands, Mr and Mrs Nawfel sat in the front and I sat in the back, behind the passenger seat, opposite their 16 year old son Zayd, who turned to look at me somewhat curiously, but said nothing, pushing his bookish glasses further up his nose.

I watched my family from the rear windshield, watched them get smaller and smaller as we got further and further away from the house in the village and closer and closer to my new life in the city.

The house in the city turned out not to be a house in the city, but a rambling villa on the outskirts of the city, enclosed with a 2 metre high brick fence and a heavy metal double gate at the entry. All I could think as we drove through the gate was that I could die here and no-one would know; that's how unforgivingly private the property was.

Clara was the Ethiopian housekeeper with kind eyes that contained a wealth of wisdom unspoken. She showed me to my room, a little nook off the kitchen, and allowed me to settle in, advising me that my training would start the next day.

"Training?" My voice caught in my throat as I looked at her with wide, fearful eyes.

"Why, yes dear. You'll be my little helper. And one day, you'll take my place and be housekeeper of this old house."

She was not unkind. Truth be told, she was nice and warm, and looked at me sympathetically when I told her that's not what I wanted to be when I grew up.

"Well, when I was your age, I wanted to be an actress," she told me. "Look how that worked out for me." She gave me a warm smile and continued to move around pots and pans on the stove.

"Sometimes in life, we don't get what we desire. We may plan one route, but the Almighty sends us on another. That's just the way it is," she shrugged.

"But I've worked so hard in the olive grove. To understand the land, and the olives, and weather patterns. Some day I want to buy my own olive grove, and bottle my own oil and olives. This is all I've ever wanted."

"You can still do that, my dear. You're young. You have your whole life ahead of you. But for now, you're here, so let me teach you everything I know about how to keep a house so you at least have that trade in your arsenal, hmm?"

CHAPTER 38: AUJENE 1970

Clara was the only redeeming factor about my new home. With each passing day that I remained at the Nawfel household, the ache in my heart grew stronger and I missed my siblings terribly. It seemed like I had gone to sleep and entered a nightmare, from which there was no awakening. Every day I waited for my parents to pick me up, but they never did.

Rarely did I see Mr or Mrs Nawfel. Mr Nawfel spent most days at work (he was a councilman) and Mrs Nawfel spent most days in her room (drunk or drinking or hung over). I had never really known the meaning of drunk or even drinking in the context in which it was referred to when Clara spoke, as we had never, as semi-practising Muslims, had cause to have alcohol in my family home, but Miss Clara soon availed me to the true definition of the word when she explained to me what the "devil's liquid" was.

Zayd had, up until now, left me to my own devices, stopping only casually every now and then to regard me like some spectator at an art exhibition. He stayed mainly in his room, his glasses always fixed firmly on his nose, reading or studying, or doing whatever it was he did. There came a time, though, about three weeks after I had started at the Nawfel home, and mere days after I had turned 15, when Zayd spoke to me while I was in the garden clearing glasses from the previous night's cocktails that had been held by the pool. He emerged from the house in his swim shorts, a towel flung over his shoulder, making enough noise as he strutted past that it was hard to ignore his presence. I noticed that for the first time, he didn't wear his glasses, and thought it odd that he wore them in the first place if he could so obviously see without them.

He dove into the water from a section closest to me, sending a spray of water out of the pool to splash me until I looked like a drowned cat. Taken aback, I jumped away and fell to the ground, hitting my leg on the cast iron side table and sending the glasses in my hand hurtling to the ground, now covered in a thousand little shards of glass. The ruckus was loud enough to bring Clara running, and she gasped as she neared and found a gash in my leg that was spurting blood like a geyser.

"Oh dear," she tsked, looking at my butchered leg. "What happened?" She regarded me with concerned eyes before she turned her gaze knowingly to the pool. Zayd had dunked his head under water, but Miss Clara was having none of it. She stood and called his name, waiting for him to break the surface of the water and glide over.

"Now I know for a fact that Aujene didn't splash herself and create this mess. Seriously, Zayd, what were you thinking!" She admonished him. I could see from the look on his face that Zayd, although listening, neither cared nor felt remorse for his actions. She tsked once more as she helped me up and held me under the arm, assisting me inside to have my leg checked.

"That's a pretty nasty gash, Aujene. I'll call the doctor to come and have a look at it so it doesn't get infected. You need to stay away from that boy, you hear me?" She brought her stern voice out as her concerned eyes looked at me. "he's nothing but trouble. May seem meek, but he's the devil incarnate."

CHAPTER 39:
AUJENE 1970

The days passed uneventfully as I adapted to my new home. Life went on as it had before, with Mr and Mrs Nawfel going about their lives as usual as I stumbled through my training with Clara. Zayd more or less left me alone after the poolside incident, for which I breathed a sigh of relief.

One of my favourite chores was when Clara took me with her to the farmers markets to buy the weekly supply of fresh produce. Clara was mesmerised by my knowledge regarding fruits and vegetables, and equally surprised that I was able, at my age, to pick the freshest produce without having been taught how to do it. Me, I relished being around so much fresh fruit and through these trips, felt a connectedness to the earth that I both missed and longed for.

"Maybe you do have a future in farming, after all," Clara mused as we carried our bags back to the waiting car. "I can see you have a deep seated passion for the earth. I wonder what your life was like before you came to us?"

"Much the same as it is now. I helped with everything around the house. But I have a special bond with the land. I could sit in the olive grove or the garden for hours, just thinking and watching the crops as they flourished. Anything I could do sitting in the garden, I always did. Stringing beans, cutting okra, picking mallow....all of that was done in the garden. Did you know you could use the refuse waste of all vegetables in the garden to fertilise and grow your crop? See, not many people know that," I pointed out after Clara shook her head in surprise. "I would string the beans and drop the refuse right there over the *kettayfeh*-then see them sprout larger and healthier! The garden at home was my task, and I relished it. I cleared the land and sowed the seeds, I nurtured the seedlings once they sprouted, watered them and fed them to keep them healthy. Very rarely did we need to buy any fresh produce from outside...I grew everything, from tomatoes to eggplants, spinach and lettuce. Everything you could imagine."

Clara looked at me wondrously. She was the only person ever who had looked at me in awe, mesmerised by my words. The only adult who had ever listened or ever cared enough to give me a voice. I realided this was because at home, I did what was expected of me. There was no glory or acknowledgment that I grew a garden that fed a family of 8 and most of the neighbours. There was no bewilderment that I had a green thumb (another term that Clara introduced me to) and that I accomplished, single handedly, at 15 years, what most men could not begin to accomplish in a lifetime. Where I came from, that was the norm, because we had been doing it for generations. It was inherent in our DNA that we all worked the land. We tilled and tithed and sowed and ploughed and prospered from the soil of the earth. Whereas here, closer to the city, a child's only chore was to go to school to receive an education and prepare themselves for the future.

"You're a truly amazing child, Aujene. Did you never attend school?"

"Where I come from, school isn't for girls. It's just barely for boys. Working the land is our way of life. It's expected of a boy to work the land and provide for his family. A girl helps her family around the house and on the land until she marries and has babies. That's what girls are expected to do. And even then, after she has children, most times she is expected to aid her husband in his plot of land. That's how our village is sustained. The only other notable trade we have is animal farming, cows for milk and sheep for meat." I scrunched up my nose at the thought of farming the animals and added "But I'd much rather work the land than milk the cows."

Clara burst out into laughter as we arrived at the car and slid our bags into the boot. "How about we get ourselves a nice cold drink before we head home. Would you like that, Aujene?"

CHAPTER 40:
AUJENE 1970

The thing about people who are troublemakers is they know when to stop because they've reached a threshold that could force their victim over the edge. That's how I view what happened next with Zayd. After the pool incident, he had laid dormant, knowing that Clara was onto his games and wouldn't allow him to subvert her authority or hurt me in any way.

I could almost see him, in my mind's eye, plotting and planning his next move, his smirk every time he passed me growing bolder by the day. On a day when Clara was attending to Mrs Nawfel as she lay in bed with a migraine hangover, he came into the living room as I was dusting and proceeded to move things out of their place, no doubt in an attempt to agitate and goad me into lashing out at him. When I opted to leave the room rather than force a confrontation, he grabbed my arm with such ferocity that I could feel where his nails had cut through my skin. Looking down, I could see blood seep from beneath the surface. He followed my gaze and blinked, then looked back up at me, a cruel smile spreading across his face.

"Off to run and snitch me to Miss Clara, are we?"

I shook my head quickly, suddenly frightened of what he might do, and tugged on my arm so he would release it. His hold was firm, his fingers like clamps as they dug deeper and he brought his menacing face closer to my own.

"Just let me go, please," I whimpered.

"Not a chance."

"What do you want?"

"Now, what would I want with a scrawny little thing like you?"

"Then just let me go."

Zayd refused to let me go. He held on tighter until I winced, before he thought better of allowing me to have a voice and promptly placed a hand across my mouth. I could feel my eyes opening wide in fear as I continued to struggle with him and he refused to let me go.

Finally, he removed his vice like grip from my arm, but whatever relief I felt was short lived as he wound his fingers around my throat and proceeded to squeeze the life out of me. If it were at all possible, my eyes widened even further as I shook my head, pleading for him to stop, my voice a mere jumbled whimper against the hand preventing me from screaming.

When I opened my eyes, it was to Clara whimpering "No,no,no,no,no." I could feel the earth vibrating, but later recognised this as Clara shaking me awake. Her anguished face told me everything I needed to know – it was so much worse than I could have imagined. And there was no doubt, not a single doubt in her mind, what had happened here.

CHAPTER 41: AUJENE 1970

One look in the mirror, and I could see the deep purple tones of a ring around my neck where Zayd had squeezed, attempting to extract the life out of me. My arm was torn to shreds by his nails, the blood congealed in some places. My mind, blitzed to smithereens as I rocked back and forth on the ground, with my knees tucked under my chin, refused to acknowledge what had happened.

"I don't know what happened. He just came out of no where. I didn't say a word to him," I cried.

"I know, sweetie, I know," Clara soothed, shushing me against her chest.

"But why did he do that to me? I've never done anything to him."

"I don't know what's in that little devil's head, my dear. I won't let him come near you again. If he comes into a space you're in when I'm not there, you make every effort to leave, you hear me?"

"I tried Clara. I really tried. That's why he grabbed me, he wouldn't let me leave."

Clara pulled me back and regarded me with freshly worried eyes. She surveyed the damage to my arms and winced painfully as she looked at my throat. "Thank God I found you in time," she breathed. "Dear Lord, what am I to do with that little terror?" she said with an exasperated sigh, more to herself than to anyone else. I neglected to remind her that the "little terror" had just turned 17. If anything, he was not showing signs of slowing down his dastardly ways; rather, his evil ways seemed to be escalating.

CHAPTER 42:
AUJENE 1970

If Zayd had meant to destroy me with his constantly alternating mood swings, he was doing a damn good job of it. After the incident where I had almost died and my skin still bore the scars of his nails, there came a time of complete and utter civility where he basically left me alone and went about doing his own thing. Sometimes he would happen across Clara and I chatting in the kitchen and would throw a smile my way or compliment the way I was doing something. I would notice Clara's eyes shift sideways as she watched him mistrustfully but said nothing. It was only when he started commenting on my vegetable garden that the magnitude of the evil he possessed within him was finally realised.

My garden was what Clara termed a mid city paradise, spanning a length of the side fence that rivalled any grower's garden. I had planted silverbeet and lettuce, carrots and tomatoes, peas and cauliflower. A multitude of vegetables that at first glance took one's breath away and held a person captive to time as we awaited the outcome of my crop. From my end, spending every last free minute I had in the garden brought me incomparable joy and happiness as I watched the bounty of my hard work to come to life.

Then one day, in the blink of an eye, it all changed. Zayd deliberately sought me out as I tended to the garden, removing weeds and watering the newly sprouted bulbs, a smile plastered across my face as I nurtured my crop, proud of myself for having done it all on my own.

"Why do you like spending so much time out here in the garden?" he asked, and if I didn't know better, I'd say he was an angel.

"What, gardening?"

"Your hands are soiled with dirt. Girls don't usually do this sort of work," he commented. If I didn't know better, I'd believe God had removed the old Zayd and replaced him with another. But the thing about vipers is they always strike when you least expect; it.

I shrugged by way of explanation. "I don't mind. I like the outdoors, planting things and watching them grow."

"You seem to be good at it, too."

I smiled at the compliment.

"You know, people actually attend universities to learn how to do what you're so seamlessly doing."

"I think some people are just born with a green thumb," I told him.

"Is this what your family does?" It was unusual that he suddenly seemed so interested in my family, as he had never really been curious.

"My family has worked the land for years."

"And is this where your future lies? Working the land?"

I shrugged again. "Does anyone really know at our age where

their future lies?" I asked. "What I do know is I will always want to get my hands dirty in the soil, planting and growing things."

"I've never been interested in growing anything." Zayd told me. My inner self smirked knowingly – I already knew that Zayd wasn't very big on growing anything aside from his ego. He was more about destruction.

"It's not for everyone," I told him, in a bid to make him feel better.

"But it looks like you were born to toil in the earth," he proclaimed, pointing at my soiled hands again.

I said nothing and continued to pick out weeds as he loomed above me and watched. I could see a furious curtain of questions swarming his brain as he watched me. It was like I sat before two different Zayds – the Zayd that was trying to suppress tyranical Zayd by trying to be nice, and the Zayd that loathed that other Zayd for trying to be nice. The two Zayds were at war with each other, tugging at an invisible rope to be one or the other.

"Maybe you could teach me to do some gardening," he said, leaning forward eagerly.

I leaned back on the heels of my feet, my knees coated in wet soil, and regarded him carefully. One could almost believe his attempt at sincerity.

"If that's what you want," I said, not really wanting to accommodate any of his requests. If anything, Clara had warned me to stay away from him, and under this roof, for me, Clara trumped all others.

"When do you want to?" he asked.

"How about next time I'm out here," I said, making a mental note to come out to the garden only when he was at school to avoid spending more time with him.

"Sounds like a plan," he remarked, excusing himself politely and taking his leave.

The next day, Zayd came home with a rabbit that he let roam wild around the garden. Within minutes, the beautiful garden where I had expended most of my energy had been decimated and the crop lost.

I stood at the edge of the garden looking down at my garden sadly as Zayd stood off to the side with his hands in his pockets, a grin spanning the length of his face as he watched the expression on my face turn from disbelief to horror to resigned sadness.

I fell to my knees in the soil, taking a clump of earth in my hands and watching as the grains sifted through my shaking fingers. My teary face looked up at the sky, seeking mercy and patience, then turned to watch Zayd as he watched me, a look of satisfaction parading his lips as I felt the weight of his cruelty fall upon my shoulders like a tonne of bricks. I silently cursed him to a lifetime of hardship and misery, wishing I'd never set eyes on him or this Godforsaken house in which he lived. And there in the shade of a disappearing sun, I mourned the loss of the only thing that connected me to my roots and gave me some semblance of hope for better days to come.

Clara was beside herself when I walked back into the house with tear-stained cheeks that still glistened with the salt of the earth. I was devastated and the torture on my face was so apparent, she could not overlook my sadness without crumpling into herself at my grief. She took in my soiled knees and my dishevelled hair from when I had grabbed clumps and pulled, sobbing pitifully. My vacant stare now bore down on her as she engulfed me in her arms, a look of consternation on her face as she looked out the window toward the garden and saw Zayd standing there.

"Dear God, what has he done now?" she muttered, almost to herself. She held me close, a fierce determination emanating from her as she started to curse the ground that Zayd walked on.

"Lets go get you rested," she said, leading me away from the kitchen and into my cramped little room.

She tucked me into the bed and told me not to worry about the sheets getting dirty, we would change them tomorrow. She announced she would be back in a few minutes with some soothing lemon tea to calm my nerves.

Clara closed the door behind her as she exited, leaving me to wallow in my bottomless well of pity. I wondered what, if anything, she would say to Zayn. The common theme at the Nawfels was that Zayd was pretty much untouchable. Both parents were practically absent, leaving him to his own devices, without repercussions or reprimand when the occasion called for consequences. And that was when I became acutely aware of something I had previously overlooked; either the Nawfels were afraid of their son, or they simply didn't care.

CHAPTER 43: AUJENE 1970

Clara and I became quick friends. Even though the woman was old enough to be my mother, she took me in under her wing and treated me like I was her own daughter. She was patient while she taught me household chores, and excited every time I mastered a new recipe that I had been attempting at her request. Clara often marvelled at how relatable I was, displaying a maturity way beyond my years. Sometimes, she told me often, she forgot that I was not her age, and many times she would apologise for sharing with me her troubles which were beyond my age of understanding. But this came from a place where she treated me as her equal, not as a subservient. I was so in tune with her needs that I fell so effortlessly into the role of what she was missing most; a daughter and a best friend.

She taught me chores that I hadn't learnt at home, which I mastered quickly. Mother had always said I was better equipped to run the land than to run the house, and so had given me free riegn over the garden and the land and assigned the household chores to the siblings who seemed more adept at home duties. Of all my siblings, I was the one who communicated best with nature and the earth. But now, as I sat with Clara stringing beans, it seemed I had finally broken down one craft to merge the two and become successful at both.

She and I sat at the kitchen bench, stringing beans and chatting excitedly like old friends as we prepped the day's lunch.

"How does your mother cook these beans, Aujene?" Clara asked me, curious. It was a well known fact that recipes differed slightly from village to village. From village to city, there was often a bigger variation on the ingredients and the method of cooking.

"She tried to teach me many times," I laughed, recalling my mother and the times that we had spent in the kitchen. "I know she blanches the beans in hot salt water for 30 seconds to avoid that stiffness in the beans."

"Hmmm, that's a new one," Clara said.

"She fries onion, garlic and tomato with a sprinkle of chili flakes before adding the beans and tossing."

Clara's eyebrows shot upward in excited surprise. "My mouth is watering just considering that combination," she remarked.

"It's truly a nice recipe. Mother makes amazing fried beans."

"Maybe we can try your mother's recipe this time," she smiled, and I beamed, looking forward to the aromatic smell that would fill the house with all the combined ingredients.

Zayd came in then, standing by the table as we continued to string the beans. Clara watched him with a hawk eye, wondering what he was up to. I thanked the lord that he was away at school most of the time, but on the rare occasions when he was home, he was an absolute menace.

"What's wrong, Zayd?" Clara asked.

Zayd shrugged and looked down at his feet, trying to act innocent but by no means succeeding.

"I'm bored," he proclaimed.

"Well, I would ask you to help us out, but we're almost done here," she said, rising to take the bowl of beans to the kitchen sink.

No sooner had Clara got up and turned her back than Zayd was behind my chair, his hand fisting a lock of my hair. I yelped painfully as my head snapped back, the sudden movement taking me by surprise. A sweltering heat engulfed my head as I felt my hair nearly tear from my scalp. Clara screamed and there was the loud banging of something smashing against the floor as my eyes focused on the ceiling. Everything happened in an absolute blur, my mind numb with pain and shock, then relief as my hair was snatched out of Zayd's hands and doused in something cold. I heard two simultaneous loud bangs, and later I would learn that two things happened at once; Clara pushed Zayd away from me with such force that he went crashing into the door, and I was so overwhelmed and confused that I toppled sideways with the chair and my shoulder made contact with the floor.

Later, much later, with the beans forgotten and the laughter of earlier dissolving into the annals of history, Clara would tell me the story of how Zayd had set my hair alight. He had simply taken a lighter, pulled my hair back viciously, and proceeded to set my hair on fire. If not for Clara's quick thinking and even quicker action, the damage would have been far more extensive that the scorching of the ends of a few strands. The mere horror and unexpected nature of what had happened had been enough to send me into shock, and I sat on my tiny bed and rocked back and forth, allowing my tears to fall in cascades down my cheeks.

I couldn't understand why Zayd hated me so much. No-one, that I knew of anyway, had ever hated me with such fervour and enough malice to set my hair on fire. What had he hoped to accomplish? Surely, he didn't mean to kill me? I asked Clara.

She had looked at me sadly as I continued to whimper but couldn't answer my question. All she knew for sure was that Zayd was obviously a very disturbed young boy and in the absence of much needed adult supervision, she couldn't turn her back on him.

CHAPTER 44:
AUJENE 1971

I stayed at the Nawfels for a year. A whole year in which I lived on tenterhooks, always waiting for the next incident to happen. Expecting my imminent death around each and every corner I turned. Breathing a sigh of relief when Zayd was away at school during the week, holding my breath at the weekends when he was home and using me as his entertainment.

Whenever he was home, Clara constantly warned me to stay close to her at all times. She often went back and forth through the house to check up on me and ensure everything was okay. Zayd, for the most part, made himself scarce, but would at other times pop up out of no-where when I was deeply immersed in my work, and drop something heavy to create a thud that would startle me. Then he would simply smirk and walk away. He never said a word, although he seemed to thrive on my fear.

For all her efforts, there were times when Clara couldn't constantly be at my side. Understanding this, I did my hardest to fend for myself and not give in to the fear (Clara advised me that was what Zayd wanted-my fear), keeping a watchful eye out for him so I could make a mad dash away if the need arose.

The only time Clara was ever away for me for any extended length of time was when she had to tend to Mrs Nawfel, whose forays outside her bedroom were becoming few and far between. On one such day, almost a year after I had been brought to service the household, Mrs Nawfel woke with a particularly bad migraine and Clara reluctantly left me alone to attend to Mrs Nawfel's bath and administration of medication.

"This may take a while, dear child," she told me, fussing with her apron distractedly. I could see that she was frustrated by Mrs Nawfel's worsening condition and her lack of willingness to help herself. "You run along and wait for me in your room; I'll collect you once I've seen to Mrs Nawfel's needs."

At 16, I still had no firm sense of time, but she must have been gone only a few minutes before I heard a key turn in the lock. In mere seconds, Zayd was in the room, standing before me, his hand firmly glued against my mouth. Forget what I said about fear; it's one thing to say it and wish it, but when you have a hand at your mouth silencing you and menacing eyes peering into your face, there's no way not to be overcome with fear.

Zayd sort of snarled, snickering, like he'd finally found just the right opportunity to wreak havoc and inflict chaos on my poor tormented soul. I struggled to throw his hand off me and scream, but he had a super strength I was not accustomed to.

"Don't. Make. A. Sound," he sort of rasped, before he whipped out a scarf from his pocket and gagged me with it. I could feel the tears as they fell from my shocked eyes and onto his hand as he hurriedly tied the scarf behind my head. All of a sudden, he viciously turned me around and grabbed my hands behind my back, and even as I struggled and kicked at his feet, he managed to bind my hands and render me helpless.

I could hear him laughing, a low throaty chuckle, as he turned me around yet again to face him. I cursed the size of the room- a single narrow bed that barely held my frame and a small desk and chair more apt for use by a 6 year old. The room was so small and claustrophobic, it caused my heart to palpitate in sheer fear as I noticed his physical proximity to me. This room wasn't made for two. It was so spartan, there wasn't even anything there that could aid me in fending him off.

Zayd looked at my wide eyes and seemed to pause, thinking. About what, I don't know.

He raised a hand, picked up a loose strand of my hair, and held it up to his nose, sniffing deeply as he inhaled my scent. The scent of fear. I watched as his eyes fluttered closed momentarily, and then as he opened them, his pupils dilated and his nostrils flaring. He traced a finger down my arm, and my eyes followed his finger, afraid of what was to come next. He traced all the way down to my wrist, lifting my hand and bringing it toward him, placing it between his legs.

My silent scream was buried in the folds of the fabric across my mouth, my head shaking back and forth as my eyes pleaded with him to stop. He pushed my hand firmer onto his shorts. He was hard. I was afraid. He could smell my fear and he seemed to enjoy it. This small, gangly, weird boy with the bookish glasses atop his nose-never in a million years would I have thought him capable of such things.

Zayd stepped away from me momentarily, and I almost sighed in silent relief as I started to calm down, but all too soon, as he looked at my face and took pleasure in my tears, he dropped his shorts and I could see his bulge bursting forward, on prominent display as it slapped against his thigh. He wasn't wearing underwear. He stood as bare as the day he'd been born, stroking himself as he edged toward me. My tears came harder and faster, my body shaking fearfully in recognition of what was to come.

In one quick movement, Zayd grabbed my arms harshly, dragging me toward the bed, where he fell on the mattress and pulled me on top of him. He righted me so I straddled him, struggling and squirming for him to let me go. I could feel his hard bulge as he thrust through my clothes, dry humping me. The constraint of the gag ensured my mouth was dry and my protestations became whimpers. I could feel Zayd's efforts picking up-he thrust harder and faster, his eyes becoming glazed as he continued his assault on me. He took my chin in his hand and lifted my face, squeezing my cheeks viciously as he clenched his teeth and panted. All of a sudden, he pulled the gag down away from my mouth and said "Now, scream for me, bitch." And I screamed.

I let out a blood curdling scream that I was sure could be heard the next street over.

CHAPTER 45:
AUJENE 1971

That night, as I lay sobbing on the bed, my legs curled up to my chest, Clara came in and set down a travel bag.

"Aujene," she said softly, pulling my hair away from my face. "Aujene, we're leaving."

"Leaving? Where?"

"Come on, you're going home."

Clara brought me home that night, my things (what few possessions I had) neatly folded into a duffel bag. She had a suitcase by her side also. She had had enough of the Nawfels and was going to seek employment elsewhere or go home. But first, she brought me home. She held me the whole way home in the taxi, wiping my tears and soothing my back while she reminded me that I was strong like a rock and could not let this one experience define the rest of my life.

My parents were surprised to see us when we arrived in Tul Ghosn in the dead of night. The taxi idled outside waiting for Clara as she sipped her tea and advised my parents I belonged with them, and not to send me back to the Nawfels.

"It's no place for a young girl like Aujene. Her place is here with you. Please don't make the mistake of sending her back there. I, too, have ceased my employment in that home and will be moving on."

As she rose to leave, I clung to Clara with fearful eyes, sad I wouldn't see her again.

"You will be fine, my girl. You belong to the land and the earth. Maybe someday life will be kind to us and we will meet again." She smiled and turned to walk away, the taxi picking up speed as they drove away.

No-one ever spoke about what happened at the Nawfels. To maintain the honour of the family name and our reputation, no one ever spoke of my time in the city.

My mother looked at me with sad, grief-stricken eyes. I knew what she was thinking-that she had lost not one, but two of her daughters.

My father, he barely looked at me at all.

They knew something had happened, but no one asked. We weren't a family of deep talkers. We didn't share our pain. We sort of swept things under the rug and hoped they'd go away rather than dealing with them.

CHAPTER 46:
AUJENE 1971

Everything was different after I came back. I wasn't gone that long, a little over a year, but in that year that I was gone, everything changed. My mother and father were different people. It was like I left for a year and walked back into a stranger's home when I returned.

Even my friends, they laughed and cried, and carried on as they always had. They remarked on the changes in me. Withdrawn, quiet, different, were just a few words they used to describe me. And in all reality, I had changed. They remained the same. But I had changed. I went away and that experience changed me. My mother lost Farida and that changed her. My father lost Farida and subsequently, he lost everything because of his actions. He lost my mother. He lost me. And he lost his soul.

The days seemed like an endless blur. For the rest of the world, life went on. Time passed. Things went back to normal. For my mother, time seemed to have stopped still when Farida disappeared. She couldn't remember, from day to day, what she had eaten, nor what she was doing when we found her standing at the edge of the garden looking down into the murky water of the stream. She could not follow the string of a conversation without losing her train of thought and suddenly starting a whole conversation unrelated to the current one.

I settled back into my home life as though I had never left. Farida was still gone and I had just lost a year of my life serving a family whose son had all but decimated my youth. I shut out that time in my life, opting to ignore the pain raging through my memory and the ache in my heart at Clara's separation from me. I threw myself back into the land, growing and sowing and reaping and nurturing, my mind switched off but for the living, breathing crop in front of me.

Yet life went on. The children grew and the seasons changed. There were the sounds of preparations and excitement as our neighbours celebrated their children's weddings. The whole valley would be filled with the thumping of the *tabal* and the flute that old man Nizam played as a courtesy at every wedding. I could tell, with news of such events, even though we didn't attend, that mother would be envying the hand of fate that had taken her daughter and stripped her of her chance to see Farida as a bride and a mother.

There was only one time where I truly saw any sort of serious emotion flicker through my mother. It was just over a year after Farida went missing and we received word that Farouk was getting married and would be parading his new wife through the main street of the village to introduce her to the community. Although it was tradition that a groom would walk his bride through a village until they reached their marital home, there were always concessions to be made depending on circumstances. My mother didn't understand how he could be so insensitive as to allow this to happen, considering he would be walking right past our front door, not knowing whether or not Farida was alive or coming back and not taking into consideration the feelings of grief that still plagued his old fiancee's family. To compound things, Farouk's mother came to visit and invite us to the wedding.

"Have you no *shame*?" my mother hissed.

"But Haji Tala, Farida is gone and my son seeks to marry," the old lady explained.

"Have you *no shame*?" my mother roared, causing Farouk's mother to flinch and retreat. "To marry is one thing! To parade his wife before us and remind us how little he cared about Farida is another!"

Farouk's mother quickly sought her exit and left the house in a flurry of curse words as my mother screamed and ranted at her retreating form.

Mother was bed-ridden for days after that, her heart a broken mess. She didn't understand how people could forget and go on with their lives so effortlessly after such a tragedy and couldn't reconcile in her mind that everyone had just given up on Farida. Everyone believed she was never coming back.

CHAPTER 47:
AUJENE 1971

It was Little Mahmoud who found her. Little 12 year old Mahmoud with the misshapen head, the uneven teeth and bulging eye. Most of the younger kids in the village mocked him and threw stones at him, bullying him for his appearance. An appearance he was born with, made worse by his idiot mother who mistreated him.

The older children all looked after him, treating him with the humanity that was a right upon every person. Especially the older girls. With their maternal instincts, they looked out for him and allowed no one to bully or take advantage of him in their presence. Ironic, then, that it would be Mahmoud who skipped through the orange grove and onto the second water well, no longer in use because it had apparently dried up, kicking stones as he sought a quiet corner in which to hide from the constant barrage of abuse being hurled at him.

The first thing he noticed was the stench. A foul odour permeating the well as he neared it. And as he got closer, his mouth falling open in a silent scream, he unconsciously understood the smell and too many things became clear in his head. A swath of heavy fabric gathered around the body of a young woman, her face swollen beyond recognition and her dark hair tumbling out of her scarf. Atop her chest, a lumpy bundle swaddled against her chest. No movement, her eyes closed but so obviously extinguished of the life they once held.

There was no mistaking the little white flowers on navy fabric that covered the girl-Mahmoud would know that dress anywhere. His voice came out, something between a wild howl and a keening pitch, as he stumbled backward, then turned on his heel and ran at manic speed all the way back to the village to ignite the fire that would rage through the valley and tear our lives apart.

My mother howled. She screamed. She scratched her face. She pulled her hair out as she screamed *"Binti. Ya binti.* Farida. *Binti."* She literally went crazy with grief.

No mother should ever have to see that.

No mother should ever have to bury her child.

Even with the stench, Farida having been out in the open for an uncertain amount of time, my mother refused to bury her without washing her body first. The older ladies washed her, made prayer above her body, swathed her in the customary white burial cloth, and prepared her in death.

We marched in, one by one, to say our goodbyes and bid our sister Farida farewell. Still in shock, we looked at her in disbelief, our eyes stinging with tears, our hopes and dreams crushed beneath the trampling feet of men unknown, as our mother continued to wail and destroy herself over Farida's body as it was prepared for burial.

Three things were for certain:

Although we knew not where, Farida had remained alive for almost a year after she'd been taken.

The bundle swaddled to her chest had been a baby, a boy born prematurely and placed in a sling against his mother's heart so they could be buried together.

The baby, undoubtedly, had been Farida's still born child, the blood and material caked between her legs evidence that she had very recently given birth.

CHAPTER 48: AUJENE 1972

It was after Farida was laid to rest that my mother slowly started to go blind. My father refused to get her a doctor, telling her it was all in her head-she had done it to herself. She would tell me she saw things in shadow...sometimes she could make out a face, other times the image was too blurred for her to recognise anyone or anything.

The ladies of the village, pitying my mother, all claimed it was due to seeing her dead daughter's body-it was her brain's way of shutting out what it had seen. Yes. Some things could never be unseen.

Even Rabiaa, still mourning the disappearance of her own daughter, visited with my mother, and spent endless hours in her company; even if they had nothing to say to one another, as was often the case, a world of silent conversation took place between them as they shared in their common grief. Rabiaa, stalwart Rabiaa, pitied mother yet silently thanked God that it wasn't her own daughter. Why wouldn't she-any mother would. Yet I knew she pitied her more than anything else. She shared in our grief while at the same time, although holding out hope that her daughter was still alive somewhere, she basted in her own fear that her Farida would meet a similar fate.

◆ ◆ ◆

My father was merciless. He had no *rahma*. He was especially hard on me. Sometimes he would call me Farida, mistaking me for his missing daughter. Everyone understood why he would make the mistake; we had looked so much alike, we could have almost been twins had it not been for the three year age gap between us. However, my father had always treated me differently to the way he treated Farida. Many years later, after he was long gone, my aunt Yumna explained to me what my own mother had not had the heart to share with me.

I was supposed to be born a boy. Abu El Banaat's long awaited boy. But instead, I was born a girl, and from the moment I took my first breath, my father had resented me. His brain could not reconcile nor understand the cruel hand that he had been dealt, and that's why, the girls that were born after Farida were emotionally exiled. Two girls he could deal with. Three was acceptable. But anything after three was banished from his heart and set into the background of his life. I was the unlucky fourth girl.

"A shame if ever there was one," my aunt Yumna explained, looking at me longingly. "In character, you're the child that most resembles a boy. You're strong, and smart, and you understand the earth. You're a tomboy and you're nimble on your feet. You don't like the usual things that girls like...opting to play with marbles and dirt rather than dolls and jewellery. You're everything a boy should be, but you're a girl. That's your curse." Her eyes softened as she looked at me sadly. Aunt Yumna loved me to death, and no one could deny that I was her favourite niece.

So it was my father's longing to have a boy to carry his namesake that cursed my life. I was his proverbial punching bag as he took out his frustrations on me. Nothing I did was ever good enough, no matter how hard I tried to please him.

CHAPTER 49: FARIDA 1972

Nothing happened in our village, in all small villages, I suppose, without everyone finding out. Keeping secrets in little tight knit communities was near impossible. Things that happened, no matter how ordinary, always got found out. And the ordinary sometimes became extraordinary.

The day I came home, Hassan drove me up the winding gravel road that led to my parent's house. It was the main street of Tul Ghosn, our little village, and little had changed in the years that I'd been away. Little Khaled, now just over a year old, bounced on my lap as the car jumped up and down in its meandering toward our destination. The road was so demolished, full of potholes and loose rocks, that the town folk often joked that it was quicker to walk than drive up the main strip for how slow cars had to go to avoid busting a tyre.

As we drove along, more and more people came to their doors to watch this strange, shiny new car as it made its way through their village. I could see some people squinting, as though daring their eyes to admit to what they were seeing. I know some people looked at me and gasped, especially those that had known me in my past life.

"Do you want to stop?" Hassan asked, looking over at me as I looked at a woman on the side of the road who had seen me and promptly dropped a tray of beans. I shook my head in response and we continued on. I knew that people would have a lot of questions. From time to time, Hassan had relayed to me the latest news he had heard about the village and the general consensus was that I was long dead.

"Thank you for letting me come," I whispered, not looking at him. From the corner of my eye, I could see that he had turned once again to look at me, but my focus remained ahead as we neared ever further toward my old family home.

"There's no need to thank me. You've proven yourself beyond measure; you're one of us now."

There was a long stretch of silence until we finally reached the big red metal double doors leading into my parents' home. The village was now brimming with people at their front doors, silently curious as they watched the events unfold. I could see my great aunt, the town gossip, leaning over the railing of her second floor apartment above, looking, but as though not actually seeing, not understanding what her eyes were showing her as I stood at the door with Khaled latched to my hip. Hassan rapped loudly on the door then stood to the side with his hands fisted against one another in front of him in military fashion.

It was my mother who answered the door, who stood there looking through me, seeing but not seeing. Khaled squeaked, and I watched carefully as her head moved towards the sound, but again, she looked straight through Khaled.

"Mama? *Shu sarlek ya mama?*" I cried, moving into her. The woman who had aged years since I'd last seen her raised her hands in surprise, fumbling to hold onto something. I saw the precise moment that her back went ramrod straight and she perked, turning her face to the side, then into my neck, where she took a deep sniff and stumbled back.

"*Meen?*" she asked, fearful. "F...Farida?"

"*Ana* mama, *ana* Farida," I laughed and cried as tears rolled down my cheeks. Whatever had happened to my mother that she couldn't see me was bad, but I was so happy to see her, I fell further into her arms as Hassan grabbed Khaled from my arms and told me he'd look after him.

I heard my sister Aujene calling to my mother, asking who was at the door, at the same time that mama moved out of the entry way and I came face to face with Aujene, who I could swear stopped breathing the moment she saw me.

"Farida..." she whispered. "But how...*Subhan Allah Subhan Allah, la Illaha Illa Allah.* How are you here, *ekhti?*"

Hassan took this moment to usher me into the house rather than remain on the main road with all the neighbours' curious gazes stripping us of our privacy. I heard the gentle thud of the door behind me as my mother took my hand and led me through the breezeway and into the garden. She walked gingerly, her feet shuffling and her back hunched a little where it never had been before. I realised that in the three years I'd been gone, my mother had aged immeasurably.

We sat in the garden, the beloved garden where I'd spent my younger years. Khaled squealed at the sight of a chicken and Hassan let him down to chase after it.

"Mama, this is my husband, Hassan," I said, putting my hand on his knee. "Khaled is our first born." I looked after the little boy as he laughed and ran happily through the garden.

"Aujene, *layki ya binti*... Farida *rej3et*," my mother explained to Aujene, who I could see, although dumbstruck, knew it was me.

"Mother lost her eye sight," Aujene explained. "She sees things as shadows now. It happened after we buried you." There was an accusatory tone in my younger sister's voice.

I looked down sadly, hurt and ashamed that my parents had had to go through such torment, not knowing how to tell them the sequence of events that led us to this moment and prevented me from coming earlier.

"Where have you been, Farida," Aujene asked, "and who did we bury thinking it was you?"

I proceeded to tell them the story of how I was taken from the olive grove by a local Bedouin clan and kept in a bunker for many weeks. The close call I had when the kidnappers realised they had taken the wrong girl and had to "dispose" of me, because they couldn't return me without getting themselves killed. How one of the guards had broken from the clan and informed a nearby clan of my imprisonment, and the Shaikh from that clan had stepped up, out of a sense of duty to do what was right, and proclaimed that he would marry me.

"This created an unexpected-but not unwelcome-resolution to the problem at hand, and a wedding was hastily organised and we were married before the eyes of God and the bedouin village to which Hassan belonged."

"I don't understand," Aujene reiterated "so who did we bury in your dress?"

I took a deep breath and let out a sigh. This was not news I wanted to deliver, for although it would make them happy to know that I was alive, someone else's heart would be broken with this deliverance.

"I wasn't the Farida they were after. God damn the curse of Farida," I said, rolling my eyes to the sky and shaking my head. "All this over a name." I paused to catch my breath and felt my heart sink with every word I uttered as my mother's tears rolled down her cheeks and she whispered "Poor Farida. Poor poor Farida."

"They took another girl. Another Farida. Rabiaa's daughter. Again, she was the wrong Farida. She wasn't as fortunate as I. I don't know where they kept her for the duration of her captivity – I had already married so I didn't know she was there until the gatekeeper came to let Hassan know that there was a dead body in one of their fields that they had to attend to. Hassan took me to see her afterwards, telling me he believed the girl was a neighbour in my village, and perhaps I would like to say a prayer for her." I looked over at Hassan with gratitude in my eyes. Although this was not the life I would have chosen for myself, I was still alive thanks to Hassan. He didn't have to marry me. He was not obligated in any way to me – yet he had saved me and he was the reason I was now here.

"She died during childbirth. I found her naked, the baby across her chest, still attached by the umbilical cord. A baby boy. She couldn't have been more than a few hours gone. I couldn't bear to see her so violated and alone. I cut the cord and dressed her in my best dress. The navy dress you sewed for me, Mama. The gatekeeper promised to bury her, but I guess she somehow made her way back to the village."

"Little Mahmoud found her by the empty water well," Aujene explained. "It broke his little heart. She'd been laying out there for days and the only thing to identify her was her dress."

My head slumped forward in sorrow, the pain lancing through me like a thunderbolt. Of all the things that I had gone through, I was still here. The other Farida was gone and would not be returning. When I thought of the pain and torment she would have endured in her short life, my heart was crippled with sorrow and remorse that I was the lucky one that managed to survive.

"I looked for you," my mother said. "I looked and looked and looked, but lost all hope after we buried...." My mother looked off with a glassy stare as something held her attention "Poor Rabiaa..." she began "she will have to reckon with her grief all over again when she learns what has happened to her daughter."

CHAPTER 50: AUJENE 1972

My father came running home as soon as word reached him that Farida had come home. He ran all the way from the olive grove, arriving in a breathless mess as he flew in through the front door like a hurricane. He had heard, but did not quite believe, that a woman bearing a striking resemblance to his missing daughter Farida had come knocking on our door. Some of the children relaying the news swore on their life that it was Farida, and my father had initially scoffed at such a suggestion, putting the childish chatter out of his mind. It was only when the news had spread like wildfire throughout the grove, cemented by eyewitness claims by several grown men, that my father began to consider the impossible. Realising there was only one way to confirm or debunk the rumours, he ran all the way home to discover for himself that which had stirred up such excitement in the village.

I had never seen my father's face so tormented as when he laid eyes on Farida as she stood in the breezeway looking out for her son as he ran around the garden in circles. Mother was preparing lunch, and Hassan, stoic Hassan, stood by closely watching the events unfold as my father entered the house. I knew exactly what Hassan was afraid of.

My father's face morphed from relief to disbelief, then finally settled on fury. He alternated between emotions as he battled his inner torment over the situation with which he was faced.

"*Baba,*" Farida breathed.

Before we knew it, father was charging toward Farida with a venomous glint in his eyes. Hassan, who had most likely remained on the outskirts of father's view til now, stepped in front of my father, a steadfast mountain of a man preventing the inevitable. Hassan stuck his hand out and offered an introduction, while Farida moved to stand beside her husband. Hassan raised his other arm like a barrier to keep Farida behind him and it was not lost on him that my father did not shake his hand.

"I've heard about you," my father released a heavy breath. "You belong to the Badu tribe of Dhar Khamra."

Hassan merely nodded his head once and continued to watch my father wearily, expecting him to strike at any moment.

"Then you know exactly who I am. And what I stand for. Farida is now my wife. She is therefore under my protection."

"Your wife?!" my father roared. "Under your protection? Then where are all your men that will protect you as you protect her from me!"

Hassan, in the face of my father's yelling and rage, remained calm and spoke at almost whisper level as he relayed to my father, in words, the damage he was prepared to inflict on anyone that dared to betray his family.

"I don't need to be protected, Abu El Banaat. My family name and crest are protection enough. Know that if a single strand of Farida's hair is hurt, the entire Badu tribe will rain down on this village and destroy everything in it, both living and dead."

I could see my father's fingers twitch at his side as he considered his options, none of which worked in his favour.

This was a matter of honour. He was considering the elders' anticipation of an explanation for Farida's absence. He was considering the whispers and accusations of the neighbours. He was considering what failures would be allowed to slide unpunished, thus setting the stage for future generations to accomodate the same sin and agree that this was now a "new tradition." Their whole way of life would be dismantled. Their values eroded. Their customs and traditions twisted to fit a narrative that was devoid of morals and ethics.

"Farida has been in my care since she left you. She was intact until she entered our marital home and her honour was maintained at all times. She is now my wife and therefore part of the Badu tribe of Dhar Khamra. Past conflicts with our tribe have not ended well, Abu El Banaat. It would serve you well to bless our marriage and announce to the elders that Farida is now under the protection of the House of Damour."

I could see my father's nostrils flaring as he questioned the matter of Farida's honour. I looked at Farida, who in turn looked from my father to Hassan, where her eyes settled in soft waves of happiness. It was so obvious that Farida was in love with Hassan, it made one wonder if she had gone willingly with him that day in the olive grove. But how would she have ever had the opportunity to meet Hassan? I wondered, when we had been joined at the hip.

"The elders won't let this go so easily," my father explained. "Honour, above all, is the one thing that cannot be negotiated on."

"What happened, my daughter?" father asked. "I want to know everything that happened since the day Farida was gone," he said, turning back to Hassan.

And so, there came to pass many an hour as we all sat and Hassan relayed the story – brutally honest in every little detail, of how it had been a case of mistaken identity when the Waqas tribesmen collected Farida, how he had felt it was his duty to spare her the horror of an unjust death, and all the in-betweens of life as it happened during Farida's absence.

We took turns passing Khaled around, his cheeky laugh and big grey eyes mesmerising us all into a frenzy. I played with one of his ringlets, winding my finger through the chestnut brown strand, watching it bounce back after every pull. The boy was beautiful in that manner which only children could possess. Soon enough, his head fell to one side against his shoulder and I realised he had fallen asleep. I carried him to the nearest room and placed him on a mattress by the door so we could hear him if he woke.

"People will be asking questions," my father proclaimed, as my mother brought out a lunch of fried eggplant, cauliflower and potato with assorted dips and sides. We huddled around on the *haseeri* and proceeded to eat in a quiet silence laced with tension.

My father was not appeased with Hassan's version of events, no matter how honest and credible it had been. He worried about the questions the elders would have, but most of all, he was concerned about his standing in the village. Families who had broken with tradition had been exiled for doing much less. Honour was the highest level of accountability, and he wasn't sure how Farida's re-emergence would affect our standing in the village.

My mother's sole concern was having Farida back. She was

ecstatic that her daughter had returned, and was already planning, in her mind, at least, family dinners and reunions to introduce a married Farida to the wider family. Khaled, too, created within her a peace that radiated from within her as she followed his shadow through the garden. Even without her eyesight, she could sense that he was a stunning boy.

Before my father had arrived at the house, she had taken Farida's face in her hands, her shaking fingers traversing the planes of Farida's skin as she smoothed the skin to memorise each and every valley and dimple. Her hands moved to Farida's hair, gliding under my sister's scarf, trailing down the length of her hair, now to her waist, as she recalled the many hours, a lifetime ago, where she had sat brushing Farida's hair down her back. My mother had smiled-if anything, she was satisfied that Farida was healthier than ever and in all likelihood, living the kind of life that every girl deserved to live.

Next, mother had moved to Hassan, pausing before she raised her hands to his face. Hassan had taken her hands in his own and lifted them to his cheeks, and my mother had closed her eyes, feeling her way across Hassan's face until she had learnt every avenue and every indent in his face. She had trailed over the light smattering of hair on his cheeks and chin which created a 5 o'clock shadow, his wide cherry coloured lips and his long curled lashes that had so often beguiled women wherever he went.

"Hassan is light," I had told my mother. "Much fairer than we are." My mother smiled, her mind understanding an inside joke no-one else was privy to.

Now my father sat, a grumpy old man, still trying to work out in his head the next step in the unfolding saga of Farida and her new husband as he lapped at tahini sauce with his freshly baked bread.

"I have arranged a meeting with the village elders," Hassan said, in what seemed to finally allay my father's fears. "My elders will be meeting with them tonight. You have nothing to worry about."

My father merely looked at him, staring dumbfounded at the man who sat opposite him. Hassan barely ate, I realise, so unlike the men we were constantly exposed to. My father dropped the morsel in his hand as his face clouded with fury.

"Are you saying I am incapable of handling family affairs without your help?" my father roared.

"On the contrary, Abu El Banaat. It was out of respect to you and your village elders that I sought this meeting. This will hopefully eradicate any animosity between the two tribes, and build bridges that will enable us to continue trade and support each other's goals."

At this, my father softened. It was always about the bottom line for my father. And just like that, as we sat around the *siffra*, my father's appetite returned with a vengeance as his mind carried him into a world where we did endless trade with the Badu and our livelihood and finances flourished due to this newfound union. Without a doubt, his mind already 180 miles ahead, my father would eventually take credit for introducing Hassan to Tul Ghosn.

CHAPTER 51:
AUJENE 1972

In our village, two things dictated your status and earned you respect.

Money.

And power.

My father had neither. Nor would he live to see either in his lifetime.

Instead, he was known in the village as Abu El Banaat, or "father of the girls." After he married my mother, they had six girls in rapid succession, without a boy amongst them to carry the family name. A great shame that my father carried like a heavy weight on his shoulders. However, he was not only known as the father of the girls because he had spawned only female offspring, but also the father of the most beautiful girls in the village. We all had the same exotic look that my mother sported, with dewy skin that was softly sun kissed with all the time we spent outdoors. Our dark hair blended perfectly with our equally dark almond eyes to create perfect symmetry, and our full lips danced with the song of youth.

My father was a man with a vain streak. If he couldn't elevate his status with wealth (he had none) or power (not even close), he used the one tool he had in his arsenal to stand out amongst the men who easily overshadowed him. The one tool that gave him even a semblance of power: his daughters.

When I was just barely 17, finally recovered from my time at the Nawfel household, suitors started knocking at our door. My two older sisters were already married and well on their way to producing babies. Farida was gone-and returned-but no longer on the waiting list for suitors, and two younger sisters were not quite ready for marriage yet. But my father decided that I, at 17, was just ripe for the picking and proceeded to entertain all manner of suitors at our home, on an almost daily basis, in his attempt to filter the best opportunity that would elevate him into the upper echelons of society.

Suitors came from near and far; some acceptable and some not so much. But he entertained every last one of them, including those that requested a second and third visit. I had two pretty dresses that rotated between the nightly visits, and too late I noticed that some suitors who had come several times had seen me in the same recycled fashions several times over. Not that I minded nor cared; it was merely an afterthought, a realisation that struck me as we entertained another suitor who had brought with him a rockmelon as an offering on his first visit.

The thing about my father was he entertained every single enquiry, but when it came to decision making, he couldn't do so out of fear that a better opportunity was just around the corner. My opinion was never asked for and was not considered important. All that was required of me was to greet the visitors at the door, prepare and serve the *Ahwi,* and keep my mouth shut as I sat with the guests looking pretty. I soon came to understand that my father, an uneducated man, was terrified that if I opened my mouth to speak, it would become apparent that I was also uneducated, a trait that the best of suitors avoided at all costs. Little did my father understand that educated men wouldn't necessarily be looking to marry a 17 year old girl.

As per my mother's instructions, every night after the guests left, I would take off my dress and hand wash it, wringing it well to hang and dry in anticipation of another visit. Eventually, the two dresses became three when my older sister gifted me one of her old dresses that no longer fit her after childbirth.

The suitors continued to knock on our door. Generally, all came through a referral;"We heard you have a girl ready for marriage" or "We come to seek your daughter's hand in marriage." Everyone had something to offer. But father seemed not to be too happy with what was being offered.

At night, as I collected the *ahwi* cups and wiped down the coffee tables, I would hear his criticisms as my parents discussed the "lucky family that was fortunate enough to visit us tonight", as he would put it. "This young man walks funny" my father would complain, and tell my mother to send word to the family that there was no *naseeb* for him with his daughter. "This boy is shorter than our daughter; it's traditional that the man is taller than the woman," and I would roll my eyes behind his back. The list of reasons to decline a prospective suitor kept growing until I felt half of the village had been turned away as unsuitable suitors for me.

"This boy lives from a village too far away, from a family whose heritage is doubtful…"

"I don't think this suitor is the right one; he has manicured fingers like a girl."

"His family works the land. What can they offer us?"

My mother had a reply to each and every one of his grievances. She was a simple woman with simple tastes who saw the world as one flat plain. Everyone was the same, and she believed that no one human was better than another. I smiled at her with pride as she quipped back after every excuse my father put on the table, but her latest, after my father stressed tonight's visitors were farmers toiling in the land was my favourite.

"So do we," she replied. "What can we offer them?" It was one of my mother's boldest moments, and I could see the old her shining through the armour she had built around herself. My father merely scoffed and turned away from her, knowing there was nothing he could say to counter what she had fired back at him.

CHAPTER 52:
AUJENE 1972

They called him the hunter. Everyone knew who he was because he was the oddity in the village. He carried one rifle strapped across his chest and another around his neck and sat in the trees in the plot of land across from the olive grove hunting birds all day long. He was a good shot, rarely missing, birds falling from the sky and landing at our feet as we tended to the crop. When that happened, you knew the hunter was around. When he ran out of bullets, he would pull out a sling and some rocks which he'd start aiming at the birds.

He had the misfortune of being the only male child of a woman who was on her fourth marriage after his father passed away prematurely. Her current marriage was to a man 15 years older than her who was a tyrant if ever the village had one. His father's premature death ensured that Samer was kicked around and constantly abused by his mother and his stepfather, as well as his three sisters' husbands. After his father's death, his mind a blur of all the possibilities in life that would now never see fruition, he had taken to the streets and fended for himself as best he could. The irony was that when his father died, he had land rights over almost a third of the land in the north, a fact that was not lost on people who saw Samer walking the streets in torn clothes and worn shoes. Subsequently, the land would be tied up in estate litigation for decades, but in the meantime, Samer sat in his usual tree and shot bird after bird whilst singing brooding, woeful ballads.

The hunter had occasion to see me tending to the olive grove. Later, he would tell me I was the most beautiful thing he had ever seen. The day after he saw me in the olive grove, he was knocking on our front door in the evening requesting a meeting with my father.

"But, my son, traditionally boys do not come knocking on prospective wives' doors without their parents," my father had explained to him, holding the door ajar to prevent his entry.

"Away with tradition!" Samer cursed. "My father is no longer with us, and my mother is bed-ridden."

"Where are your sisters, their husbands? Your stepfather could come in your mother's stead..."

"Abu El Banaat, I am a man of my word. I have seen your daughter yesterday, and knowing you are entertaining suitors, urged upon myself to request her hand before she could be betrothed to another."

Although agitated, he felt sorry for the boy, and saw no harm in accepting him into our house to share a cup of tea with him. My father set aside his tradition and opened the door wider for Samer, who took off his shoes which were worn down to the soles and entered the home.

My father called for me to make the tea and I obliged, bringing it to the living room where they sat bantering about anything and everything. My father took a liking to him immediately. Me, not so much.

Samer saw fit to drop subtle hints about his family's fortune (no money, just land-land as far as the eye could see) and made a point of reiterating that he would be building a grand home on the family plot where his children could run around and be free. There was, he remarked, more than enough land in the family to build an entire kingdom a hundred times over.

My father seemed impressed, to say the least, and when he enquired about how Samer would fund the build, he advised he would be commencing work in a massive transport company in the city the following week, even though he had no cause to be looking for work, seeing as the family trust was more than enough to sustain the family for generations to come.

I could almost see the moment that my father's eyes lit up with dollar signs, and wondered at how easily this boy had come into our home, sans family, and so swiftly tackled my father's feeble mind and sold him a load of bullshit. I knew then, without a doubt, that my father was sold on Samer and had made up his mind who my future husband would be.

Even as my mother argued with him to be reasonable after Samer had left his position on our couch after hours of conversation with my father (most suitor visits only lasted up to an hour), my father could not be swayed in his conviction that Samer was just what we needed in our family. Not only did he come from a wealthy family and would one day be extremely rich, but he was also starting a new job in a big company that would undoubtedly see the young boy escalated to the highest ranks of authority in the company due to his family's standing in society.

My mother argued with him endlessly, reminding him that money should not be a driving factor in who he chose to betroth their daughter to, but my father, ever stubborn and set in his ways, was steadfast in his conviction and would not back down.

"You haven't even met his mother yet," she whispered.

"I've met her in passing. Pleasant woman. Plus she won't be marrying his mother, she's marrying him. And you heard him, he has hopes to travel to Australia. AUSTRALIA!" he breathed, almost awe struck. "Can you imagine what that would mean, if your daughter were to go to Australia, then pull us there one by one? There would be no need to work the land because in Australia, money pours on you just because you are in Australia. It's a whole other world!"

My mother shook her head as she realised there was no getting through to him. "I don't want my daughter to move far away from me," she announced. "I've already lost one daughter; I won't sacrifice another!"

"You're not listening to me, Tala!" my father said, shaking my mother by the arms. "We will follow her there. After she is settled, she will send for us and we will follow. So you see, you will not be far from her for long. This is what we've been waiting for," he said, trying to convince my mother that this was the right thing for everyone.

My mother turned her face away from him, and I could see that she was ashamed to even look him in the face. Even with her poor eyesight that was ever dwindling, I know the clearest she saw of anyone was my father. For even though she may have seen him as but a distant shadow in her eyes, the power he wielded over all of us was enough for her to recognise him anywhere.

Neither said anything further as we collected ourselves and headed into different directions of the house. I realised it was close to midnight and slumped onto my bed in defeat. 5 hours. It had taken 5 hours for Samer to convince my father that he was the man for me.

CHAPTER 53: AUJENE 1972

I didn't want to marry Samer. My father wanted me to marry Samer. But I didn't want to marry Samer. Father cursed and cussed and screamed at the top of his lungs, bringing my sisters running to see what all the commotion was about as he stood over my cowering figure calling me an ungrateful burden. He called me every name under the sun, slapped me several times because he was "slapping sense into me", and went for long stretches without talking to me, even when I asked him a question in an attempt to strike up a conversation. His silence punished me, knowing that it would affect me and my deep seated need to be an obedient child. It hurt, the pain igniting in me a sadness so terrifying, I thought my heart would give out and I'd cease to be, obedient or not.

One day he was particularly angry, especially after Samer had told him that I'd deliberately been avoiding setting a date for the wedding. My father was especially vicious, calling me the devil's spawn, his hand smacking so hard against the side of my head that the force sent me hurtling towards the wall. I curled up in a ball and started to cry, my tears rushing down my cheeks as I silently prayed that that would be the end of it. But he advanced on me again, this time grabbing me by the hair, pulling me this way and that, huge clumps of my hair still woven between his fingers as he flung me to the ground. He flicked his fingers loose until the hair floated like wisps of clouds to the floor, not batting an eyelid at the damage he'd done as my head throbbed in pain and I continued to sob incoherently.

"You will do as you're told!" he roared.

My mother came running in and put herself between us as he reached out to attack me again. With a sweep of one hand, he pushed her out of the way and stalked towards me again, squatting down to my level and pointing a finger in my face. I could feel the snot dribble down, staining my chin as my lip quivered. "You will marry Samer," he stated, matter-of-factly "you will be his wife and abide by what he says. You will travel with him and bear his children. Eventually, when the time comes, you will take us all there to start new lives."

I turned my face away and cried some more, shutting my eyes in pain as his words struck my heart. Like always, he was dictating my life. Who I would marry. How I would live my life. What would be required of me. I tried to think back to my older sisters, tried to remember if they had had the same experiences when it had been their turn to marry. Had they had the same restrictions? I couldn't remember. But a strong numbing sensation started to rise within me, spurning me on as I focused on my father's words and the torment and pain he inflicted on me.

"Stop Amjad, the girl has had enough," my mother whispered, tugging at his sleeve as she wiped at some blood at the corner of her mouth. He pushed her away with such force, she once again went hurtling to the floor, her head hitting a coffee table. I could see the pain etched on her face as she winced and mumbled, putting her hand to her head and drawing blood. As I saw my mother laying there, pain emanating from her body, something in me snapped and a red tinge crossed before my eyes as my heart started to palpitate.

"Mother's hurt," I whispered. "Let me help her," I begged him.

"Help her?" he hissed. "You want to help her? Then marry Samer and get us out of here!" he snapped.

"Isn't it enough that you already gave me away once?" I asked, all sense of obedience dissipating as I straightened against the wall.

My father's eyes widened at my disobedience, his head shaking in disbelief that I would bring up my time with the Nawfels.

"That was for your own good!" he hissed.

"Like this is?"

"You insolent child!" he screamed, grabbing my hair again and pulling it down so his face loomed right above mine. "You stupid, wicked girl. You marry Samer, or you leave here in a coffin."

CHAPTER 54: AUJENE 1972

The wedding was the most elaborate farce I'd ever seen. I wore a white dress and my sisters helped with my hair and makeup, my father insisting that I wear fire engine red lipstick. It was an odd request, but I realised later that it was Samer's request, but when he had suggested it, it had fallen on my deaf ears, so he had asked my father to ensure I wore that red lipstick. He also insisted on red underwear, and my face must have turned a deep crimson with embarrassment when my father instructed me to wear the cheap red set he had purchased from a passing Syrian saleslady. My mother had refused to tell me, and told him to leave it up to me what I chose to wear, not believing that he would actually take the matter up with me.

I sat on the *barzi* next to Samer, in my white dress with my fire engine red lipstick, a fake smile plastered on my face. Samer took my left hand and squeezed lightly, a real smile parading on his lips. Silent tears pierced my heart, threatening to explode forth out of anxiety. Just the thought of him touching me was enough to make my skin crawl.

The *tabbal* was a thudding tempo challenging the beating of my heart as it rose above the noise of the wedding guests and the sound of the *zalagheet*. I could see my mother greeting more guests as they arrived, my father strutting like he was the town chief, and my sisters mingling with their friends in the crowd, whispering little secrets about which boy they felt was the best looking amongst the guests.

My mother in law didn't like me much. I saw her standing amongst the guests, a scowl on her face as she looked at me then turned back to the woman standing beside her, whispering something to her. She shook her head then made her way towards us as I braced myself for the onslaught that was definitely coming my way. There had never been an occasion where I had run into her when she didn't berate and denigrate me and make a fool out of me in front of other people.

"*Shu ya arous*," she started, a sarcastic tone lacing her words. "*Ma lakayti gayr hal hemra elhamra?*" She was asking me about my red lipstick, and why I hadn't worn another colour.

"This was your son's choice," I said sweetly, confident that this time her ire would be directed elsewhere.

She looked at her son out of the corner of her eye, then slanted her gaze back to me, her eyes blazing with contempt. This woman was never going to let go of the fact that I was supposedly "taking her son from her." I would have liked to tell her that she could keep her son all to herself if that suited her better.

"All the women are talking," she said, watching me for some sort of a reaction. It was as though she was spoiling for a fight and wanted me to engage her in conflict.

"That's what women do at weddings," I told her. Again, my voice was dripping sweetness as I tried my hardest to kill her with kindness. My nonchalance seemed to enrage her as she humphed and looked from me to her son again. Samer, I realized, had remained quiet, avoiding the conflict even though he knew his mother was trying to pick a fight.

"*Aajbak ya Samer?*" his mother asked, turning to her son "*mar-*

tak labsa lawn el sharameet."

I could feel my face burning up, and I was sure my cheeks were now the same colour as my lips as I sat with my mouth gaping open, staring dumbfounded at my mother in law, who had literally just told me I was dressed like a whore. I looked to Samer, who merely laughed at his mother and smiled, then replied *"Ma'alash emi,* tonight she's my whore."

CHAPTER 55: AUJENE 1972

When the older girls in the village talked of their wedding nights, there was often giggling and sighing and explicit descriptions of what went on. It was a sort of tradition for the brides to share this useful information with the other girls, to tell us what our mothers wouldn't tell us. I had been lingering around during some of the conversations that took place, especially in the olive grove, and believed I knew enough about what happened on a girl's wedding night. I had often turned my ear the other way, tuning the girls out, but sometimes I had caught bits and pieces that I know held on to for dear life. I needed to know what would happen. And I needed to prepare for what was to come.

Most of the girls had stated they'd been afraid and nervous, but with some fondling and kissing, had relaxed enough to do the deed and enjoyed it. Maybe not the first time, but eventually, as the couple started to explore one another and understand their mutual needs and desires, they enjoyed a certain measure of excitement when they lay side by side.

My wedding night was anything but joyful or exciting. And truth be told, it was the total opposite of what I had heard the girls portraying happened to them on their wedding nights.

Samer had rushed to rid me of my wedding dress, fumbling with the buttons clumsily, then, growing impatient, tearing at the fabric of the dress until the buttons had popped and flown across the room. I had looked at each button as it hit the floor, my heart thumping heavily to the beat of each button that fell away from the dress. It was too late to tell him that the dress was borrowed and would need to be returned.

He pushed the collar of the dress down my neck and pulled the sleeves away from my arms. He struggled to get the dress down past my waist, and I stood mute, watching him as he fought to get the dress off. There was minimal skin contact in his rush to reveal the body under the fabric of the wedding dress. There were no warm and fuzzy kisses, or whispered words of welcome or endearments in his haste to undress me.

As soon as the dress fell in a heap at my feet, he rushed to remove his own clothes and pushed me towards the bed. I looked at him, doe eyed, dreading what came next and hating him at the same time. He didn't give me words of encouragement or hold my hand or lead me gently into the unknown. Instead, he sat me on the bed, then gave me a gentle push, covering my body with his own as he buried his head in the crook of my neck. His face moved back and forth against my neck, in a strange manner that I could not make sense of. Not kissing, not hugging, just sort of wiping his face against my skin over and over again.

I could feel the bulge between his legs as it nestled against my thigh, and he started to stab it against my skin, as though he was aiming for something, but not quite finding it. I knew the basics of anatomy. I knew what was supposed to go where, and he being older than me, I'm sure he knew, also, but for a while, he just kept poking his member at my thigh, in almost the same place over and over again. Later, I would realise the bruises that had formed on my thigh were from his poking and prodding.

I grunted as his body weighed heavily against my own, my

breathing laboured as I struggled for air. Eventually, he moved, rising onto his knees and looking down between his legs. Without aplomb, he took his penis in his hand and guided it to my opening, laying back down over me as he gave one sharp thrust towards it. I hissed through my held breath as he continued to breach through my opening and a stabbing pain surged through me. The pain was like nothing I had ever felt, like a sharp rod was piercing me, and I felt my insides being torn to shreds as he gritted his teeth and continued to push his way through with violently sharp jabs.

"*Layyyysh*," he hissed, through gritted teeth, and I could feel his frustration as he tried over and over again to breach me. Why. He wanted to know why. He let out a heavy breath, reared back, then surged forward and broke through my entry, thrusting once, twice, three times then settling within the depths of me with a spasm of hot liquid as he slumped on top of me.

My tears rolled down my cheeks unchecked, and for once, I didn't care about containing myself or being the strong, silent type. I needed to let out my pain. I felt like something had been stolen from me. I felt like I had been violated and abused. Samer shifted without saying a word and got up, heading toward the bathroom. I held my breath and waited, expecting him to come back momentarily. Instead, I heard the spray of the water as he showered. I sat there in silence, waiting, for what, I don't know. But realising that in all the stories told by the brides that came before me, none had so much as nearly compared to what had happened to me on my wedding night.

CHAPTER 56:
AUJENE 1972

After my marriage to Samer, I was quick to understand a few things.

First, that our marriage was not an ordinary one. I didn't know why Samer had married me – he showed me no affection and was not altogether interested in sharing anything with me except a bed. And even then, he took constantly without so much as giving. Without fail, each and every time that Samer would touch me, the experience would mirror our wedding night. There was never any affection, nor kissing, nor touching outside of him stripping, mounting my bruised body, and shoving himself into me with one deep and violent thrust. It would all be over in a matter of minutes, and I would be left lying on the bed feeling battered and bruised. My thighs were constantly bruised from his violent thrusting. I could even feel my insides were bruised. I was in constant pain and agony after each time, and would get into the shower as soon as possible to wash him off me and to gain some alleviation from the pain he inflicted upon me.

At times, I would brush my hand against his elbow in a show of affection, which he inevitably always ignored. He spoke little, unless he wanted something, and was not much for conversation whenever I posed a question.

The second thing I understood, and this most likely was tied in with the first point, was that Samer was a taker, not a giver. He would take everything that was offered to him, and then some, but he would never give. And he would never offer. Not that I wanted anything from him, but simple things like washing detergent. He would tell me to do the washing without detergent, explaining that the sun would sanitise the clothes. He was never giving of his moncy. He was an opportunist and would leap at each and every opportunity, but didn't want to do the hard work to get there.

I knew that I was never going to be happy with Samer, and when I voiced this to my mother, she turned to me sadly and started to cry, silently agreeing with me yet knowing that I would undoubtedly spend the rest of my days with him, albeit unhappily.

CHAPTER 57:
AUJENE 1973

As we got older, my father became more of a tyrant. Or maybe it was that when we were younger, we just didn't see it. I noticed he kept away from my younger sisters. Possibly because they were not yet age appropriate for marriage, I wasn't sure. Me, I was his constant punching bag. As was my mother whenever she stood up for me. The older girls were now married, living in their own homes, the responsibility of their husbands, so he didn't much involve himself with them.

My mother was my only salvation. I would complain and cry on her shoulder, missing her smell and her food and her company, missing everything about her as I relayed my unhappiness to her. We sat at the small table in the kitchen, sharing in our combined misery as we chatted.

"What are you two whispering about?" my father asked one day, when he walked in on us talking about Samer. I had just stopped crying and my eyes were swollen with sadness as my mother comforted me.

"Nothing," I whispered, drawing away from my mother. By now, I knew not to bring up Samer in a negative way; father absolutely doted on him and would not hear a word that would besmirch Samer's good name. I wondered where my father got the impression that Samer was a good man, and an even better husband, because it definitely wasn't by way of my reference.

"Not nothing," my father pressed, slamming a tray onto the kitchen counter. "What were you talking about?"

"Would you like some tea?" my mother asked him, rising to put the pot on the stove in an attempt to change the subject. Without warning, my father grabbed my mother's arm and pulled her toward him, looking at her menacingly. He reached up and pinched her cheeks with his thumb and forefinger, pressing his nails into her skin until there were two indents on each side of her face. My father lifted her face to look in her eyes and spat his venomous words at her.

"You were talking about something when I walked in," he said. "What were you talking about? And don't you lie to me, Tala."

I knew that mother would lie. She would always protect me, no matter the cost to herself. And lately, she'd been doing so much protecting, I worried how much her poor heart could hold.

"Aujene is upset because she knows she'll miss her family when she leaves for Australia. They lodged their papers with immigration today. It won't be long now."

My father pushed my mother's face back with such force that she stumbled backward and almost fell. He continued to look at her, wondering if she was telling the truth, yet knowing there was no real way he could prove or disprove her explanation.

"Is this true?" my father asked, turning his gaze toward me.

"We lodged the papers today," I told him.

"And why are you sad, going to a new life? A better life. There's a lot of money to be made in Australia," he said, his greedy little eyes shining as he got a far away look on his face.

"I don't want to leave Lebanon," I told him, knowing instantly that once again, I had said the wrong thing. For this was definitely not what my father wanted to hear.

"And why not?" my father screamed. "You fight against every good thing that happens to you!"

He staggered toward me, pointing an accusatory finger in my face. "A good husband? You don't want to marry him. Go to Australia? You don't want to leave Lebanon. Be a good wife? You want your voice to be heard. What is with you and your ungrateful disposition?!?"

My father continued to bellow at the top of his lungs, his eyes bulging as they did when he was angry. But not just angry, he was furious. He couldn't contain the anger surging through him, and he lifted me by the shoulders to my feet, until I was standing before him, shaking in fear. For all my bravado, the one person who could actually decimate me with fear was my father. He had always done so.

"What will it take to make you happy, hmm?" he asked, and I shrunk back from him, afraid what he would do next. Would he dare hit me now that I was married, as he had prior to my marriage?

"Amjad," my mother whispered, a warning to lay off as she touched his arm in an attempt to pull his attention away from me. She knew him far better than I did, and she predicted, with astute clarity, what would come next. My father shrugged my mother's hand off his own and continued to advance on me.

"I'm going to go home now," I announced, turning to leave. But he merely pulled me back, his angry face warning me not to walk away from him.

"Tell me what will make you happy?" my father asked, and I could see that he was waiting for my answer and expected one. When I didn't answer, I could see the wheels turning in his head as he plotted his next move on the chessboard. "Will you be happy if you left Samer?" my father asked, accurately guessing exactly what was in my head. I saw my mother gasp and shake her head in warning behind him, her eyes imploring me not to respond. I pursed my lips and looked down at the ground, not answering him, which only made him angrier. He was spoiling for a fight, and would get one before the day was out.

"What! Will! Make! You! Happy!" My father screamed, enunciating each and every word. "Do you fancy yourself a divorced woman, hmm?" he asked. "Would you be better off without Samer? That lying, cheating bum who thinks he's got us all wrapped around his little finger," my father said, for once describing Samer exactly as he was, the first cruel words he had used to describe his son in law. And I fell for it hook, line and sinker, nodding my head in agreement. His words were vindication that he had always known that Samer was a worthless piece of scum.

The slap came out of nowhere. Strong enough to send me hurtling toward the wall, where I slithered in a messy heap and folded into myself. He was upon me within seconds, showing me no mercy as he continued his tirade. My mother screamed and flung herself into the melee, putting herself between us, and I could hear a crack as my father's hand smashed into her and sent her flying to the other side of the room.

He advanced on me again, winding my hair around his fist as he lifted my face to his own and hissed at me. My father was a tyrant. He could get angry. But this was a completely different and more violent man than the one I had known before my marriage.

"You ungrateful little bitch!" he simmered, his spittle hitting me between the eyes. "Day in and day out, I have to contend with the degrading moniker Abu El Banaat."

Slap.

"My name was dragged through the mud with your sister Farida and my standing deflated even before it ever began."

He administered an even harder slap, then retracted from my heaped body and stood above me.

"I have to live in this Godforsaken village and put up with the whispers and the rumours and the name calling."

He administered another harsh slap, then a kick to my gut that led me to howl out and curl into myself.

"Amjad!" my mother screamed, lunging at my father again. But this time, when he made to hurl her off him, she held on for dear life, ripping the sleeve of his shirt as she clung to him and tried to push him away from me. Even in my pained and delirious state, I could see blood gushing from my mother's mouth, and later I would learn that the crack I'd heard had been her teeth. He had broken two of her front teeth.

"Ungrateful, that's what you are!" he hissed, trying to climb the wall of my mother's weight as she pushed into him, shoving him away from me. "Instead of being grateful that God has given you this opportunity to help us, you spit in my face with your ungratefulness!"

After a few more choice words, he finally turned on his heels and left the room, and my mother, ambling in pain, came to my side and attempted to help me up.

"I can't, mother. The pain is too great," I complained, unable even to sit up.

"It's okay, *ya binti.* I am right here. Lean on me."

I shook my head and tears started to roll down my cheeks as I started to moan and groan, my hand spreading across my stomach where my father had kicked me. My mother looked at my stomach, then gasped, the blood dripping onto her chin as she looked at the ground behind me, then moved my dress to the side, as though looking for something.

"Oh, God," she whimpered. "*Ya Allah! Ya Allah, binti!*" and as my mother's screams and cries became the static at the end of a long tunnel, I laid my head to the ground and lost consciousness.

CHAPTER 58: AUJENE 1973

Later, I would find out that I had miscarried my first child. I hadn't even known that I was pregnant. It was early days, the doctor said, maybe six or seven weeks, but it was a child nonetheless. A piece of me that I had lost. To be honest, I'd never considered the possibility of children with Samer, but obviously this was bound to happen, and regardless of my relationship with my husband, I did still want to have children one day.

My mother was beside herself, afraid that she would lose me for all the blood she saw gushing underneath me as I lay there on the ground. My father had tried to see me. I'm not sure if it was to redeem herself, but I had refused him. I didn't want to see him nor speak with him. Even Samer had interceded on his behalf, but I had stood my ground and refused to see him, announcing that there was no valid reason on the face of the earth that would change my mind.

It was as if one day he had been, and then he was no longer. Even as the days inched towards our travel date years later, I still refused to see my father. Although it pained me greatly to avoid my family home, my one connection to my mother and my siblings, I took back my sanity by erasing him from my life and depriving him of the chance to play a role in Aaida's life. For, if there was any lesson to be learnt from my time as a child in that home, it was that there was no world in which I could allow a man like my father into my children's life.

CHAPTER 59:
FARIDA 1974

"Are you ready?" Hassan asked, rubbing at my belly.

"My bags are already in the car," I smiled, excited that I was accompanying him on this trip to Syria. He had suggested we drive to Syria on a shopping expedition and spend a leisurely weekend there before the baby was born, a chance at which I had jumped to spend more time with my husband, away from the village that seemed to always occupy his time with official matters.

My mother in law, by now my greatest advocate, had insisted on keeping Khaled with her while Hassan and I had a few days to ourselves.

It took us almost two hours to get to Aleppo, where we checked into a hotel and changed before going out for lunch. Syria was renowned for many things, not least of which was their food. The country was a major exporter of its rich aromatic spices which, when added to their minced lamb and rice dishes, or their lahme bi ajeen, or even their grilled kifta, lent itself a miraculous burst of spicy flavour that could not be contested anywhere else in the Middle East.

I had never been to Syria, and now as we drove through the city streets, I marvelled at the gorgeous history behind the architecture and the street vendors who promised everything from fresh lupins to homewares. The city was an eclectic mix of new and old, bright and bold as we meandered through the slow moving traffic until we got to our destination.

The restaurant was located in a small boutique hotel in downtown Aleppo, in a suburb called Azizíyeh. Syria was really as far as I had travelled outside of Lebanon, and I continued to be amazed by the beauty of the country as the people welcomed us warmly. It seemed wherever we went, people knew we were not natives of the country and treated us like long lost friends. After lunch, Hassan took my hand as we walked the street in comfortable silence, the hustle and bustle of the thriving city leaving me awestruck as we wandered aimlessly through the street.

"I have some friends I'd like you to meet," Hassan confided, as we entered into the grounds of the beautiful Aleppo Public Park and strolled around enjoying the greenery of the mass of land that attracted thousands of visitors a day. "I know this trip is supposed to be just me and you, but would you like to meet them?"

"Who is it," I asked?

"Allow me to surprise you?"

I scrunched up my face in question and nodded, excited yet somewhat apprehensive that I would be meeting some of Hassan's friends, when in the few years that we'd been married, he hadn't introduced me to many.

We stopped by a sweet shop and picked up an assortment to gift Hassan's friends before heading on foot to our destination. When we reached a home with soaring turrets and winding stairs that led up to a fancy garden, I looked in appreciation at the magnificent elms that towered over the home providing much needed shade.

A lady who couldn't have been a day over 60 years greeted us at the door, welcoming us in warmly, hugging Hassan close and kissing my cheeks three times in greeting.

"Sahar is one of our oldest family friends," Hassan introduced us, as we walked into the house, his hand on the small of my back.

"The kids will be down in a moment," Sahar explained, looking towards the stairs.

We sat in the lounge room, sipping *ahwi* as Sahar brought Hassan up to speed on the latest news in Syria.

"My dear, you are glowing with the aura of pregnancy," Sahar commented, looking at me warmly. "There is nothing more beautiful than a pregnant woman."

"I second that," Hassan agreed. I blushed as a sudden commotion from the direction of the stairs caught our attention and two young boys barrelled into the room, jumping in a heap onto Hassan as he reached for them.

It was when the children excitedly referred to Hassan as *"khalo"* that my breath stopped and my gut twisted. The children were so obviously identical and their resemblance to Hassan so uncanny, my mind swirled with all the implications of who they were. I didn't have to wonder long as two more figures came bounding into the room, swiftly making their way toward us. Without consciousness, I felt myself rise slowly, shock registering on my face as I came face to face with a beaming Zelekha. Before I could say anything, one of the twins bounded towards the woman and pulled at her dress, calling, "Mama! Mama! *Layki, khalo hawn...*"

Zelekha wrapped me in tight arms and covered my face with

kisses as I looked over her shoulder at Hassan, who stood with his hand on one of the boys' shoulders, watching us. He knew he'd have some serious explaining to do, and it seemed, by the way that the boys were fluttering around him, that they were accustomed to him and he had visited with them many a time. I mused at how well he had kept the secret, never once uttering Zelekha's name after that last trip years before when he returned home and commanded that no one was to ever utter Zelelkha's name in the house again.

"We have a lot to talk about," Zelekha said, her wise eyes tracking me as she moved to greet her brother.

The man who'd been standing behind her introduced himself as Talal, her husband, before Sahar ushered me and Zelekha out onto the balcony. "You two girls have much to discuss. Let the men have their space, I will bring tea then take the boys out into the garden for playtime."

I watched the boys as they tumbled behind Sahar, their squeals and laughter echoing throughout the large house. They were such happy, vibrant boys, and it twisted my heart that my own son was so far away and couldn't meet his cousins.

"Does your mother know you're here?" was the first thing I asked after we sat down.

Zelekha looked at me politely and smiled. "She has always known," she confided. "Mother has been to visit me a few times."

"She kept it from me," I whispered, turning my head to watch the children as they ran through a spray of gardenia trees.

"The only way this could have been successful was to keep this secret in the bosom of as few people as possible. Hassan only agreed to it because we swore we would stay away."

"But your traditions," I argued. "Your mother is the main component of this story, and she upholds tradition with an iron fist."

"Most traditions. On the tradition of honour, she and my brother agree. Some cases are so extreme that they require upholding the tradition. But a lot of our traditions which place us in these predicaments are very outdated. A tradition that sees me betrothed to my first cousin from the moment I open my eyes to the world is not a tradition. It's a crime."

"Yet that's what happened."

"I never wanted to marry Musab. In fact, I couldn't stand him. But tradition amongst the badu dictated that first born daughter of one brother be wed to first born son of the other. It's an old tradition, carried on through the generations, and one that many a person has tried to change. The elders hold on fiercely to our way of life. A select few don't agree with the tradition; to keep the peace, they uphold it the best way they know how."

"And Hassan? He was furious when you left."

Zelekha shrugged in nonchalance. "He had to be. It wouldn't do for the head of the clan to forgive this sleight. So he came searching for me – and he found me. Pretty quickly, too. Hassan has always been the diplomatic one in the family. He listened to what I had to say and told me he would return the next day with his answer. He made me promise not to run away again, and I didn't. I waited for him the next day, and he returned and set out for me the terms of our agreement."

"Agreement?"

"As far as the world knows, Zelekha Damour is dead. Her brothers found her in Syria, where she is now buried. Only a select few trusted friends know what really happened."

"Musab?" I asked. "He accompanied your brothers on all their trips.

"Hassan has lot of business in Syria. There was no need for them to be together every waking hour. So he never knew."

"Our clansmen visit Syria all the time, aren't you afraid what would happen if someone recognises you?" I asked, my eyes widening in horror. "Not only would it affect you, but your family also-the tribe believes you died at the hands of your brothers."

Zelekha shook her head and looked out toward the distance with a faraway look in her eyes. I could see the mist of tears as they shimmered before they fell sadly against her cheeks.

"I can never go back there, and I miss the village with all my heart. But I don't live here either." Zelekha looked down at her lap sadly, and I could see all the years that she would miss... next to her mother, her children playing with her sibling's children, watching the world transform with those she loved. Zelekha was truly alone, and I pitied her the choice she'd made, which in turn led to her being an outcast.

"I'm like a true Bedouin now-living in Jordan. Moving from one town to another to maintain my anonymity. I come to Syria only on occasion to meet with Hassan or Waleed. Sahar has maintained our safety every time we've come to Aleppo; she is a true friend and inspiration. We're in the process now of securing visas to Turkey, where we will move and make a better life for our children after the baby is born. Sahar has family there who have offered to help us with the relocation and securing work for Talal."

"Are you happy, Zelekha?" I wanted to know if the choices

she had made were worth it. I, on the one hand, didn't have a choice in marrying her brother, but that had worked out for me better than I expected. My marriage to Hassan was beyond anything I ever could have imagined or desired. I wanted to know if, having her free will to make the choice to either leave or stay, had she made the right decision?"

"Happiness is a state of mind, Farida," she started. "I'm sad that I'm missing out on a future in Dhar Khamra, but I'm happy with Talal. He treats me well, and as you've seen, we have two beautiful boys that we adore. Financially, we are just barely making it, but with thanks to the mercy of Allah and Hassan's support, we have wanted for nothing. He continues to support us even now, giving me the weight of my share of each season's crop."

I sat back in my chair and looked at Zelekha. The years had changed her somehow. She was softer, sadder, a little fuller in the cheeks where once her face was long and sleekly narrow. Although I was happy that she was alive and well, I couldn't quite believe how Hassan had been able to keep this secret from me for all these years. How had he been able to hold it in? Without ever allowing a word to slip out?

"We'll have dinner together," Zelekha said, tapping on her heavy belly and snapping me out of my thoughts. "It's a girl," she told me, "and we're due at about the same time."

"You didn't tell me," she whispered, an accusatory tone in her voice.

Hassan turned to look at his wife as he unbuttoned his shirt. "I didn't tell anyone."

"Your family knows. Those who matter know."

"You're here now," Hassan said, coming to stand in front of his wife.

She ran a hand down his naked chest, then reached for one of his hands, taking it in her own and inspecting his palm. She lifted it and kissed right in the middle of his palm, then raised it to her cheek, rubbing her face against his skin as she closed her eyes and breathed in deeply. Hassan's thumb swiped at a single tear that escaped from her eye, and she looked at him, her soul overwhelmed with the depth of her love for him.

"I didn't tell you for any other reason than the fact that I wanted to spare you, Farida. I know how close you were to Zelekha."

Farida nodded her understanding and told him she was glad that Zelekha was alive. "But it hurts that you didn't think you could trust me enough to tell me."

Hassan sighed and looked at his wife. "We come from two different worlds, Farida. Regardless how I feel about you...felt about you at the time I found Zelekha...I was the man who basically gave you no out except to marry me in order to save yourself. When I probably could've done so much more but I was selfish. I also didn't think you'd understand-that my sister had actually left of her own accord and I had let her get away with it, while I kept you shackled to me all those months."

Farida shook her head and advised Hassan that he was look-ing at the situation all wrong; she would never begrudge Zele-kha her escape to freedom, nor her life. "It was good seeing her," she told him, "but I'm saddened that her children and ours will not grow up together."

"Maybe one day, there will come a time, when centuries old traditions will no longer dictate the way we live our lives, and

Zelekha will be able to return to her rightful home. You know this is something I'm working on and have been for years. This is one tradition that's going to take time to break."

Farida looked down at her feet sadly. "Maybe in our children's lifetime," she whispered.

CHAPTER 60:
TALA 1974

If the choice had been mine, Amjad would not have been my choice of husband. No. My choice would have been Said. Tall, lanky Said with the dazzling smile and goofy glasses, who made me laugh and told the best stories. But tall, funny Said had not been prepared for marriage, and by the time I was of marrying age, my father had already started shopping around for would be suitors.

That's how it was done back then. A few suitors would visit, putting forth their case, and the father would choose the one he considered most eligible for his daughter. The girl rarely, if ever, had a say in who she would be married off to.

Such was the case for me. Father chose Amjad because Amjad was a good storyteller. By that, I mean he spun a good dance of dreams and aspirations. He appeared ambitious and pledged that he would one day elevate his status to such an extent that all the village people would be seeking his approval. My father, of course, feeble minded man that he was, fell for Amjad's drivel and promised him my hand in marriage. You didn't deny your father's wishes in those days. It simply was not on for a girl to renounce her father's decisions or go against the grain.

And so, I was married to Amjad, who worked the land when we married. He worked the land five years later. And he continued to work the land well into our marriage. Although ambitious, he had no way of fulfilling his ambitions, and lived out his life in a sort of rut that was neither here nor there. Eventually, he would turn his ambitions toward his daughters, marrying them off to the highest bidder in feeble yet unsuccessful attempts to elevate his status in society.

Needless to say, father came to hate him eventually, Amjad having reneged on his oaths and proclamations that he would one day conquer the world. However, hate him or not, divorce was not a solution and so I remained married to Amjad, Abu El Banaat, well into my twilight years, never having loved him or even grown fond of him. Ours was the sort of relationship where one simply reconciled themselves to their fate and lived out their days in hollow emptiness.

I lived my life in a sort of solitude. I was one, and my family unit was the other. Although I loved and cherished my daughters, the life I had lived with Amjad had disjointed me to such an extent that I sometimes felt like an outsider looking into a stranger's world. The girls suffered through this, often exclaiming about my absence from their lives. Although physically present, somewhere along the line, I had mentally and psychologically checked out. Although present, my mind would be a million miles away, entwined in a world far far away from Amjad, where I was happy and doting and a proper mother to my daughters.

I was lucky enough to have six girls in rapid succession. I was not lucky enough to have any boys. Amjad often berated me for this accursed situation, stating that it was entirely my fault for not giving him any sons to carry on his lineage. As though having children somehow came with a manual and I changed the settings to ensure that I would bear him only girls. As though I had a choice...

The two older girls were lucky enough to get out early. Although also not my first choice for husbands, they had somehow ended up with men that nonetheless cherished and respected them, and the girls ultimately spent as little time as possible in the presence of their father. I realised, much later on in life, that their husbands had understood what Amjad wanted of suitors and had simply told him what he wanted to hear. For that little transgression, I was glad, because at least at the end of the day, I knew that my two daughters were well looked after and taken care of.

My poor Farida had gone through an injustice no girl should have to go through, but ultimately, and against all odds, she had ended up married to a man who absolutely adored and revered her, and was willing to go to the ends of the world to make her happy.

Aujene had not been so lucky. Poor Aujene had born the brunt of her father's wrath, married to a man so beneath her who sought sought to repress her and bury her independence. Samer had never been worthy of Aujene. And he had been the thorn in my family's side since the day he'd entered the family home. And Aujene – Aujene and Aaida had paid a hefty price, forsaking their happiness and well-being to make Samer happy.

CHAPTER 61:
AAIDA 2014

I had the most vivid dream. For many many years, it was the same dream over and over and I couldn't understand why this dream returned to my consciousness night after night. It was but a fleeting vision, of myself falling, upside down, in an arc, from a bridge and towards a dark mass of water. That's all I saw. I always woke before hitting the water, my body saturated in sweat and my heart jumping like a beating drum. The dream never had an ending. Nor did it have a beginning. But I knew it was a significant element of my past.

The dream haunted me well into my teens and far beyond that. It enveloped all my daily transactions and embraced my fears head on, ensuring I missed out on two essential life adventures. Water. Heights. They were the worst of the worst. I had a robust fear of water and an even unhealthier fear of heights. And try as I may, I could not come to put my trust in anybody that would aid me in overcoming these two fears.

CHAPTER 62:
AAIDA 2014

I was a grown ass woman and couldn't get into a pool long enough to swim. I couldn't climb a ladder without feeling as though I was falling.

I remembered being a nine year old, and attending the local swimming pool with the school to do swimming lessons. I was so afraid to get into water. All my friends, who stood beside me trying to gently coax me into the water, couldn't understand what I was afraid of if they were all there to help me if I got into trouble. I shivered in fright and shook my head; I couldn't do it.

I stood at the pool's edge, looking down at the water, flanked on either side by two or three friends. They all dived into the pool in unison to demonstrate there was nothing for me to be afraid of. Rodney, a blond hippie style boy in his early twenties was conducting the lessons, and now he stood behind me and asked me what I was afraid of.

"See, they all jumped in and nothing happened," he laughed. "Go on, take a dive…" and with that, he took me by surprise and pushed me into the water. I flailed and twisted and turned, doing something like a handstand under water before I straightened and broke through the surface of the water, spluttering water and gasping for breath. One of the girls next to me held my arm and waded with me to the edge of the pool as I stared up at Rodney in contempt, willing him to disappear. By now, he was howling with laughter, proud of

himself and confident in his work that he had taught another child to swim.

"That was not fair," Matilda told him.

"She needs to learn to swim," Rodney protested, not putting up much of a fight.

"In her own time. It should have been her choice," she defended, as we hauled ourselves up the stairs.

"This is Australia! We're surrounded by sea! She needs to learn how to swim," he proclaimed.

"She doesn't need to be bullied into it," Matilda said, grabbing my hand and leading me away.

"We should report him," she said, as we changed in the locker room. I shook my head and wiped at my tears. Matilda looked at me with pain in her eyes. She was the one true friend who defended me at every turn. The one who carried my pain and burdens and had my back any time I needed her.

"I don't want to get him into trouble."

"So what, you'll just drop out of swimming classes?" she asked. "Last year, you had a stomach bug every Wednesday that we had swimming. This year, you're attending, but you're not doing much swimming. You need to learn to trust the water, Aaida."

"You're giving me the same speech Rodney did," I accused.

"Maybe so. But I'm not pushing you over the edge," she reminded me.

CHAPTER 63: AAIDA 2014

"What happened on that boat?" I asked, taking my mother's hand in my own and holding it up to my cheek. "Mama, I need to know."

"What will knowing change?" she asked me softly, a pained look in her eyes.

"It may not change anything, mama, but I have unresolved trauma and I need to deal with that."

My mother breathed a heavy sigh, patting her hand on my thigh. I could see she was reluctant to tell me, but she knew that something had to give.

"All my life, everything that came before you, nothing matters. What matters to me is that you became my life, my one and only focus, and I would do anything to protect you."

"I know that, mama, but I need to know what happened to make me this way."

"You say it like it's a bad thing," she accused, turning her body to face me. "It's not that big a deal that you can't tolerate water."

I sighed, exasperation evident in my tone. "It's not that I can't tolerate water, mama. It's that I can't get into the water long enough to learn how to swim. Yet I really want to be able to swim and float on water while I look up dreamily at the sun as it kisses my skin. I want these things."

"Sometimes, Aaida, not knowing gives us more peace than knowing."

CHAPTER 64:
AAIDA 2014

I sat with my back straight against the wall. My body planted firmly on the floor as I slid down and looked up at the ceiling in resignation. There I sat, my back plastered against the wall, for how long, I did not know. All I knew was that my heart clenched and my soul bent out of shape, a dark cloud enveloping me as my mother's confessions nose-dived through the past and straight into my brain, nestling there like a ferret scrubbing at a long lost memory.

She had warned me. She had tried so hard to protect me from the truth, knowing it would literally crush me. But I had to know. I was adamant that she open up to me and tell me all her secrets. All her long buried, tightly held secrets.

I died. I drowned. I lived. I survived. But I didn't. For what sort of a survival was it if I lost almost everything on that boat?

A brother. I had a brother. A baby brother. Who drowned. He didn't make it. Yet I did. A newborn, barely out of his crib. Snatched from my father's hands by the raging waters hell bent on taking prisoners. My mother could have lost two children that day. She almost lost two children. But God took one and gave her one back. But how easily life could have turned out differently for her…

And nothing was ever the same between my mother and father after that. That's the straw that broke the camel's back.

My mother never got over my brother's death, nor the nonchalance with which my father faced the death of his son. She hated my father then, I knew that. And she hated him even more after he disregarded what had happened with me and Faisal and had not dedicated so much as a waking hour to resolving the issue that had befallen me. Instead, he had gone about his life as before, staying up late playing cards with the men and literally disregarding anything to do with me.

I understood now. I finally understood. What my mother had been fighting all her life to hold onto. What she had fought so hard to let go of...

CHAPTER 65:
AUJENE 1977

We had to take a boat over to Cyprus from Beirut and then on-wards towards somewhere called "Australia". The oceans were heavy with swell, seagulls squawking above, delivering, in a way, a premonition of things to come. All around me, people threw up as the boat rocked and swayed in the heavy seas. I clutched Aaida close to me, trying to hold her down. She had always been an active child, and at three years, she was strong willed and had a mind of her own, never bowing to anyone's directions.

I looked toward my husband Samer, resenting him for the hundredth time for subjecting us to this torment. I hadn't wanted to leave. I had wanted to stay in the midst of my family, amongst my siblings, in the village with the olive groves and the water wells and the wild flowers that sprouted season by season on the mountain tops, encasing the village with bril-liant hues of yellows, blues and lilacs. I wanted my plot of land, to grow my olives and figs from which I would pickle my own jam and make my own oil.

I wanted to grow old with my siblings and my parents, sit with them at the table where they ate and laugh with them as we grew and endured everything that life had to throw at us. For, even though Lebanon had erupted into civil war, in my heart, what was to come, was tenfold worse than what I would face in my country of birth. The severing of ties with my family, akin to the severing of my limbs, would be my downfall.

Samer held onto the baby rocker with 8 month Yacoub in it, struggling to keep it from traversing the length of the deck. I could see and feel his frustration, but he said nothing, knowing that to do so would send me into a tirade of curses and "I told you so's."

The rocking and swaying of the sea continued to propel people forward, jerking their bodies forward and then slamming them back into the boat. One particularly bad swell spiraled the water several metres through the air and sent it crashing over the occupants of the boat, drenching them in seawater from head to toe. I gasped as the water rained down on us like a torrential downpour, catching me by surprise. In that instant, I lost my grip on Aaida and, temporarily blinded by the water slapping my face, couldn't see anything in front of me as the boat tipped heavily to one side, sending most of the occupants reeling and sliding down the slippery deck and into the murky water of the Mediterranean sea.

I lurched forward, grabbing blindly at anything in front of me as I tried to grasp Aaida above the screams and yells of the other people onboard but found myself clutching only at empty air. And just as quickly as the boat had swayed and tipped to one side, it was flattened back down onto calm seas as though nothing had happened. Some would say it had been the hand of God that had reached into the sea and urged the water forward to spray over us and wreak havoc on the boat. Others would just call it bad luck. Whether or not you were a believer, that day, on the heavy swells of the sea, as we travelled across the channel toward Cyprus and a better life, something miraculous happened...

I looked around the eerily quiet boat. Half of the people that had been on board before the spray were no longer there. I ran to the railing and looked overboard – some of the crew had already thrown rubber dinghies into the water and several people were either swimming towards them and climbing onboard or being dragged from the water and into them. I saw a boy, maybe 17, climbing the rope at the side of the boat nearest me, and as he came closer, I could see the fabric of Aaida's shorts peeking out from under his arm. She looked like a drenched ragdoll, hanging limply from his arms, and I stood there, my mouth open in a scream, but with no sound. It was like I had lost my voice. My mouth gaped open as I saw my beautiful daughter, my precious little pocket rocket, her face pale and starting to turn blue, her body lifeless as he set it down on the deck and took her pulse. All I could wonder was where he had learnt to do that. He sat back on his heels and looked at her, shock on his face, then looked up at me and shook his head. And just as I fell to my knee in exasperation, he started to pump her chest and breathe into her mouth, willing her back to life. For what seemed like an eternity, the young boy exhausted himself, pumping her chest-at one point, I was sure I heard a crack, pumping away and resuscitating her until, by the will of God, she spluttered and threw up an extraordinary amount of water as he turned her to her side.

Afterward, still in shock, I sat with the boy on the deck as he pushed Aaida's hair back and smiled at her in silence. She smiled back shyly and took the stuffed giraffe he offered her, holding it close to her chest.

"I'm Omar, and I'm going to be a doctor. That's all I've even wanted to do-to save people."

This is what he told me when I asked him how he had known what to do after he pulled Aaida from the water. He started at the beginning, explaining to me how the swell had tossed him overboard with a number of other people; he had been lucky, he proclaimed, because he was a strong swimmer. Others had not been so lucky. He had tried to pull as many people as possible out of the water, but once he had found Aaida, he had made his way back to the boat carrying her under his arm.

Saving people was all he'd ever wanted to do, almost as though he had been born programmed that way. Living in the city, he had not been isolated from the world like we had been, and had dedicated every waking hour of non-study to watching television programs that had anything to do with doctors and reading medical journals which had been sent over from Canada by his uncle Dawoud. I asked him why he would be travelling to Australia when he had an uncle in Canada, and he explained to me that Canada already had a magnificent doctor in the form of his uncle Dawoud, and he had wanted to go somewhere he could make a definitive change.

As he held onto Aaida's pinky with his own, my daughter's favourite game, I watched him in awe and made abundant Dua that this young boy would have a long and rich life and see his dreams to fruition. I owed him my life. Never in a million years would I, Aujene, of Tul Ghosn, have known what to do to revive my daughter had Omar not been there.

I looked around for Samer; this was definitely a story worth sharing, only to realise he was not there and I had not seen him since the boat had tipped over. Instantly, my heart skipped a beat as I stood hurriedly and looked toward the people being pulled up from the dinghies. And there stood Samer, aiding the survivors of the swell as they came onboard, himself drenched all over, obviously after having been submerged in the swell. As though he knew I was watching him, he turned and looked my way, and facing me, spoke of the horror of what had happened without uttering a word. In that instant, I understood what had happened-God had taken one child, but given me back another...

CHAPTER 66:
AUJENE 1977

The thing about grief, what they don't tell you, is that it doesn't go away. It is all consuming, encompassing everything and anything in its orbit. It manifests itself, compounding the pain and anxiety of your loss. I felt Yacoub's loss deep down in the depths of my soul and mourned his death painfully, wallowing in a bottomless well of self-pity. My breasts grew heavy with the milk that was meant for my dead son, and the heavy weight of my full breasts only compounded my pain, reminding me that I was missing a part of my heart.

Cyprus didn't diminish any of my pain. If anything, it aggravated it once we landed on ground and I felt the pain of a missing child, like something akin to a missing limb. After the boat rocked and swayed and drowned my life, I remained numb and unfeeling.

Samer did his hardest to bring me out of my funk, but failed miserably, as I held him ransom to the pain lashing my heart. It was his fault we had been on that boat. His idea for us to leave our beloved country, by any means possible. His responsibility to protect and nurture us as a family had fallen flat as our hopes and dreams drowned that day on that boat in the middle of the Mediterranean Sea.

With no family in which to seek comfort, I withdrew into my own shell and started to resent my husband even before we reached our final destination. Most of the people on board that fateful trip had lost someone to the swell, so there was no comfort to be found amidst the wailing and torment of others who had shared in our journey. Meanwhile, Samer had gone on about life as though nothing had happened, regaling other travellers with stories of his experiences in the war before we left our ravaged country. At night when I lay curled up in a ball on the bed that just barely accommodated two people, with Aaida folded into my side, he would seek out other men from the old country and they would play cards well into the night and into the early morning. Their screeching and yells could be heard down the hallways of the old inn where we stayed, holding our collective breaths as we awaited a flight out of Cyprus to Sydney.

Four days later, we boarded a plane and said goodbye to the jewel that is the middle east as we headed out to the plains of Australia. Aaida sobbed every chance she got, her heart sweltering with pain as she gasped for breath and cried for her grandmother, her jeddo, every name she could recall from her life in Lebanon. She wasn't the only one...I yearned to turn back the hands of time and go back to a time when I was safely ensconced in my family's home, before Samer, before the war, before our self-imposed exile.

The thing about Samer is he didn't care. About anything. He was indifferent to anything going on around him, his feelings so switched off, you would think he had none. Even when we arrived at our final destination in Sydney, standing with our meagre belongings; all our worldly possessions crammed into two small suitcases which were each only half full. My father had insisted to Samer we take two suitcases instead of putting everything in the one and minimising our luggage, laughing we would need the two suitcases to fill them with all the money we'd make in Australia.

And now we stood in front of a small brown brick bungalow on the corner of a street, knocking on the door of the contact whose number my brother in law had given us. There was no answer, and so we stood, waiting, unsure what to do, waiting for the door to open.

Aaida, who had been slumped against my shoulder sleeping as I used one of the suitcases as a makeshift chair now opened her eyes and started to wail, her howl bringing people out of the nearby houses to see what the commotion was about. Samer snapped at me to shush her, even while I was already trying to do so, his hand constantly moving to his mouth as he went through cigarette after cigarette.

"She's probably hungry," I told him, realising it had been hours since any of us last ate.

"Can't she just wait?" he asked, irritation lacing his words.

I looked at my husband carefully, rage seeping through my skin and radiating from me as I mustered the will to hide my emotions and clamp my mouth shut.

"Wait for what?" I asked him. "Are you actually waiting for someone to turn up here and feed us? Is this what you've brought us here for?"

"Well, what do you want me to do?" he defied.

"Figure it out. You were the one with the big dreams and bright idea to come here, so figure it out!," I snapped. "It could be hours before anyone comes home and you want us to sit out here in the blistering sun without any food or water? If the girl is aggravating you now, she'll be stabbing you through the heart pretty soon."

I turned away from him in disgust, silently cursing my father for having married me to such a spineless man. I hugged Aaida to my chest, settling her, rewinding the past few years of my life in my mind to pass the time.

◆ ◆ ◆

I envied Farida, for although she had been stolen from us, she had a stroke of luck and married a man that worshipped the ground she walked on. Their life, filled with the laughter and joy of tiny feet, was comprised of a relationship built on love, friendship, and mutual respect for one another. I couldn't recall a time when I had seen Hassan and hadn't marvelled at one of the kids climbing up their father's shoulders, Hassan's eyes glistening with the soft lustre of happy tears.

My mother, who had endured so much as we grew up, had fought so mercilessly with my father, denouncing my marriage to Samer, to no avail. I could still see her in my mind's eye, stomping her feet as my father grabbed her arms and shook her relentlessly, leaving deep welts in her arm from the ferocity of his ire. There was no way, he told her, no way on this earth that Aujene would not be married to Samer – this was the best opportunity for a new life that had come their way, and he was not going to let this stroke of good fortune pass him by. And especially after she started to go blind, seeing things in shadow, he treated her miserably, any semblance of compassion he'd once had by now long gone.

My father, whose words continued, to the very last minute before we left the village for the port, to warn me against doing anything foolish. Although I still hadn't allowed him back into my life, his constant past warnings had continued to haunt me. He had big plans for the family, and those dreams were riding on my coattails, he had told me. Eventually, with my help, the whole family would migrate to Australia and be enormously rich, so I was to be a good little girl, an obedient and subservient wife, and not to do anything to upset the balance of nature.

I scoffed now, as I sat watching the sun gather behind clouds as the day slowly came to a close and there still wasn't a soul in sight of the house.

"Did you even notify them that we were coming?" I asked, finally, wondering why the owners wouldn't be home if they were expecting us.

"Was I supposed to?" Samer asked, and I looked at him dumbfounded, my heart a swirl of emotions, none the least of which was murder. I could have killed him where he stood just thinking about his response. And that, right there, was one of many examples that Samer was not a normal functioning human being. He didn't like, nor did he hold, any responsibility toward anything, and he lived by a sort of code where he actually believed that things which should actually be planned out would miraculously work their own way out.

"You'll need to go for a walk and find Aaida something to eat, otherwise next time she cries, she'll tear her lungs out. And we need water."

Samer looked up both ends of the street, unsure where to start. His hands in his pockets, he turned this way, then that, then doubled back again and looked at me.

"The street is closed on that end. Best to start at the open end up there," I said, pointing to my left. "I think I saw what looked like shops around the corner when we first arrived."

"Do you want to come with me," and it was more of a plea than a question of whether or not I wanted to go.

I shook my head."The thought of carrying her in my arms again as we walk is too exhausting. We'll wait for you here."

And with that, he turned on his heels and walked up the street, his head turning to admire the nearby houses with their lush green plants and rose bushes.

I had not had a chance yet to take in the surrounds, my eyes half closed with exhaustion as I sat in the sun waiting for the day from hell to end. The houses here were different, that was apparent immediately. Where in Lebanon, most of the houses were cement rendered, square blocks which all resembled each other, Sydney held an eclectic portfolio of homes made from dark brown bricks piled on top of one another, and fibro planks that sat in straight lines upon each other to hold the houses together. The homes seemed small, the lands on which they were built even smaller, as I inspected the house that our feet were parked in front of. By the side fence of the home, there seemed to be a long driveway, what I would later realise was termed an alley, lending the house the impression that it had been built on land that was larger than it actually was.

Samer returned shortly, two bottles of water in his hand, and what looked like fried chips in butcher's paper. I stirred Aaida awake so she could eat, but she only pecked at the food, complaining that she wanted tayta's food. I set her on my knee and proceeded to tell her a story of a little girl on a far away adventure, hoping to appease her enough that she would eat something. I made the story up as I went along, and Aaida listened attentively, asking me questions about the little girl as I continued to relate the adventure.

It was almost dark by the time a man and a woman appeared walking down the street. They stopped when they neared us, greeting us and explaining that this was their house, and we were blocking their gate; how could they help us? The woman looked up in horror as we told her who we were and she realised we had been sitting there in front of the house for the better half of the day.

"*Ya haserti!*" she implored. "Why didn't you tell me you were coming? You sat here all day? In this heat? Poor baby," she cooed, lifting Aaida from my arms. "You must be exhausted, come in, come in," and she welcomed us into the house like we had always meant to be there.

"My husband and I both work, all day every day," Jannat told us, and I could immediately sense that her husband wasn't much of a talker, but she chattered about enough for the both of them.

"We've been here for six years, and we like it here. God didn't bless us with children, but we have been lucky to look after others when they relocate from Lebanon," she explained. "At the moment, there is no one staying with us, so you can stay as long as you want."

Samer spoke up before I could say anything. "We only need a few night's accommodation," he told Jannat, "during which time we will be looking for work and our own home."

"You take as much time as you need." Jannat patted his hand in a motherly fashion and smiled warmly at me. She ruffled Aaida's hair, trying to entice the girl down from my lap, but Aaida, unaccustomed to strangers, simply stuck her finger in her mouth and began to suck. And that was the start of Aaida's nervous tic, which would take us years to overcome.

CHAPTER 67: AUJENE 1981

Samer's original promise-that we would only be in Australia for two years, to make some money and set up a better life for us, had flown right out the window with all my hopes and dreams to be reunited with my family in Lebanon in a reasonable amount of time.

We stayed with Jannat and her husband for three years and eight months, with Jannat acting like a mother to me and an overly attentive grandmother to Aaida. If it hadn't been for Aaida, I don't think we would have stayed as long, but the young girl had sought-and found-comfort in Jannat's arms and had quickly established a connection with the older woman.

Samer had argued incessantly about us moving to our own home, but this was one argument I would not cede to him. Whether we paid rent to Jannat or another landlord, what difference did it make? I asked him, knowing full well he was actually fuming that he couldn't have full control over me while we remained in the company of Jannat and her husband.

Jannat became sort of a mother figure to me, inspiring me in ways in which my own mother hadn't. I could tell she didn't really think much of Samer, believing me too good for him, and it was so obvious that the feeling was mutual. Jannat's husband, too, soon took a shine to Aaida, and I would often, on the days he felt like talking, hear him chiding Samer on his attitude and nonchalance towards me, as well as the lack of time he spent with Aaida. Soon enough, Samer felt he was being persecuted, and took double shifts at the bakery to spend as little time as possible at home. Which didn't bother me much, as it afforded me time away from his persistent nagging for us to move out.

I was lucky enough to find work in a local factory that manufactured clothing and textiles. Jannat introduced me to some of her neighbours, who were all eager to help out with Aaida when I was working, in return for my services helping them with chores around the house. Soon enough, I had built up a network of friends who guided me, consoled me, and shared in my misery every step of my agonising journey in the *ghorba*.

On the work front, I was quick to make friends. Being one of the youngest in the factory, I was the oddity. Barely 21, fresh faced, no English, with a child…most of the other factory workers were also refugees, but none had endured what I had endured and none proclaimed to understand the hardships I had faced, but all were sympathetic, and again I found myself surrounded by a strong support system of like-minded females who sought to alleviate some of my burdens.

By the time the afternoon would roll in, I'd head home toward Aaida, missing her with a soul crushing urgency, she being the only solid thing in my life connected to my past, my present, and my future. I would grab her under the arms and swirl her around, listening to her delightful squeals as we teetered on the brink of dizziness and collision.

"She was such a darling today," Amna said in her thick Southern Lebanese dialect one afternoon as I picked my daughter up from her house after work. "She helped me in the garden-it seems she really enjoys the outdoors."

"Just like her mama," I mused, smiling at the old lady. She wore an apron around her waist no matter the time of day.

"She loves to potter around in the garden, but little one does not like to bake," she laughed, scruffing Aaida's hair. Aaida stood watching the interaction intently. At four years, she was wise beyond her years and had already picked up basics of the English language and some Greek, owing to her time spent with some of Jannat's neighbours. I would watch the women interacting, Lebanese, Greek, Egyptian and be confounded as to how they would understand each other with a mere few words of English interspersed with their mother tongues. Whereas, Aaida would watch them in awe, her eyes widening at the women's mannerisms, the way their hands lifted and turned to enunciate what their tongues could not, and the way they laughed and interacted with one another. She would watch and listen attentively, talking only when she knew she wouldn't overshadow anyone else speaking, because she didn't want to miss a word that was said.

Aaida, from an early age, was a listener. She listened to people talk. She listened to their stories as they told them. She felt people's pain as they explained what happened to them. She was so in tune with people's feelings, I often felt like she felt their pain right along with them. She listened, she heard, she felt, and then she committed all their stories to memory.

By the time she was a five year old entering kindergarten, Aaida was fluent in Arabic, English, and Greek. She kept listening. And learning. And feeling. Then she would come home and babble in her sleep *"ti ka nees, kala"*. I was grateful that everyone had taken to Aaida and had taken her under their wings. It had been just what she needed after our migration from Lebanon, aiding in our settling in beyond measure.

CHAPTER 68:
AUJENE 1981

The day that Samer dug his foot into the ground and announced we'd be leaving Jannat's house and moving into our
own purchase-not rental-was the day I knew I'd run out of
steam. There was no longer a reason for us to stay with Jannat
when this door had opened to us, and I remember that of the
few houses that we'd looked at, the one that had appealed to
me most was the one that was two streets away from Jannat's
house and the friendly little community of which I now was a
part of.

Samer had sought to move to the other side of the suburb,
where my interactions with the women would have been very
limited, especially as I didn't drive. But my only ace had been
that I needed these women to help with Aaida's care while I
was at work, otherwise I would not be able to contribute to
the financial maintenance of our new household. My husband
had looked at me out of the corner of his eye, weighing up
what I said against what I really meant. But when I shrugged
noncommittally and told him I didn't really care and that I was
happy to spend more time at home with Aaida, my act paid off
and he relented, putting down a deposit on the house the very
next day.

Still, I had sacrificed so much in buying this house. It was
situated on a narrow block, a single face house on a 300 metre
block that left little room to establish an orchard. There was an

apple tree, and a strip of soil on which I was able to grow my own lettuce and tomatoes and eggplants and parsley and mint. Enough for our little family and a little left over to share on occasion, but nowhere near what I had anticipated my forever garden would look like.

I maximised every inch of land I possibly could to get the best yield and the best garden in the area. There was a patch at the front of the house where I planted a lone olive tree, and watched it blossom from a fledgling to a bountiful asset that serviced our home. Along one backyard fence, I planted a passion fruit and watched as it crawled over to our neighbours house and they asked what it was. On the other fence, I planted a grapevine, and marvelled at it when it didn't give me grapes, but it gave me enough grape leaves to spread amongst my friends whenever they wanted to wrap dolma. Thanks to my little vegetable patch, I was able to recreate the dishes from back home with produce that wasn't always readily available in the local shops.

I was in awe as I watched Marika make her beautiful *Yemista* and introduce us to a culinary explosion like no other. On another occasion, I made *Koussa Mehshi* to illustrate the similarities between our cultures. Megan, who lived over the fence divided by my passionfruit, remarked she was experiencing a culinary revolution as she cut her first koussa and deposited a generous portion into her mouth. As she cut further into her zucchini, it went flying like a torpedo across the room after she failed to cut into it properly, the spoon slipping so the juice went sloshing all over the table. There was a pregnant pause as Megan sat with her spoon hovering in mid-air and the ladies all stopped what they were doing, looking at the zucchini that had flown across the room then back at the tomato juice that now trickled down the plastic table cloth and onto the floor. Amna, bless her soul, was the first to slice through the tension, letting out an uproarious laugh that filtered through the room and infected each and every lady present until they all folded over themselves and cackled like hyenas. After our laughter died down, a few of us wiping at our tears, we all worked in unison to clean the messy koussa and clear the table of any debris, a collective symphony of women coming together to build bridges and become lifetime sisters.

"I've never had anything like that," Megan stated, and we could all see her senses were tantalised by the fusion of flavours we had set before her.

"Ahhhh, what do you Aussies know but bangers and mash!" Marika joked, slapping Megan on the back. "We need to teach you to make real food."

CHAPTER 69: AUJENE 1981

By now, as we settled into our new home, almost four years had passed since we'd initially arrived in Australia. Samer was still pulling double shifts at work, doing one shift at the bakery and another on the assembly line at a car manufacturing plant. I still worked days at the textiles factory, while Aaida attended school and was now in the second grade. At school, she flourished, excelling at everything she did, her academic level far superior to that of the other students. She was an inquisitive child, constantly asking questions in her quest for knowledge. I learnt the basics of English, and this was in large part thanks to Aaida. Never having set foot inside a classroom myself, it had been difficult to grasp this alien language that everyone seemed to speak so effortlessly, but with a lot of effort and determination, and Aaida's insistence that she speak to me only in English, I was able to grasp the basic fundamentals of the English language so that I was able to fend for myself. The other women marvelled at how hard I worked to better my language skills in an effort to fit in more easily.

And the more I learned the language, the more my independence grew. The more I became self-sufficient and my self esteem rose. At the factory, I worked alongside a long line of men and women from all walks of life. Some Turks, a few Italians, some Greeks, a handful of Lebanese, and a few Europeans as well. I was fortunate enough to be popular with the non Arabs, which meant I was able to pick up the English language even quicker, until eventually I had grasped the language so well that Jannat's husband had taken to calling me "el bolbol", which meant sparrow, but was also used as an affectionate term for one who spoke much and did it well. He was in awe of how far I'd come in terms of adapting to my new environment. Even Samer, who also worked with pre-dominantly Anglo Saxons, therefore having more ample opportunity to learn English, viewed me with a sort of envy I had never encountered from him before.

Having come to a country like Australia, where everyone was predominantly Anglo Saxon, with fair skin, light hair and coloured eyes, I had stuck out like a sore thumb with my dark hair and even darker eyes, which were slanted like almonds. The women all called me the exotic beauty, and although they may have thought of me that way, to the Australians, I was still-and always would be-one of the others because I didn't fit the mould of what an Australian looked like.

I had started at the textiles factory on the bottom rung, putting my heart and soul into every task and working diligently to complete orders well before the timeframe allocated. While most of the women had befriended me and were nothing short of nice, some of them grumbled that I worked too fast, and wanted to know why I was doing that-we were getting paid by the hour, so the faster we finished, the less we got paid. I tried to argue that that wasn't necessarily true, as there were still always new tasks opening up. Since they weren't sending us home when a task was completed, what did it matter, but they would only scoff and tell me I didn't know what I was talking about.

For the men, however, it was a different story. Initially, the interest they had shown me had instilled an envy in most of the other women as the men turned their undivided attention toward the "exotic beauty from the middle east". Some of the couples that worked side by side at the factory had gotten into fights with each other over what the wife would perceive as "unwarranted attention toward the new girl." A few of my female friends had remarked about how the men were paying me too much attention, and I had to be careful, as not all attention should be welcomed. I had ignored anyone and everyone, opting to focus on my work and keep to myself. Yet with this focus came even more unwanted attention, as the males watched me carefully, in awe of the way I worked, developing a healthy respect for my ethical approach and professionalism, and started to treat me with a newfound appreciation.

CHAPTER 70: AUJENE 1983

One day, after a few years at the factory, there was a flurry of sudden activity as employees from a different run burst into our work area and promptly proceeded to make noise and fuss about clearing fabric remnants from the floor. I saw the commotion out of the corner of my eye and continued to work, turning my focus to the sheath of fabric before me.

"What happening," one of the Europeans said in a nasally, high pitched voice. She was a bottle blond who never attended work without a full face of makeup caked onto her skin.

"Boss is coming," one of the Anglos replied, stubbing out his cigarette on our floor, then bending to pick up some fabric but neglecting to remove the butt from where he'd put it out.

I saw the factory manager Stewart emerge through a side door a little while later, followed by a few others as they entered our floor, and continued on with my work, minding my own business, which was my usual practise unless I was called upon. I could see that a few of the workers on our run had stopped to gawk and throw out comments as I continued to work, ignoring all else as I sought to complete the task at hand. It was only when the machine I was handling came to a standstill that I lifted my goggles and raised my head to look at the controls. Stewart had switched the machine off and came to stand in front of me with the other men. He noticed everyone else had stopped working and urged them to turn back to their work and continue what they were supposed to be doing.

"This is Aujene," Stewart said, speaking to a tall lanky Anglo who wore spectacles. He was so tall, I had to tilt my head to look up at him. The man nodded in my direction, then turned to Stewart, as if to ask a silent question. "She is our latest addition to the department and is fluent in both Arabic and English."

The tall man smiled widely, and I could see that Stewart had told him exactly what he wanted to hear.

"How do you do," he asked, and I merely nodded my acknowledgment.

There was a quiet silence and I surmised that he was the factory owner, but they said nothing more as they stood there for mere seconds, then moved on to the next table. I supposed they were conducting inspections of the factory and the workers, but couldn't be too sure, as this was the first inspection of its sort since I'd started at the plant.

A short while later, Stewart came out to call the employees to meetings in his office. He took some people in individually, and some as groups. I assumed the owner was there also, but this was just an assumption as I continued to work in comparative silence while all the other employees buzzed with excitement around me. I tried but couldn't read their expressions when the employees emerged from the office after their meetings, returning in silence to go about their work as they had been doing before. When asked, they merely shrugged and said it had been a sort of "meet and greet" and I wasn't entirely sure that I was familiar with that term, but I shrugged and continued my work.

I was the last one to be called to Stewart's office. I was also one of the few that was called in alone. A few of the women eyed me suspiciously, and I could see the bottle blond European with her fluff of ridiculous hair and flamingo lips as she snickered and muttered something under her breath when I walked past her.

"Take a seat, please," Stewart said, directing his hand toward an empty seat in front of his desk. The tall lanky man sat there, his hands clasped together on the desk in front of him. "This is Mr Spears," he said, finally introducing the stranger who had today thrown our whole production line into disarray. "He owns this factory and a few others," he explained.

I remained silent, opting to listen and take what I could, rather than give anything that was not requested.

"Stewart is very impressed with your strong work ethic," Mr Spears started, his eyes crinkling into a kindly smile. Claims you're focused, driven, and a hard worker."

"She's the hardest worker here," Stewart chimed in, somewhat proudly, like I was the product of his own brainchild.

"Stewart's never let me down. He's a good judge of character, and he did a good thing when he hired you. Our production levels are up 13%, and this is by no small measure because of you. Here at Cynthetix, we like to take care of our own and reward those that work hard to advance the business."

"I'm just doing what I get paid to do."

Stewart shook his head and stepped forward to reply, obviously to say something in my defence, when obviously, there was nothing to defend, as it appeared that Mr Spears was already sold on my solid performance. "Other employees disappear to the toilet for hours on end. I know there are some that sit in there and read the paper and still expect to get paid. They have no scruples," Stewart said, somewhat seething.

"This is something that should be regulated," Mr Spears said, looking at Stewart. "If you're still having issues with employees not doing their work, but production is up so high, it means the only anomaly here is Aujene – she's producing enough to cover all the time wasters."

Stewart nodded solemnly, obviously agreeing. I had never thought of it that way, but when I heard someone else pointing this out, I realised something was really wrong if it had been up to one woman alone to pick up everyone else's slack.

"I'll help in any way I can," I announced.

Mr Spears smiled. "This meeting is not about you helping," he told me. "It's about acknowledging your hard work and rewarding you for it. Effective immediately, you will receive a 20% pay increase."

I gasped, not really understanding what he had just said.

"Not everyone who was called in here received a pay hike," Stewart explained. "In fact, Mr Spears wanted to meet the staff and get a feel for where the company is at."

"Your performance here at the factory has been exemplary," Mr Spears remarked. "That is why we're offering you the pay rise. And the opportunity to be factory manager at one of our outlets when we relocate to Melbourne next year."

The news that the factory would be closing its doors in a year hit me like a tonne of bricks, so much so that when I emerged from Stewart's office with a stricken look on my face, there was no need for me to act out my misfortune as I crossed the floor to my table; everyone simply assumed I'd received the worst news and no one ever asked for clarification. And I let them believe what they chose to believe.

Stewart had explained that no-one knew yet about the reloca-tion. They wanted to discuss it with me first and offer me the head position. They met with all the other employees and had shortlisted those that they believed were worthy of a position at their Melbourne plant should they wish to relocate. No one else was given a raise, and they requested that I not discuss this with any other employee, as they rightfully predicted that this would cause more angst among the workers and I may end up feeling alienated.

I went about the rest of my day completing my work, at the same fast pace as usual, regardless of the grief emanating through my soul. I loved my job at the factory. I cherished the time I spent with my co-workers, and my hard earned pay that I took home at the end of the week. The fact that I was offered a head position was a huge accomplishment, one I never would have considered I'd be eligible for in a million years, but I was proud that my hard work had been recognised and grateful for the raise that acknowledged this recognition. There was, how-ever, a sinking feeling as I considered the implications of the factory closing. I would lose my job. There was no way that Samer would ever leave Sydney. He loved his perfectly struc-tured life of work, play, play, work, play. Whereas, I wanted to remain in work, but this would no longer be possible unless I left the state. And that was as near to impossible as you could possibly get.

CHAPTER 71:
AUJENE 1983

Samer was dumbstruck when I told him the factory would be closing the following year. He didn't understand why they would relocate when they seemed to be doing so well, and he was adamant that we would not be moving to Melbourne. I hadn't yet told him about my raise, and I watched on reluctantly as he dragged me into a debate I really didn't want to be a part of.

"You'll just find a job somewhere else," he decided, shrugging his shoulders in finality, as though his words solved all our problems.

"You know it's not so easy to find a job," I reminded him.

"Well, you'll look until you find one."

I looked at him, irritated that he was so lax about my depression over my job. I was also upset that he was so adamant that I work. I mean, what if I didn't want to work? And so I tested the waters, but obviously I said the wrong things, because by the end of the argument, he was absolutely fuming.

"What do you mean, you might not go back to work?" he asked, frowning.

"It means, I might want to stay at home and look after Aaida. I'll go to school to better my English and do a course. I might learn to drive, even," I beamed with aspirations.

"Don't be so ridiculous!" Samer admonished. "We came to Australia to make some money and go back home. All the things you want to do are going to cost us money, not make us money."

"You wanted to come to Australia to make some money," I reminded him. "You promised it would only be for 2 or 3 years, yet here we are 4 years later!"

"We should have enough money soon," he told me.

"But enough money for what, Samer? I give you my paycheck without ever opening it. Where does all our money go to?"

Samer's eyes widened in disbelief that I would ask such questions. "I told you! The money is sent to Lebanon, where it will be safe with my mother until we return and build our house there."

"Don't you think we've already sent enough?" I asked. "I'd like to buy some new furniture for the house."

"Our future in Lebanon is more important," he told me. "Why would we buy new furniture here if we're not going to be here much longer?"

He looked at me like I was an idiot, and I backed down, but only slightly.

"Well, I'm working just like you are. I think it's only fair that I have a say in where our money goes."

In a heartbeat, Samer was up on his feet, shoving me into a corner and looming above me. I had never seen him so angry, and I was frightfully aware that he could so easily hurt me and no-one would be the wiser. He raised a hand, and for a moment it looked like he would hit me, but then he fisted his hand and plunged a pointed finger at my chest as he roared at me.

"I need you to stop hanging around these foolish women who fill your head with rubbish about how women are strong and independent and have a voice. I am the man in this house, and we will live the way I see fit!" he bellowed, his eyes turning red with rage.

I shook my head and tried to speak, but he only slammed a hand against my mouth to shut me up, continuing to raise his voice and tell me all the ways he was king of the household and I was basically a maid to cook and clean and do things his way, as well as contributing to the household expenses by working my hands to the bone so he could "invest" our money wisely. He had our best interests at heart, he reminded me, and he was building a future for our family. He made it sound like he was the sole breadwinner, the master of the relationship, the one who would lead us to strong financial freedom.

The reality, I realised, was much much different. There was no equality in our relationship, and there never had been. We both worked, but I was still expected to come home and clean and prepare meals, and wash and press his clothes, while he came home from work and put his feet up on the ottoman and read the paper or watched television. After dinner, I would clear the table, do the dishes, then peel and cut him a plate of fruit, before preparing Aaida for bed. At night-time, I was expected to be a lover. And in the morning, I would pack his lunch alongside my own and walk 15 minutes to drop Aaida off at school before walking in a different direction for a further 10 minutes to catch the bus to my workplace.

Every day was a case of rinse and repeat. And every Friday, I would come home clutching my pay in an envelope and hand it to him as he requested. Every single pay. Every single dollar. So after this conversation, I did the unthinkable. I would hold the envelope over a pot of boiling water until the seal popped open, then extract the 20% raise I'd been given and squirrel it away. I would use Aaida's glue to seal the envelope back up and hand it to Samer when he came home. He never knew that I got a raise. And he was none the wiser that I was stealing from my own money.

I listened carefully to the stories the other women told about their joint finances with their husbands. Jannat and her husband had sent plenty of money back home, but she could see where that money went. They had finished building their home and planned to go to Lebanon every few years to holiday with family. Others held their finances in joint accounts that both husband and wife had access to. Even some of the women who didn't work still shared access to funds with their husbands. They all had relationships with foundations built on trust and equality and common sense. Whereas Samer did not want me to question where our money was going, who held on to it, or even what the big picture was. Lebanon had become a distant memory and it didn't look like we would go back any time soon.

CHAPTER 72:
AUJENE 1983

The only respite I got from Samer was when he was out playing cards. Samer spent many a night away from our home, having his get togethers with his friends, where they would stay up until all hours playing cards. On some occasions, I joined him and spent an enlightening time with his friend's wives, chatting and sharing stories and experiences about our time in the mother country. These events were rare though, having felt like I was an outsider to this elite group of women. Fights and arguments would often sprout up between Samer and me, where he accused me of being stuck up because I refused to join his nightly games nights regularly.

These were the nights when I would take advantage of the empty house and invite the girls to our home, where we would sit around eating a different cultural delicacy on every occasion, laughing well into the night until our happy tears streamed from our eyes and Aaida would come running at our riotous noise and laugh herself into a stupor watching us acting silly.

There was a bunch of us ladies, and although we weren't always available at the same time, there was always enough of a group to create an atmosphere worthy of kings and queens. Jannat, my adoptive mother, who never left my side, no matter what was required of her. Amna, who lived four houses down from Jannat and hailed from the South of Lebanon. Marika, the Greek, who was steadfast in her belief that food solved every problem, and could prove this by the inches added to her waist on a yearly basis. She lived in the same street as Jannat and had been one of the first women I'd met when we came to Australia. Megan, the married yet childless Australian woman who lived right next door to us and took to our group like it was a lifeline. Sayeda was a Syrian woman who had migrated to Australia with her three children after her husband had taken a second wife. Her husband had started kicking and screaming for their reunion ever since she'd come to Australia. She swore that karma was her best friend, and took comfort in the knowledge that he would never set foot in her adoptive country.

And now Najla had joined us. Beautiful, carefree Najla, who like me, had not come to Australia willingly, but was now etching out a life for herself and her family. We were her first friends, obviously being the most dominant visitors to her husband's store as it was the closest one to our homes, and she clung to us for dear life as a means to have her own life away from the family and the shop.

"Ahhhhh! Here comes my greatest competition!," her husband Sam would laugh whenever I walked into the store.

"There will be no more competition once I master how to grow the mango tree!" I would counter, laughing along with him.

He was a robust man with a gentle soul and kindly features who embraced the community with a sort of fatherly concern as he tried to settle his family into their new Australian routine. His main concern had been his wife Najla, who had been homesick ever since she'd landed in Australia, and whom he couldn't bring out of her depression. Eventually, he suggested that she come to the shop and help him out as a means of keeping busy and not dwelling too much on the past or missing her family that was situated thousands of miles away. At first, she sat in a corner and just watched sadly as people came in and out of the store, but eventually, I noticed how she would perk up whenever another woman from the home country would enter the store and banter with Sam. Still homesick, she would join in the conversation and her velvet eyes would transport to another world as she reminisced of her old life and her family back home.

I could see the toll that Najla's depression was taking on Sam as he questioned if he had done the right thing in bringing her here to Australia.

"She can't be limited to home and the shop," I told Sam, one day when Najla had foregone her daily trip to the shop.

"I don't deny her anything," Sam argued.

"I know that, Sam, but you work long hours, every day of the week, spending more time here than you do at home. That's got to be affecting her."

"That's why I told her to come to the store with me. So we can spend more time together. But even that, it's not working." He looked down sadly and shook his head, obviously at his wit's end.

"It's still not enough, Sam. You need to spend time with her away from the shop. Away from other people. If that's not possible because you're still trying to establish the shop, you need to find something to keep her busy so her mind is not working against her."

He lifted his shoulders in defeat, as though to tell me he was out of ideas.

And that was how Najla had come to be a part of our circle of friends. Gently, gently, I had drawn her into one of our meetings and she fell into a comfort she had not realised was long gone. She came to Australia with no relatives or friends, no sister to lean on, only an absent husband who was trying to build a new life for them. The women became her sisters, her friends, and her confidantes, sheltering her from the depression which had ravaged her since her arrival in our midst. And this is how we formed our little circle of friends and a lifelong sisterly bond that could not be easily broken.

CHAPTER 73:
AUJENE 1984

The thing about Megan was she was so willing to listen and accept change and try new things. She did not look at us in that funny way most third and fourth generation Australians looked at us, scrunching up their noses at things they did not understand. Instead, she embraced our differences, and if anything, hungered for the opportunity to learn more about our cultures. She participated in any and every group event we organised, and was always the first to put her hand up and accept whenever we suggested we try something new. We had even taught her to wrap dolma leaves, which she loved doing. The nightly get togethers we had to wrap kilo upon kilo of dolma proved to be an exercise in fun, laughter, and hilarity which none of us ever missed.

The same couldn't be said about Megan's husband, Wayne. Where Megan was bubbly and happy and open to new ideas and ways of life, Wayne was a staunch opponent of the refos. He looked down his nose at us as though we were something putrid to be thrown out with the garbage. He wouldn't eat our food when we offered it, and he tried to prevent Megan from mixing with us at every turn. Our row house was so narrow and so close to the neighbouring houses, we'd often hear him shouting up a storm as he told Megan not to attend the nights get-together with those refos. People put down such behaviour as being due to lack of education and ignorance. But the thing was, Wayne was as educated as they came. And he worked in a bank, where he had to deal with all manner of cultures and ethnicities. Yet he still had a chip on his shoulder when it came to dealing with "the others."

Beautiful Megan continued to join our meetings, while her husband Wayne continued to rant and rave on about how Megan would end up a wog like us if she hung around with us long enough. He would not be swayed, no matter what we tried. Eventually, things came to a head when we realised that Wayne was a drinker, and not only did he constantly belt Megan with a verbal tirade, but he also started to abuse her physically.

One day, Megan didn't show up to our nightly meeting, nor the day after that, nor the day thereafter. I knocked on her door in the afternoon after work, before I knew Wayne would be home, but even then, she did not answer the door. I stood on my back stoop and watched her as she quietly watered the garden, her back turned to me, but when I'd call her name, she'd quickly switch off the water and run inside without so much as a glance my way.

Eight days after she first missed one of our meetings, Megan knocked on my door as I hosted a meeting with the girls. She stood quietly, her left hand circling her right arm as it fell by her side, a sheepish grin on her face. She seemed to be embarrassed to be there, but I just threw my hands up in the air and grabbed her, dragging her into the house as though nothing had happened and she hadn't been missing or ignoring me.

The ladies were momentarily dumbstruck as Megan entered the living room behind me, and I hoped that the anxious lift of my eyebrows was enough to tell them to act normal.

"Let's eat, shall we!" I said, clapping my hands together to break the ice. For no matter where Megan had been, no matter where she was going, the unspoken rule in my home had always been that my home was open to everyone at all times, no questions asked. I grabbed her hand and led her to the table, the other ladies standing and following excitedly. "Boy, are you all in for a treat today!" I exclaimed.

CHAPTER 74: AUJENE 1985

There were long stretches of time when Megan would go into a self imposed exile and isolate herself from us. We came to expect these episodes, and accepted them, albeit reluctantly. We knew that there was something bothering Megan, but we just didn't know what that was. Of course, we all had our theories, which were constantly being flung around loosely. They ranged from the timid mood swings to the more aggressive battered wife, but no one ever asked. It was an unspoken agreement that if one of us had a problem, we would discuss it when we were ready.

The day we found out about Megan's problem was the day we were all sitting around discussing our hopes and dreams for the future. Najla was asking if anyone was interested in-or knew anyone that would be interested in-working in the fruit shop. Sam's work had picked up to such an extent he was now thinking of taking up the lease next door and extending the shop so he was trading in not only fruit and vegetables, but also Arabian herbs, spices and other convenient products not previously accessible in Sydney. Marika chimed up, informing us the local yeeros shop had asked her to provide them with more of her home cooked foods, so although she would have loved to help, she was in no position to do so. Amna came forward and told us the factory her husband was working at was closing down, so this job would be a godsend. And she was also happy to work alongside her husband if he allowed it.

Just then, the doorbell rang and I hurried to answer it. Rarely did we have visitors during our night time catch ups, and by this point, we had become accustomed to Megan not joining us. The times she did attend were a blessing and full of joyful laughter as we all slid easily into comfortable female companionship.

But nothing could have prepared me for Megan knocking on my door, her right eye busted and bruised, almost swollen shut. Even I, usually the one most likely to hide my emotions well, could not disguise the surprise and subsequent horror on my face. I pulled her in and led her to a corner near the door, Jannat's sing song voice calling down the hallway asking if everything was alright.

She had made a pitiful attempt to mask her bruises with makeup. Layer upon layer of concealer to hide the shame of her abuse, but the damage was too extensive to simply be buried beneath foundation.

"I'll be just a minute," I called, knowing we had precious seconds before the women, concerned at my extended absence, would come looking for me.

"Are you okay?" I whisper asked. Megan nodded her head and pursed her lips, then shook her head and looked away in shame.

I didn't have to ask what happened. Maybe I didn't want to know. Maybe I already knew. I surveyed the damage to her eye and realised what a mess it was, the skin around the corner of her eye broken and swollen red.

"I'll go," she announced, regretting that she'd chosen this moment to come.

"No," I shook my head. "But they'll have questions." She nodded her agreement and followed me into the living room.

Jannat gasped when she saw Megan, and Amna lowered her face in pity. Najla looked horrified and the remaining women took Megan and guided her to a couch, where they sat her down and proceeded to rub her back in consolation.

No-one said anything for the longest time. Megan sat doe eyed, staring at nothing in particular as she closed her eyes and surrendered to our silent support, women standing in solidarity with each other.

"This is a safe place for all," I began. "I don't think I have to remind any of you that whatever is spoken between these walls stays between these walls, and no one is obligated to share anything they don't feel they are ready to share."

"This probably doesn't happen in your community," Megan whispered.

"Honey, this happens in every culture. There are no exceptions to men behaving badly," Jannat replied.

"I see your husbands," Megan whispered. "Working. Always working. Making a better life for your families. I don't see them hurting you."

We all looked down shamefully. Everyone had their burden. Yes, Megan's husband smacked her around, but my husband was absent. And when he wasn't, I led a miserable existence with him lacking the sense of responsibility a man should possess. Jannat's husband was a great man, but he was weak. He never spoke up, leaving all the decision making to Jannat. Sometimes a woman just wanted to not think. Sayeda had left her husband because he'd left her for another woman with three young children to look after. Everyone had their burdens, but when it came down to it, some burdens were easier to carry than others.

The women waited in silence for Megan to say something else, for fear that they would say something that would further inflame her wounds. When she said nothing, and the women were at a loss as to how to direct the conversation, I clapped my hands together and smiled, informing them of a special treat tonight.

"I know just the thing that will cheer us all up!" I exclaimed, rubbing Megan's back in a soothing manner. "You guys need to meet my friend Nuran-she's Turkish, and she brought a tray of authentic Turkish baklava!"

There were enthusiastic murmurs as the women collectively responded, looking forward to the sweet taste of filo pastry and crushed walnuts drowning in a sugary syrup. "Come Megan, I just know you're going to love this!" I said, leading her to the table.

CHAPTER 75:
AUJENE 1985

Looking down sadly, I remembered the last time I saw Megan, with her battered cheeks and her eye swollen like a grape. She had taken a particularly bad beating that day. I remembered Wayne banging on our front door, screaming at the top of his lungs for us to open the door for him. His accusations that we had infiltrated his marriage and turned Megan against him. His reluctance to back down and away from the door when I told him Megan wasn't with us. He had fumed and cursed and called us every name under the sun, and as he did so, long buried memories of my father rose to the surface, and I understood, like a sudden awakening, that Megan's abuse at the hands of her husband wasn't all that different to the abuse I'd suffered at the hands of my own father.

Wayne had continued to rant and rave, a few of the neighbours emerging from their homes to see what all the commotion was about. Aaida, fearful and concerned what he may do, had the presence of mind to phone Jannat, who came running from two streets away and faced him like a tornado, yelling that she was going to call the police if he didn't remove himself from our property. He had backed down, but only so far as the public footpath, where he stood and looked at me with venom in his eyes, informing me that if he found out I had been hiding Megan, he would come back and make me pay dearly.

Later, I would find out that Megan had been visiting with her mother, and Wayne had forgotten this fact. The minute he left our house and went back into his own home, he had started drinking, so that when Megan did come back later that evening, he was wild eyed and drunk out of his mind.

In his drunken state, he couldn't recall the conversation where Megan had informed him about her whereabouts. He couldn't see straight, nor could he let her absence slide so easily. He beat her to within an inch of her life, then quickly proceeded to pass out, his vomit caking the carpet beneath him where he fell.

The last time I saw Megan, she was battered and bruised and beaten to a pulp. She had come to me, her mascara running down her bruised and battered face, fingernail tracks marking her face and her left eye the size of an engorged red grape. She looked at me helplessly, and I opened the door for her, allowing her in. Megan fell into my arms, sobbing like a child, her ravished cries echoing through the silence of the house.

For once, I was grateful that Samer was at work and Aaida was sleeping, so neither would have to bear witness to the travesty that had landed on our doorstep. Nothing I could have said would have made the situation better. Instead, I filled a bowl with warm water and wet a cloth, touching it to her cuts and bruises to clean her face and reduce the swelling. Her hair was a mess, and from the way it was tangled, I could see that Wayne had gone hard on her head, pulling her strands so fiercely, they had formed a mess of spidery clumps on a head that was ordinarily styled neatly.

In time, her sobs stopped and were replaced by steady gulps of air as her shaky body rocked with the dance of defeat.

"He's going to kill me," she whispered, looking right through me more than at me.

"Shh…" I replied, wishing her to stay calm and not be over-whelmed with sadness.

"He's going to kill me," she whispered again, and I knew, in the depths of my broken heart that shattered for her, that her premonition was more than likely an accurate one. Every time I saw her in this condition was worse than the last time; Wayne's violence seemed to be escalating and it was only a matter of time before he lost control of himself and really hurt her.

"You need to save your strength," I told her.

She whimpered and cried some more, bending over her stom-ach in pain, her sobs becoming more pronounced. I wondered why she was clutching her stomach, and hoped he hadn't hurt her anywhere else.

"Megan?"

"I can't have children," she gasped.

"Come now," I admonished "You don't know that." But she only lowered her face and shook her head, biting her lip as more tears continued to roll down her cheeks.

"I was pregnant," she told me, and my hand, of it's own vol-ition, stopped in mid-air as I stared at her in shock. She nod-ded, more to give herself strength to go on than anything else.

"What happened?" I asked her, almost too afraid to know.

"It was a few years ago. I miscarried."

"You can try again," I reminded her, but Megan only shook her head.

"He came home in an exceptionally bad mood. He was so

angry. I still don't know, to this day, what he was so angry about."

I pushed her hair away from her face and put the cloth down, taking her hand in my own as I supported her in her journey to divulge her secrets.

"I tried to protect my baby, I did," she gasped. "But he just kept kicking me over and over and over."

I closed my eyes in resignation, sympathy for my friend overwhelming me. I had to remain strong and supportive for her, but hearing her tell me about what happened to her was breaking something in me that I knew I could never recover. It was dredging up old memories and phantoms that I had believed long buried.

"Do you know what it's like, to know that you have a dead child in your stomach, and that you'll have to go through a forced labour to remove that child? Do you know what it's like not to be able to save your own child? I never forgave him, but still I stayed. Hoping for...what, I don't know." She lifted her hand helplessly then dropped it back in her lap.

I closed my eyes in pain and felt the thread of tears as they escaped from the corners of my eyes, lacerating my heart.

"Everything that came after..." she started again, after a long exhale "resulted in me not being able to conceive. I lost the only child I'd ever be able to have."

"They could be wrong," I grasped at straws. "You could get a second opinion."

She shook her head and looked at me sadly. "I know I'll never be able to have a child. And even if I could, would I really want to bring a child into this life?"

"Who doesn't want to have children?"

"Someone who's married to a man like Wayne."

"Let's concentrate on getting you better now," I suggested.

Megan grabbed my hand and squeezed it. She looked at me with wide eyes, imploring me to listen and understand what she was trying to tell me.

"You've been an amazing friend to me, Aujene. I'll never forget your hospitality."

I shook my head and looked at her in confusion, silently asking her what she was talking about. Like she understood exactly what I was asking her, she took a deep breath and sighed heavily.

"Aujene, if anything happens to me," she began, and I shook my head, not understanding, but she squeezed my hand again, urging me to allow her to finish talking. "If anything happens to me, you tell the police, you tell my family. You tell anyone that will listen that it was Wayne."

"Megan, what are you saying?"

"Will you do that for me?"

"Why can't you just leave?" I asked her, fearful for my friend.

"I've tried that, Aujene. He finds me every time." I nodded in understanding. "You have to tell the police it was Wayne. I know he'll try to say I left or blame someone else."

"Will they even believe me?" I asked her. "He's your husband, I'm just your neighbour."

"There's a recess behind the rear balcony stairs where I keep my diary. I've kept meticulous notes regarding my marriage," she added, grabbing my hand with a sort of desperation I had not previously seen from her. "It's a sort of ledge, at the back of the third stair up."

"Do you really think it will come to that?" I asked her.

"You don't know what he's capable of, Aujene. There's no leaving him. The only way out for me is in a coffin."

"Don't say that," I whispered.

"Please Aujene, you have to promise me. If anything happens to me, you make sure everyone knows that he did it. It's the only way I will get any semblance of peace from my grave."

CHAPTER 76:
AUJENE 1985

When the police knocked on my door four days later to en-quire about Megan's whereabouts, I knew that she was gone. A heavy sadness cloaked me and I spiralled into a deep de-pression from which there was no return. I heaved heavy sobs of desperation as I sat and listened to the police tell me that Megan was gone and they needed to ask me some questions. I walked them into the living room, where they sat and asked me generic questions like my name and how long I'd been liv-ing in the house. Who did I live with, and what did I do for work? How well did I know the neighbours, and what was my relationship with Megan?

"Would you consider Megan a friend?" Officer Daly asked. I noticed that his height caused him to sort of sink into the couch.

"I would say we are friends," I replied, wondering where their line of questioning was going.

"Good friends...or acquaintances?" the female officer asked. From her tone of voice, I could see that Officer Bowtitch was going to try to break me.

I shrugged. "I don't know what you would define as a good friend or acquaintance. I consider her as more like a sister. Does that answer your question?"

The two officers looked at each other knowingly, as though to silently relay to one another that they had a smartass on their hands.

"Why are you asking all these questions? Has something happened to Megan?"

The concern in my voice was genuine, and I could see from the looks on their faces that they were tossing up whether or not to tell me the news. The female officer spoke up before the male did, ostensibly to navigate the line of questioning in a different direction and hopefully get a confession out of me which would close the case and make this the shortest investigation in the history of mankind.

"What makes you think something has happened to Megan?" she asked, looking at me suspiciously, and I bit my tongue, sucking my upper lip into my mouth at my stupidity for having walked right into her trap. The officers continued to watch me while I remained silent for endless minutes, saying nothing. Officer Daly finally spoke up, realising I probably wouldn't give anything away without receiving something from them first.

"We got a report from a Candace Fisher that her daughter Megan Cummings is missing. She didn't turn up to a lunch date with her mother, nor did she call to explain. Mrs Fisher has been worried because Megan hasn't been answering the home phone."

"Well, have you checked with her husband?" I asked, before I could realise what a stupid question that was. Of course they would've checked with her husband.

"Mr Cummings, ironically, sent us to you. Apparently, Megan spent almost every waking hour over here," the female officer piped up.

I looked at both officers dumbstruck, and I could feel my brows knitting in a curved line above my eyes. "Would you mind if I get some water?" I asked.

"Oh, I'll get it," Officer Bowtitch stated, and I pointed her towards the kitchen.

She returned with a glass of water and I sat sipping quietly, realising it must look to the police like I was buying time to get my story straight. Finally, I put the glass down on a nearby table and sighed deeply, looking back at the officers.

"How can I help?" I asked, and the two officers looked at one another in surprise, so obviously not expecting that I would be so forthcoming with any information.

"How well did you know Megan Cummings?" the female officer asked.

"Well enough to welcome her into my home."

"When did you last see Megan Cummings?"

"Last Saturday night." I kept my answers short and relevant, as much to the point as possible without offering additional information. I could see that this was irritating the female officer, who no doubt was expecting a chatty female.

"Where?" she asked, taking notes.

"Here." The two officers looked at each other. I could see it was so obvious they had decided the female officer would lead with the questioning, hoping I'd be more open to conversing with another female. The male officer now shifted in his seat, another obvious signal between them that something had to give.

"We know she was your friend," Daly started, much to the ire of the female officer, who seemed offended that he had taken the reigns. "We just want to find her to give her mother some peace. Her husband said you might know where she is."

"Why would he say that?" I asked, shaking my head. "We may be friends, but she lives with him. If anyone knows where she is, it would be him."

"That's true," he mused, but he says he hasn't seen her since last Saturday night, when you say she came to visit you."

I gasped in disbelief. "She's been missing since last Saturday?" I asked, and he nodded his reply.

"I would think that you would have noticed her disappearance," Officer Bowtitch chimed up "seeing as you were friends and all and she lived right next door."

"I haven't seen much of her lately," I replied. "She would go long stretches of not visiting."

"Yet you'd still see her in passing?" she asked. "Coming or leaving the house? Going shopping?"

I didn't understand what she was getting at, and frankly, I was starting to resent her accusatory tone. I turned my attention towards Officer Daly and directed my reply to him, conveying that my conversation with the female officer was pretty much over. She not only turned beet red, but I also noticed the male officer straighten his back as though he had received vindication for her hijacking the initial conversation.

"Megan came to see me on Saturday. She stayed for a while, then she left. I haven't seen her since."

"Why does her husband think you have something to do with

her disappearance?" Officer Bowtitch, obviously more irritated by my ignoring her than she appeared, tried to jump into the questioning again, but I continued to ignore her, directing my answers toward the male officer.

"I don't know what he thinks or why. I don't know where Megan is," I replied, my eyes settling on Officer Daly. I was proud of myself for having kept my cool throughout the ordeal.

"It doesn't seem like you're concerned about your friend's welfare," Bowtitch jumped in, her voice still ringing with a tone of accusation. She also came off as aggressive when she addressed me, and I made a mental note to ignore her completely until she left.

"If you don't mind," I said, looking at Officer Daly sympathetically "I'm not comfortable with the way that Officer Bowtitch is interrogating me. If there's nothing further, I'd like you to leave now."

"You don't want to find your friend!" Officer Bowtitch exclaimed, incredulous that I was basically kicking her out of my home, but grasping at straws to conceal her lack of professionalism.

I showed them to the door, where Officer Daly gave me his card and asked me to call him if I had any further information as Officer Bowtitch climbed into their police patrol car.

"I'm extremely sorry about that," he apologised, before placing his hat on his head. "Do you mind if I come again with someone else if our current lines of investigation don't pan out?"

I looked towards the squad car and saw Officer Bowtitch scowling at us, and if only looks could kill, she would have sawed me in half with her daggers.

"Megan's not missing," I told him.

He took his hat off again and squinted his eyes at me as he furrowed his brows.

"Do you know where she is?" He asked, and I shook my head in response.

"But I may know what happened to her."

CHAPTER 77: AUJENE 1985

True to his word, Officer Daly returned the same afternoon with another male officer who he introduced as Officer Jenkins. The new officer was a baby-faced blonde with pock marked skin, and looked like he was barely out of diapers, let alone straight out of the police academy. He introduced himself and sat quietly, listening and interpreting the conversation, then committing our conversation to paper as he took notes. Sometimes, his hand would hover above the notebook, his mind deep in thought, and I could almost see his brain concocting questions he would likely ask if the investigation was his.

"I apologise again for the aggressiveness displayed towards you by Officer Bowtitch," Officer Daly sympathised. I waved him away and asked them to take a seat.

"You said you may know what happened to Megan Cummings?" he picked up, as he settled into the couch, the same place he had sat earlier.

"Megan came to see me on Saturday. She was in a bad state…"

"How do you mean?" he asked, cutting me off.

"She had been badly beaten. By her husband."

"And you know this how?"

"She told me. It wasn't the first time. But she was terrified it would be the last time."

"Mr Cummings seems to think you're involved with his wife's disappearance."

"Well, of course he would. That's convenient for him," I pointed out, and he nodded his agreement.

"Tell me what happened on Saturday, the last time you saw Megan."

"She appeared at my door. It was late…maybe close to midnight."

"Who else was here?"

"Just me," I responded, and I could hear the wheels churning in his brain. *No one to corroborate my story.*

"I may have been alone, but I have plenty to prove what I'm about to tell you."

He smiled widely, as though proud that I would not let him down.

"She knocked on my door and her face was beaten to a pulp," I looked down sadly. "I'd never seen her this bad. Wayne had been extremely drunk and got out of control. But it was different this time, because she kept telling me that he would kill her. She was frightened for her life."

"And you're sure she fingered her husband, Wayne Cummings, by name?" he asked.

"Yes. He was a violent man. He came banging on our door a few times, kicking and screaming for his wife. Most of the neighbours witnessed these incidents. He didn't like that she had any friends, especially not the strange types that looked and spoke different."

Officer Jenkins tsked and shook his head, disbelief registering on his face as he comprehended the meaning behind my words.

"Megan was terrified that Wayne would kill her. She was so fearful for her life. Every time she came to me, battered and bleeding, would be worse than the time before. I knew, too, that the escalation in violence could only mean one thing...I mean, how much worse would it get before it came to a head?"

"You never witnessed the violence yourself?"

I shook my head and looked at him thoughtfully, wondering whether or not I could trust this officer to do the right thing. Knowing, instinctively, that if anyone could do Megan justice, it would be this man.

"I would hear the screaming through the walls. As you can see," I said, looking around the house, "these row houses are packed like sardines, so not many things are kept secret here unless you go out of your way to hide things."

Officer Daly nodded his agreement and urged me on.

"Megan told me about her miscarriage. She lost her child because of a particularly bad beating. Wayne just kept kicking her and kicking her, over and over and over again until she lost the baby." I could feel tears escape from the corners of my eyes, and grabbed a tissue to dab at them. "I'm assuming there are hospital records somewhere, because she ended up in emergency and had to go into an induced labour."

I looked at Officer Daly and noticed the look of horror on his face. Officer Jenkins had gone slack around his mouth, and I worried that he would throw up right where he sat. It wasn't a pretty story to tell, and I had hoped I'd never have to be the one telling it, but someone had to stand up for Megan against a tyrant like Wayne.

"I have a ladies meeting club that I hold here at my home most Fridays, sometimes also at other times during the week if one of the ladies is going through something and needs the company. Megan would often attend. She turned up to the meetings several times in bad shape, and the women can attest to that."

"She was open about what her husband did to her?"

"Not at first. She hid it so well, missing meetings when it would be so obvious what had happened. But then it got too much for her and she felt alone and alienated from the world. We're really all she had," I gasped as more tears came, overwhelming me and throwing my emotions into turmoil. "He didn't allow her to have friends, or to work, or to have a life outside the home they shared. And in some ways, I think he punished her because she voiced her desires to be a part of something bigger and to want more out of life."

"You mentioned that he was drunk last Saturday?"

"I didn't see him. She told me he had been blind drunk."

"So where do you think she is now?" Officer Daly asked.

"She warned me that this would happen. And she told me to let you know that if anything happened to her, to look at Wayne."

"Do you think he's done something to hurt her?"

"Now, that's a matter of opinion. But if you're asking for my opinion, and after seeing what that man is capable of doing to his wife, the answer is yes. Because he did hurt her. Over and over and over again."

"I'm a little curious," Officer Daly said. "A bit off topic here, but how did you two become friends?"

I smiled and looked up at the ceiling, a faraway look crossing my face as I recalled the first time that I met Megan.

"Well, obviously, we met as neighbours when we moved into the house here," I laughed. "But I think what you're really asking, is how were two women from opposite sides of the globe and so very different walks of life, able to co-exist harmoniously?"

He shook his head sheepishly, and Officer Jenkins stopped scratching his pen on the notepad and looked up, watching the conversation unfold between the two of us, a look of utter surprise on his face.

"Would you believe it if I told you Megan leaned over the fence dividing our back yards and sniffed, asking what the unbelievable smell was?" I smiled at the memory.

Officer Daly snorted and laughed, then asked what the smell had been.

"Vine leaves," I told him, smiling. "No one can ever resist the smell of stuffed vine leaves slow cooking on the stove for three days."

"And the reason we got along so well was that there was never any judgement. About anything. And Megan accepted us all, as we were, with our diversity and backgrounds and all the baggage we came with. She was an amazing woman."

"You talk about her in the past tense," Officer Daly pointed out. "Why is that?"

"Because Megan wouldn't just disappear," I told him. "If she's gone, she's gone for good. She wouldn't just leave of her own accord and not let her mother know that she's leaving-that woman meant the world to her."

"Can you point us toward who else would be able to shed more light on Megan and her relationship with her husband?

"Why, yes, you can hear it from Megan herself," I replied, proceeding to tell him all about the diary, it's location, and my belief that the contents would give the police the answers they needed relating to Megan's disappearance.

CHAPTER 78:
AUJENE 1985

Officer Jenkins once again accompanied Office Daly to my home six weeks later when they had concluded their investigation into the disappearance of my neighbour and friend, Megan Cummings. There were no new developments or leads in the case, and having exhausted all leads, would be handing their findings over to the coroner so that he could prepare his report.

"Findings were inconclusive, but all indications are that her husband had something to do with Megan's disappearance," Officer Daly started.

"What does this mean for Wayne?" I asked, wanting to see him suffer as he had made Megan suffer.

"Unfortunately, in the absence of a body, and no conclusive evidence of a crime, we can't bring charges. It's up to the coroner now whether or not there is sufficient evidence to indicate foul play and to name a suspect."

"That won't bring Megan back," I whispered.

"No, it won't. But hopefully, it will bring some measure of closure to her mother and those that loved her."

"Do you know where he's gone?" I asked, and Officer Daly knew exactly who I was talking about. Wayne had moved out of the row house a few weeks after the start of the investigation.

"He's relocated to the Gold Coast."

I nodded and thanked the officers for their time and keeping me informed on the outcome of the investigation. Officer Daly assured me that although their enquiries had been exhausted, any new leads that arose over time would be followed up and investigated to ensure the integrity of the case.

I watched them drive away and turned my face toward my former neighbour's house. I knew I had to switch off and move on. Because at the end of the day, when all was said and done, it was but a house, and had never been a home.

CHAPTER 79:
AUJENE 1989

My life could be divided into three chapters.

Chapter 1 - My life before marriage.

Chapter 2 – My life after marriage.

Chapter 3 – My life after divorce.

There were two life altering events that happened when Aaida was fifteen. Two events that not only changed the course of my life, but also led directly to my divorce.

The first thing that happened was my father died. I was thirty four years old. The news reached us by phone, and although our relationship had been strained and tempestuous, I still mourned him, albeit as one would mourn a stranger.

The ladies all rallied around me, complaining because I had not told them my father passed away. Jannat had called to speak with me and Aaida had told her I was upset after receiving the news and needed to rest. Before I knew it, the house was filled with women who bustled about cleaning and cooking and consoling me where no consolation was needed. For although I mourned my father, my own flesh and blood, we had been estranged and the annals of time had done nothing to diminish my resentment toward him for the way he'd mistreated me. I still had not forgiven him for so many things that had come to pass. My miscarriage, my forced marriage to Samer, my exile, the oppression, the way he'd treated my mother...

"Why didn't you tell us?" Marika complained. "We're your friends, no?"

"My father and I weren't very close," I replied, giving her a sad smile.

"He's still your father. Even if you no mourn, the heart mourns," she stuttered in her broken English, tapping on her chest knowingly, where her heart was.

"How long haven't you seen him again?" asked Najla.

"Twelve years," Jannat answered for me. "She hasn't been back to Lebanon in twelve years."

"That's a long time," Najla said. "What about your mother?"

"I've been avoiding going home because of my father, but now that he's gone, I can go back and sit at my mother's feet and enjoy her companionship in peace." My voice was a quiet whisper as I suddenly realized all the possibilities now that my father was gone. I would no longer risk his ire no matter what I wanted to do.

"Do you have plans to go back?" another lady asked.

"Soon. Very soon," I whispered.

The second thing that happened was the thing that would break my back. It was also the thing that would sever any remaining shards of a relationship between me and Samer.

Faisal played a pivotal role in our lives. The brother of one of Samer's best friends, he seemed to appear out of no where at the most delicate of times. He would often stop by in the afternoons on his way home from work or wherever he had been, asking to speak with my husband, who would still be at work. Everyone knew that Samer did shift work and kept odd hours, but he continued to turn up at almost the same time every day. It wasn't long before I realised that he had taken a liking to Aaida.

At almost 10 years her senior, and with Aaida still in high school, the notion of a union between them was one riddled with absurdity. I made it a point to send Aaida to her room whenever he was around and refused to allow him to come into the house to wait for my husband when he wasn't home.

Samer had a handful of friends who he would see on occasion and they took to playing cards, his favourite past time. On one such evening, and to appease him, I went along with him to spend some time with the wives that had gathered and attended with their husbands. Although I didn't visit with the women often, they had made it a habit to organise these get togethers so they would not grow bored without their husbands. While the women were being entertained in one room, and the men were playing cards in another room, the phone rang and the hostess called me over to speak with Aaida.

Aaida's words were a rushed jumble and I could barely understand what she was saying but in the midst of her words, I understood three things. Faisal. Came to visit. Forced himself into the house. I dissected her words, feeling as though I had been drenched with a bucket of cold water. Faisal had been here earlier. He had sat to play cards with the men. He knew that we were here at his brother's home. Why then, would he be at our home asking for us unless he had bad intentions?

Enraged, I flew into the room where the men were playing cards and looked around. Faisal had disappeared. I advised my husband that I had to leave and would call him as soon as I got home if there was a problem. I ran the two streets to our home fumbling and dropping the key on the door mat. Before I had a chance to unlock the front door, Aaida flung it open and charged at me, wrapping her arms around me as she sobbed.

I embraced her and walked her into the house, sitting her down on the couch. Her pitiful sobs clenched my heart and I rubbed her back, soothing and calming her down as she fought to let her voice be heard. In between huge gulps of air, Aaida started to relate to me the story of how Faisal had come to visit the house tonight.

"He called first," Aaida told me. "To ask me where father was. I thought it was odd seeing as they had gone to visit his brother and he lived there so I told him that's where you were."

Aaida paused and breathed deeply; she had stop start spurts where she would talk a little then stop and cry a little, her body shaking like a leaf.

"A little after he called, there was a knock at the door. He asked me where father was. I reminded him that he had already called and I had already advised him that my father was at his house with his brother. I was a little irritated because it just seemed like he was wasting my time and I was in the middle of doing a very important paper. Faisal told me he'd just come from his house and that father wasn't there so he thought he'd drop by to check if he had come home by now."

At this, Aaida started to shake her head in disbelief. "I can't believe how stupid I was. I told him to leave, that my father wasn't home and I had things to do. But he just wedged his shoe in the door and forced his way into the house. He had a smile on his face walking towards me as though we were old friends. I tried my hardest to get away from him. I pushed him, telling him to leave, screaming at him but he wouldn't budge. I knew that Faisal was interested in me, but yuck!"

I recalled Aaida telling me that several times, he had been lurking around when she got off the bus from school, and had tried to walk with her on her way home. He was there in the shopping centre anytime she was there. Everywhere she turned, Faisal was there, regardless of where she was and how unlikely it would have been that he would be there of his own accord. He appeared in places where I knew he had no business to be.

"I pushed him harder to leave but he just started to say all these things that I didn't want to hear. That I was too big for my boots, that I was too stuck up and wouldn't give him the time of day and he was fed up with it. All he wanted to do was talk to me and he was sure that if we could just talk, I would see that I had feelings for him. I told him that I didn't have feelings for him and I never would. That he was too old for me, I was still in high school and I wanted to finish my education. I wanted to live my life. He told me that there would be no problem with that, he would still allow me to finish my education. I was so disgusted. I felt so violated."

"When I told him how repulsed I was by him, he grabbed my arms and pulled me to him. I almost couldn't breathe, he was that close to me. I wished that I would die rather than to go through what he was planning to do."

"He tried to kiss me, slobbering all over my face as I tried to get away from him. I stomped on his foot and tried to elbow him in the gut but he was way stronger than me. He overpowered me and continued to try to kiss me. As I struggled to get away from him, my thoughts all jumbled and my heart beating out of my chest, all I could think was the worst case scenario. All I could see in front of me was the phone, but there was no way I could use it to call for help. I grabbed the receiver and aimed for his head, ramming it into his left side until he fell back against the wall. I may have concussed him. He probably does have a concussion. I ran out of the house and across the road to the neighbours house where I stood with Miss Marie on her stoop, upset and agitated, trying to catch my breath while I waited for him to leave the house. Miss Marie could see that there was something wrong. She tried to ask me over and over again how she could help, but I was too upset to even talk. The moment that he stepped out of the house and started walking down the street in the direction of his home, I ran across the road and bolted the door.

I let her cry and sob into my chest as I held her, exhaling a deep breath, grateful that the situation had not gone any further.

"It's ok, my love," I cooed, smoothing down her hair. "It's ok, I'll take care of everything. He won't bother you again."

I urged Aaida to lie down on the couch to rest. I grabbed the phone, calling Samer to come home as soon as possible. Samer was reluctant to come home, letting me know that he was half-way through a game and he wanted to see it through. I told him he needed to get home as soon as possible, that something terrible had happened and Aaida was upset. I could hear Samer huffing and puffing down the line, agitated that I had ruined his night.

CHAPTER 80: AUJENE 1989

Despite knowing that something had happened to Aaida, Samer didn't come straight home after I called him. Nor did he come home in the hour after that. Nor the hour after that. He stumbled into the house at 3:00am in the morning, his bladder full as he pushed past me and went straight for the toilet. I waited for him to emerge, expecting him to ask about Aaida, but he headed straight for the bedroom without asking me a thing or enquiring about his daughter.

I cornered him as he stood in the bedroom changing into his sleep wear and asked him why he had taken so long to come home. He reminded me that he had let me know when I called that he was in the middle of a game and couldn't come home there and then.

"But you were halfway through that game that you couldn't leave and by my estimation, that game should have been finished by 10:00 PM. That was five hours ago. What's so important that you couldn't be here for your daughter when she needed you?" I asked him.

Samer dived into all the reasons why he deserved to be out until 3:00 AM in the morning playing cards, enjoying his hobby, having time with his friends. He was a hard worker, he reminded me. I knew where he was and he never went anywhere else, so why was I complaining? And he was sure that the situation with Aaida had been worked out since the girl was nowhere in sight and was obviously asleep by now. Was it as serious as I had told him it was, or had I been over reacting again?

"I'm finding it hard to understand what you believe your responsibility is in regard to your daughter," I told him.

"I put a roof over her head, food on the table, she goes to the best school, what more do you want?"

"So is that what being a father is all about by your definition?" I asked him. "Aaida was attacked last night. She was attacked , in her own home, by someone we know very well."

Samer sat up in bed slowly and asked me what I was talking about.

"Faisal came here tonight," I advised him "and tried to take advantage of our daughter. We weren't here, and he knew that we weren't here, so this was deliberate and malicious. He came here with bad intentions and he would have done whatever he wanted to do had your daughter not had the presence of mind to hit him over the head with the telephone."

"He was in the house?" Samer asked.

"He forced his way into the house after your daughter repeatedly told him that you're not home. She tried to make him leave but he wouldn't. He put his hands on her. He touched her. He had his hands on our daughter, Samer, and where were you? Til 3am in the morning. I just can't fathom what is running through your head right now, knowing that this has happened and it's all your fault."

"You didn't tell me this on the phone," he accused, trying to put the blame on me.

"I shouldn't have to tell you these things over the phone. If I tell you there's something urgent and you need to come home, you need to come home. What is so hard to understand about that?"

Samer jerked his back, straightening , thunder roaring through his eyes as he thought of a way where he could turn all of this around and put it on me. But enough. I had had enough. I would no longer be coerced into thinking I was doing the wrong thing. This was not my fault.

"How many times did I ask you to talk to Faisal and tell him not to come to the house unannounced?" I asked him. "Did you ever once talk to him, Samer? This could all have been avoided if you had just drawn that line and told him not to cross it but you obviously didn't. Did you ever tell him not to come to the house unannounced?"I asked him again.

Samer was silent. I knew his silence meant his complicity. I had told him no less than half a dozen times to speak to Faisal to make him understand that it was wrong of him to show up at the house unannounced, especially when there was no male in the house. But he had never done so.

"I don't think I need to tell you, Samer, that this could have ended very badly for Aaida. I don't understand why sometimes you don't take things seriously. She is all I have. I followed you to this godforsaken country. I worked side by side with you for years giving you my paycheck as though you were my pimp. I accepted your excuses when you wouldn't allow me to visit my family in Lebanon. And I also accepted your decision for us not to have any more children. I've propped you up at every turn, respected you and supported you in every way possible, even forsaking my own happiness, but this is where I draw the line. Aaida is all I have. She is all I will ever have. The fact that you have so blatantly disregarded what I asked you to do and played Russian Roulette with her life leaves me no option. You don't want a wife, you want a housemaid. And I am no longer willing to play that role for you."

I could see the look of rage on Samer's face as my words spurted forward. At the same time, I felt like a heavy weight had been removed from my shoulders. For the first time in my life, I felt lighter, and freer, like I could take on the whole world and win. I had finally let my voice be heard. I would no longer be one man's doormat, taking on the responsibility of mother, father, and friend.

"I will not be here tomorrow afternoon when you get home from work. My bags will be packed, my clothes will be gone, and you will have this whole house to yourself, free to do whatever you want. You'll have all the freedom you need to play your cards til well into the morning hours, and spend much needed time with your friends, as these seem to be your main concerns in life."

Samer sputtered as I finished off, for once at a loss for words. He made to get up from the bed, but I held my hand up to stop him, the furious look on my face the deterrent he so needed.

"What is it exactly that you're saying?" Samer asked, seeking clarification.

"You know exactly what I'm saying. Our well has dried up and it's time for us to go our separate ways."

He frowned and looked at me as though I was mad. "What about Aaida?" he asked.

"Oh, so now you're concerned about Aaida?" I looked at him with an expression of mock horror.

"I'll let Aaida decide who she wants to be with. And best you talk to Faisal…if I have occasion to cross paths with him ever again, I will kill him with my bare hands."

CHAPTER 81:
AUJENE 1989

Leaving Samer was probably the easiest thing I would ever do. And the reason for that was that I wanted to do it. I no longer wanted to be connected to him. His nonchalance to the incident between Faisal and Aaida was the catalyst I needed to turn and walk away. Or maybe the catalyst had been my father's death. And the push had been the incident with Faisal.

He should've been the one to leave the house; it's always the man that leaves the house when there is strife in the marital home, but even there, Samer did not know his responsibility, and carried on as normal. He didn't ask about Aaida, nor where we'd moved to, nor how we were managing.

Noelle was a short petite woman who worked as a women's advocate. She had a degree in psychology and ran a shelter for abused women, volunteered at a soup kitchen, and took on numerous projects to better her community.

She also took in female boarders on occasion, and this is how I happened to meet her. Introduced to her by a friend of Jannat's, she offered Aaida and I accommodation until we could get on our feet. Although Jannat had offered us lodging, I had opted against her offer, knowing for certain that would be the first place Samer would look for us. And not that we had run away, but I didn't want him popping up here and there to make things worse than they already were or trying to talk me into going back to him.

◆ ◆ ◆

The first order of the day was for me to find work. I had to make myself useful and contribute to the community, but I also needed an income to ensure that Aaida and I were self-sufficient. Although I had been out of the work force for quite some time since the textiles factory had shut down and I had focused all my energy on raising Aaida, I was able to secure a job three days a week at a supermarket a few suburbs away. The convenience of having the bus stop a street away from Noelle also helped, and I saw Aaida off to school in the morning before I took the bus myself to my new place of employment.

At Noelle's suggestion, I signed up for volunteer work at the shelter on the days I wasn't working and every second week-end. I spent time at the shelter, listening to the women's stories and playing with the children who had the misfortune of having their lives turned upside down and were now resigned to living at the shelter. Aaida even attended the shelter with me on occasion to read to the children and help them with any learning difficulties they might have. She thrived on being able to help out, and the experience gave her a look at how the other half lived and a fresh perspective into how easily that could've been she and I when we left our family home.

I loved my time at the shelter, and time and time again, Megan would cross my mind, my mind's eye remembering with vivid clarity her dirty blond hair and all Australian features. She had been one of my first friends in my new country, and my first Anglo Saxon friend in Australia. She had spent many an hour in my home, laughing and joking with us and blending so uniquely into our family unit that it felt like she'd always been a part of it.

I found a solicitor and started proceedings against Samer, which may have been the tipping point that made him sit up and pay attention and realise the enormity of what was happening.

That was when he tried to contact me by reaching out to mutual friends who knew where I was staying, asking that we meet to discuss our situation and see if we could work something out. To which I replied that there was no way on earth that I would go back to him. This was the best outcome for everyone involved. Aaida too, could see the change in me once I had removed the shackles of my loveless marriage and sought to fulfil my own happiness with a renewed sense of purpose.

Some of the women in our community had voiced concerns... how exactly did a woman survive in the great big world without a man to take care of her? To which I scoffed and reminded them that if a woman had to rely on a man for her livelihood, there was no hope for the world. My friends, the circle of friends that had continued to meet over the years, rallied around me as I moved with purpose from one chapter of my life to another. Although they loved me as they would their own sister, and treated Aaida like their own daughter, they had no doubt that we would be okay and we would show the world that we would survive after shedding our shackles.

Samer continued to be a nuisance, knocking on each and every one of my friend's homes to ask about us after he had exhausted every avenue in trying to contact us through mutual friends. Each and every one of my friends that opened the door to him was cordial, courteous, and respectful while they maintained my privacy and gave nothing away.

It was merely by chance that he happened to find me at a local supermarket I frequented. I almost ran my trolley into him in the fresh produce aisle as I continued to fill my basket with groceries.

"Aujene!" he exclaimed, somewhat gruffly. "I've been trying to reach you."

"Hello Samer." I was nothing if not polite, the soft lilt of my tongue in sharp contrast to his robust baritone.

"Hello is all you can say?" he accused, his voice rising. I refused to lower myself to his level. He had been the master of his own undoing, and I would not accommodate his foolishness as I once had.

"You're making a scene," I pointed out, looking at the curious shoppers who had turned to watch us as they would a soap opera. He looked around, then ran his hand through his hair, letting out a low sigh. He didn't look too well; it looked like he hadn't shaved in days, his hair was unkempt and his clothes wrinkled. I mused that at one point in the past, this would have bothered me immensely, yet with a nostalgic twinge, I realised I really didn't care anymore. Samer was a part of my past I willed to stay dead and buried, never to resurface again.

"Can we go somewhere and talk?" he asked, lowering his voice. His tone, however, was one of desperation.

"What more is there to talk about, Samer? The divorce will be final soon."

"I don't want a divorce!" he hissed. "I want you to cut out this nonsense and come home with me." He set down his basket and grabbed my hand, twisting it in a way that caused me to wince. I gave him a stern look and pulled at my arm until he released it.

"Don't you dare touch me again," I hissed in response. "You no longer mean anything to me. It would serve you well to remember that."

And that was the last time I saw Samer. Shortly after that incident, our divorce decree was finalised and I heard that he had returned to Lebanon and remarried. He had not so much as tried to contact Aaida to bid her goodbye before leaving, and Aaida, although heartbroken, had put on a brave face and declared that it was for the best that he was no longer in our lives. I could see how his exit from our lives affected her...she was hurt and frustrated, nursing a painful guilt that her experience with Faisal had been the beginning of the end for our family. Although I did try to clarify, my marriage to her father was over even before it ever started...

CHAPTER 82:
AUJENE 1994

The weeks bled into weeks and those in turn turned to months. Eventually, the years crept up on us and before I knew it, Aaida had graduated from high school and was in university doing a degree in Social Services. I no longer worked at the supermarket, but had moved on to a part time job at the local municipal library, where I'd been working happily for months now. It had been a slow start but had eventually helped me immensely to further my English language skills, until I was no longer struggling to string sentences together. Granted, I may have still been a slower reader than others, but against all odds, coming from an illiterate background, I had learnt to read and to enjoy the art of reading. And I finally understood why Aaida had spent her life immersed in books; the beauty of the written word bore no comparison to anything else in life.

The rest of my days were spent at the shelter, where I had been able to secure a position as an administration worker, overseeing the day to day running of the centre. What little spare time I had I also spent at the shelter, volunteering my services and giving back to the community. Although the weekly get togethers with the ladies from the old neighbourhood had somewhat dwindled after our children were grown and we all got busy with our intersecting lives, the old guard still managed to meet at least once a month on a rotational basis.

Aaida and I had moved into a two bedroom unit one street away from our old home. Samer was long gone, having sold the house and given me my share before flying back to Lebanon, where he remarried and settled with his new wife and a bundle of kids. I thought it ironic that he had fought so hard against having any more children while we were married, while his new marriage had given him half a dozen children. At first, I had resented him for his selfishness, which had me sacrificing all my wants and needs, while he got what he wanted either way. I had despised him. With every bit of news I received regarding a newborn, the daggers slashed across my heart as I relived my sacrifices and realised I would never have any more children and Aaida would never have siblings.

He all but forgot about Aaida. A few times, he reached out to her...to what end, I don't know. But even Aaida, after having been ignored and neglected by him for years, had grown weary of his communications. He would reach out and speak with her on the phone, then go for long stretches without further contact, choosing to ignore his eldest daughter's phone calls any time she would instigate contact. I would be left to pick up the pieces of her broken heart, helping her to mend while at the same time not being able to answer her questions as to why her father didn't have time for her. At those times, I resented Samer even more, hoping he'd just leave us be and not make any further contact so that Aaida would be able to retain her sanity and I would be able to finally put the past behind me.

One day, towards the end of September, as the year wound down and the air started to thicken with heat, there was a wrap at my door and I answered with the heavy heart of someone not knowing what to expect. Perhaps Aaida had forgotten her keys at home? Jannat coming for a quick visit? Maybe even

Sayeda coming past unannounced, as she usually did, for a coffee and a gossip about what was going on in her life. I always welcomed visitors, and especially the ladies from the old neighbourhood, whose memories I clung to for dear life, for fear of the past being erased and mistakes re-written. I opened the door and blinked. Once. Twice. Rapidly. The late afternoon sun slanted through the door frame at an angle like the glow of a halo as I blinked again, then squinted and tossed my head from side to side in disbelief.

"I'm glad I found you," said a pretty blond in her early 40's.

I felt my eyes go wide with disbelief, then crumple with fear, until recognition settled over my softening face and I stammered my response as I reached my hand out to touch her, afraid it would be an apparition.

"Megan?" I whispered. She had changed, but I could see that it was her. She looked well, dressed in stylish clothes that hugged her figure without being obscene. A scarf was twisted around her neck and tied to the side, and I could see that something about her teeth had changed. She also wore her dirty blond hair in a short bob, which took years off her age.

"Could you spare a coffee for an old friend?" she asked, her smile spreading across her face.

"Of course!" I stammered, pulling her by her hand and into the house hurriedly, as though we had something to fear. She laughed at my rushed and fearful state, then put a hand at my shoulder and brought her eyes down to my own. She had always been taller than me, and with age, it seemed like she had only become even taller.

"Don't be afraid, Aujene," she commanded. "There is no longer anything for us to fear."

I creased my brows and shook my head, indicating that I didn't understand, and she took the couch by the window while I put the kettle on.

"How did you find me?" I asked.

"It was a laborious task, I can tell you that," she admitted, and I could see from the lilt of her tongue that once meek and battered Megan had turned into a refined lady with a beautiful aura and huge intellect. Wayne had held her down. What came after must have set her free. I looked at my old friend and marvelled at how long it had been since I'd last see her. The circumstances that had brought her to my door. The events that followed that ensured she would be laid to rest peacefully and that door closed.

"I moved a few years after..." I stopped and didn't know how to finish. For how did you describe someone who came back from the dead?

"I died," Megan said, laughing.

I looked at my friend once again, suddenly realising how much I had missed her. Had missed her thirst for knowledge about the world. Her eagerness to walk our path and share our experiences and her request that if we ever went back to Lebanon, we take her with us so she could see our beautiful country, as we had described it.

"I never thought I'd see you again," I whispered, setting two steaming mugs of coffee before us.

"I never got to thank you," she countered. "You played your part well, otherwise they just would have kept digging." I looked down at my feet, ashamed at the role I'd played in Megan's drama.

"I know how hard it was for you," she remarked. "You're not a liar, nor an actress – you drew on immense strength to maintain my safety."

"I didn't want you to get hurt," I told her.

"And I didn't. I wanted to come back so many times, but was always worried that Wayne would find out. I didn't actually know that he'd moved until last month," she explained, shaking her head in disbelief and getting a far away look in her eyes. "The end of this saga actually beggars belief," she told me, not missing a beat.

"What do you mean?"

"I happened upon the obituaries and found Wayne's one. Amazingly, he lived a 40 minute drive away me in Queensland. He had lived there for years, and miraculously we never bumped into each other. I didn't even know until I read that obituary. Then I had to make sure, so I asked the right questions and determined it was one in the same."

I gasped. "How did he die?" I asked.

"Ready for it? Liver disease. Man literally drank himself to death." As she spoke, I could see an easy sadness envelope Megan. For all that he had put her through, she had loved him at one stage in her life, and obviously she would have preferred things to have been different. Anyone would.

"Poor Wayne," I muttered, and she shrugged.

"How's Aaida?" she asked, in an attempt to change the subject, and for the next few minutes, I told her all about Aaida and what she was doing now. I divulged the timeline of events that had brought us to this point, and if Megan was surprised at my divorce, she didn't show it. She told me she had remarried, an accomplished dental surgeon who treated her well and made up for all the heartache that Wayne had inflicted upon her. True to her old doctor's word, she hadn't been able to have kids, which had been the sore point in her marriage with the doctor, but they had eventually adopted a boy and a girl. She showed me a picture of the glowing family, and I smiled, knowing that these two blessings had brought peace and comfort to Megan's life.

"I thought it was time to right old wrongs," Megan said, looking at me wistfully. "So many times, I picked up the phone to call you. The letters I wrote you hovered above the mailbox, but I was too much of a coward to send them. I didn't want to risk him ever finding me."

I nodded my head in acknowledgment, letting her know that what had passed wasn't important. "I'm glad you're safe and happy."

" I just wanted to see you and see how you're doing."

"Stay for dinner," I urged her "for old time's sake." And a great big smile spread across her face as she told me she would like nothing more.

AMAL IBRAHIM

PART 3

THE BOOK OF AAIDA

CHAPTER 83:
AAIDA 1989

One could say that I was my father's favourite child. If at all that counted for anything when I was an only child...

At some point in my life, my father drew away from me. Or maybe it was that he had never been close, but as a child, you don't know any better...

What I remember of my father when I was a child...

Cards. He liked to play poker. A lot. He would literally do 16 hour marathons.

Don't get me wrong...he was a hard worker who spent most of his life slaving away for others for long hours and even longer shifts. But in his down time, it was poker all the way.

I couldn't recall a time from my childhood where we went out to dinner as a family, laughing amongst ourselves and relaying stories about our daily experiences.

I couldn't remember ever getting into a packed car with my parents and driving to a destination unknown-or even known-where we would spend a few days and enjoy the company of one another. Like other families did...what they called a holiday.

Each year after Christmas and the new year, I would stream into school with the other students whom I hadn't seen in weeks and listen to their stories about what they did and where they went over the holidays. Pam would tell us endless stories about her trips to the Central Coast, and Abby would talk about every family member who had visited for their Christmas lunch, who did what to whom and which family secrets managed to finally scratch their way to the surface. When the girls would turn to me for my input, I would either shrug and tell them we had "had a quiet one" or invent some story about a few birthday parties I'd attended, rather than feeling left out.

At some point in time, around about when I entered high school, I realised there was something seriously wrong with my family unit. There was a very pronounced dysfunction that no one ever talked about.

When I asked my mother about how she met my father, there were no long and winding romantic tales of how they accidentally met and fell in love at first sight. There was no beautiful, earth-shattering love story to be told. Instead, my mother relayed the story of how my father had set his sights on her one day and had been persistent in pursuing her hand in marriage. He had sold her father the very thing her father happened to be buying, and the rest was history. Had she wanted to marry him? No. Had she loved him? A resounding no. Had she ever had any feelings for him? No. But she was of a generation where the father was the man of the house and he made the decisions. A girl's request was never even taken into account, especially in her family. She told me how her father had basically forced her to marry my father. She was sad as she told me, looking at me with tears in her eyes, assuring me that I was the best thing that had ever happened to her, and the one good thing to come out of her marriage to him.

I know that my parents were two people who never should have gotten married to each other. It was clear as day, and although I loved them both, there was a toxicity in that relationship that ensured my parents would live a miserable, loveless life.

Although my mother put her heart and soul into raising me and ensuring I never felt unloved, I could see the sacrifices that she had had to make in order for me to have a stable living environment. I could see that she had stayed with my father merely for my sake and nothing else. My father, on the other hand, hadn't sacrificed anything. If anything, he was living his best life and had everything he could possibly want or need, including control over my mother.

CHAPTER 84:
AAIDA 2016

Beirut has changed.

Lebanon has changed.

The plane touches down in Rafic Hariri Airport after a gruel-
ling seventeen hours flight time and seven hour layover, which
was spent roaming the airport in Dubai. Mother refused when
I offered to check us into a hotel, her hands folding over themselves as she waited anxiously for the time to pass by. I understood her anxiety. Her mother was old and she was eager and
anxious to see her. She had recently heard of a man who had
lost his mother as he was in a plane on his way to see her. My
mother's biggest fear was that she would be so close yet not
close enough.

A hotel stay in Beirut so we could spend the night to freshen
up before making the trek to North Lebanon was also out of
the question. Mother just wanted to get to the village and kiss
her mother's feet, so afraid that this would be their last time
together. Instead, we made the four hour trek by car to Tul
Ghosn, albeit 50 minutes out of those four hours was wasted
on traffic that had come to a standstill right outside casino Du
Liban, where traffic always went to die. I cursed and muttered
under my breath angrily that in the twenty five years I'd been
travelling back and forth to Lebanon, nothing had changed.
If not for the four hour drive to the village, I would probably

make the trip over more often.

The taxi meandered through the streets of Beirut as we headed toward Tripoli, from where we would take another taxi to the village. I watched as the countryside flew by, mesmerised by the extravagant beauty of ancient architecture and sweeping villas that belonged in another era. The main road as we flew down the freeway towards our destination was littered with deserted, half finished hotels, old cafes that were boarded up, and a string of fast food restaurants. Lebanon had been Westernised, but that Westernisation had come at a price to small businesses ravished by war and ongoing internal conflict and sectarian turf wars. In Lebanon, there lurked around every corner a disaster waiting to happen. Disaster came in all forms, including corruption, bombings, assassinations and civil unrest. There was never a dull moment in Lebanon.

The taxi driver swore and cursed when I argued with him about the fare.

"Ya ayni, I was here last month, not last decade," I argued with him, refusing to pay him the $400 US dollars he asked for the fare to Tripoli.

"Why didn't you set the price before we got in the car," my mother complained, agitated. "I thought you discussed it with him."

"There was no need, *emi*, everyone knows the fare from Beirut to Tripoli is $100, and that is being generous. At $100 an hour, he's making more money than I am in Australia!" I snorted and crossed my arms across my chest in defiance as the taxi driver refused to open the boot so we could retrieve our bags. We faced off, his voice rising as a small group of bystanders started to gather.

"I will wait here all night until you give me my money!" the taxi driver's face was a puff of saggy red skin as he bellowed at me.

The bystanders looked at him like he'd been victimised, then looked at me as though I'd wronged him. Their heads swivelled back and forth as they watched the exchange unfold and mentally took sides according to what was being said.

"And I will wait here all night until you give me my bags," I offered sweetly.

The taxi driver wouldn't let up, continuing to argue and shout as even more people milled about the taxi stand, blocking foot traffic as they were held spellbound by the unfolding drama. This is as good as it gets, people.

"*Kheir, shu fi?*" a man asked, approaching us. "I am the attendant here, how can I help you?"

"Lady won't give me my fare," the taxi driver smarted.

The attendant looked at me questioningly, silently asking me what the hold up was.

"I won't pay him because he's charging me $400 Beirut to Tripoli."

There was a collective gasp from the crowd at the number and everyone turned to look at the taxi driver, then back at the attendant to see what would happen. Everyone knew, and I was glad that the taxi driver had actually parked here, that the parking attendant's word was final when he dealt with such issues.

"Why are you charging her this much?" the attendant asked, his brows furrowing. "The Beirut-Tripoli fare is $100."

"We didn't agree on a price," the taxi driver explained. "That's my fare."

"Please just take your $100 and give me our bags so my mother and I can be on our way," I let out in an exasperated sigh. "We've had a long trip."

The attendant waited for the taxi driver to make a move to retrieve our bags, but when he stood his ground and could see there would be no give and take, he shook his head.

"Your fare is ridiculous. You can't take advantage of people simply because you didn't agree on a price."

"She didn't ask. If she had asked, I would have told her."

"Well, obviously she didn't ask because she knew the fare is $100 and wasn't expecting this."

"*Haq is haq*," the taxi driver elicited.

"Only when it is just, ya akhi," the attendant replied, his anger rising to match the taxi driver's raised voice. "You picked them up at the airport and are obviously seeking to take advantage of two women travelling alone simply because they are foreigners. But enough is enough! You give them their bags and take your $100 and be on your way."

The taxi driver raised his chin in defiance and stood his ground, not moving an inch. The parking attendant shook his head in despair and asked a young boy standing nearby to fetch the police.

"*Ya akhi, Allah ykhaleek,* we don't want any trouble," I told him. "I just want to get my mother to our village so we can rest."

"You're being unreasonable," a man in the crowd yelled at the taxi driver. "Give the women their bags and let them get to their destination before it gets dark."

"*Wallah wallah*," the parking attendant hissed, by now incensed by the driver's behaviour, "I swear by Allah, and there is no greater power, that if you do not give the women their bags and take your $100 fare, you will not have a car to drive out of here and I will feed you to the dogs."

There were yells from the crowd as the bystanders cheered on the attendant and denounced the driver, who stood by, solid as a rock and stubborn as a mule. It was only when a rock came zooming out of the crowd and landed on the car's front, creating an enormous crater in the centre of the bonnet, that the driver gasped and moved to check on the damage.

"You want $400?" someone from the crowd yelled. "Well, you should know we believe the women should get their money's worth," and as the crowd converged on the car and the driver tried to protect his main stream of income, his arm flung up into the air and his keys went flying backward onto the ground. His car was swaying from left to right and back again with the weight of young boys who had flung themselves onto the vehicle in an attempt to mollify the owner.

Even before I could blink, someone had popped the trunk and removed our bags, and my mother and I were being ushered away from the maddening crowd and into a waiting car. At his request, I handed the attendant a hundred dollar bill that I saw him stuff into the taxi driver's hand before he pushed him into his car and told him to drive away quickly and never return to the city before we drove away.

The driver who took us to Tul Ghosn wouldn't take a fare, no matter how much I insisted. He apologised profusely that we had had to go through our ordeal and wanted to show us that not all drivers were the same.

"*Na'am, ya ebni*," my mother started. "We come to Lebanon often to visit with family. We have never had such an experience until now. *Absar,* maybe there was something wrong with him," she indicated in a circular motion near her right temple as if to explain the man's actions as the work of a crazy man.

This taxi driver laughed and listened to us as we gave instructions on how to reach Tayta's house in the village.

"I hope you enjoy your stay," he said, after he had unloaded our bags and started to drive away.

CHAPTER 85: AAIDA 2016

My grandmother Tala was by now completely blind and could only identify people by her senses. She either felt you, smelt you, heard you or sensed you. So when we entered through the big metal double doors that still stood to this day, it was the click clack of my heels that brought her to the breezeway in expectation.

"Hal sawt mou ghareeb alayi," she said, her smile infecting her face.

"Kifek tayta?" I asked, my arms enveloping her, and my chin resting on the top of her head. Did I mention that over time, my grandmother had shrunk?

"Jebtelek hdiya," I told her, taking my mother by the hand, and bringing her to stand in front of my grandmother. Mother had immense pearls of tears streaming down her cheeks as she looked at her mother and the years melted away.

My grandmother held my mother's hands, feeling around her fingers for indentifiers, and finding none, reached her hands up and took mother's face in them, travelling the ridges and the fine lines until I could see the moment of recognition pop into her eyes.

"Aujene?" she whispered? *"Binti Aujene? Wlek, shu jaabek!"*

The women hugged and I watched as my grandmother inhaled my mother's scent and clung to her as though clinging to a life raft.

CHAPTER 86:
AAIDA 2016

The next day, I woke to the joyous squeals of children running riot around the garden, and women laughing boisterously outside my bedroom window. I sighed and ran a hand through my bed hair as I sat up in bed, looking at my watch and wincing when I realised that it was already past midday and my jet lag had stolen half a day from me.

Still sleepy, I staggered out of bed and washed my face at the wash basin in the corner of the room, then dressed and emerged to the brilliant sun soaked vision of my tayta's beautiful *dhar*. I was immediately surrounded by about 20 young children, all running around me, my legs disappearing amidst the ruckus.

I spotted my mother, grandmother, and a handful of my aunts sitting under the olive tree in the garden sipping tea as they laughed together and caught up on their missing years apart. I spied my aunt Farida, her arm linked with my mother's arm, the two women leaning into each other and sharing a conspiratorial laugh as they joked about something. My grandmother sat nodding her head, not part of any one conversation, smiling as her daughters surrounded her.

"There she is!" Aunt Farida called, rising from her chair to greet me. She smiled and hugged me, clutching me to her for endless minutes before she let me go again. "*Wahashteeni, ya khalti!*" she said, holding me at arm's length so she could get a good look at me.

One of my other aunts pulled out a drum and proceeded to tap on it, finding a slow and steady rhythm, and we all swayed and danced to the music, a celebration of sorts as the sisters welcomed us home and the years apart melted away.

CHAPTER 87: AAIDA & KHALED 2016

"Why did you come back, cousin?"

My cousin Khaled was the first one to ask this question of me. I settled on the swinging garden bed opposite him and looked off into the distance. It was no secret that the family had once expected Khaled and I to be married to each other. It was a union that was supposed to unite our family and strengthen the ties between us across oceans and faraway lands. To me, the idea of marrying a first cousin was one that churned my stomach to sickness, even though I knew, without doubt, that Khaled had always felt differently. It had been something he had looked forward to from the moment I had visited in the 90's when the civil war wound down and I had visited Lebanon with my mother. From the moment we'd set eyes on one another, there had been an undeniable pull that ensured we gravitated into each other's orbits.

For Khaled, his golden curls and grey eyes exploding in the light of the sun, staring at me longingly with hope in his eyes, it had so obviously been a case of love at first sight. For me, while there was a magnetic pull toward Khaled, love and marriage and a familial union was the furthest thing from my mind, least of all to my first cousin. My aunt Farida, for all that she loved me, was probably the only one who understood my reluctance to conform to family pressure and agree to marry him, and her reasons were twofold. First, although she wished for her son's happiness, the thought of her niece marrying into the family because of societal pressure was something she did not wish upon me, nor her son who would end up married to someone who had no choice in the matter. And second, she couldn't grasp the idea of her son leaving her side and moving to another country. That fear alone devastated her.

"It's nice to see you, too, Khaled," I said.

He laughed and shook his head, his curls dancing in the wind as his head swung from side to side. Even at 45 years, he had retained his youthful looks and was still in amazing shape.

"I'm sorry, that *was* rude of me," he admitted. "No way to greet my long lost cousin."

"Well, not so lost," I explained, looking over at him with a smile.

"So why did you come back?"

"Mother was in a nostalgic mood. Don't read too much into it, Khaled."

He was silent for the longest time, and I could see that he was measuring his words carefully, exhaling heavily before turning to me. There was so much unsaid in our story, and I could see, so clearly, old hurts still lingering there in his eyes. So much time had passed and so much had been left unresolved.

"How's Soraya?" I asked, changing the subject before he had a chance to bring up the past.

"She'll come to visit you in a few days when you've rested from your trip."

"Well, that's a polite way of saying she doesn't want to see me," I laughed.

"To be fair, she's tried her hardest but she couldn't compete with the memory of you."

"I'm married," I reminded him. "With children."

"And that is probably the only fact that gives her comfort," he told me. "Doesn't mean she doesn't worry that won't mean anything to us."

I scoffed and looked away in time to see uncle Hassan standing off in the distance watching us, his hands in his pockets and his mind a million miles away. Even from a distance, it was not hard to read the expression on his face. Hassan had always loved me like a daughter. He cherished his wife, my aunt Farida, and still doted on all his children, and I knew, from the way he was looking at us, his sorrow revolved around his son not living his fairytale. For even though Khaled was married to Soraya, and decades had passed since the chance of Khaled and I whispered through the air, he still had not grown to love Soraya as a man should love his wife. Uncle Hassan, having lived his storybook romance with my aunt Farida, had expected the same for his own children. And even though the majority *had* married the love of their lives, his firstborn Khaled had missed that boat.

"She has nothing to worry about," I whispered, turning back to Khaled.

His mesmerising eyes danced with soulful laughter as he looked at me, once again curiously yet silently asking me what had brought me back into their midst.

"She seems not to believe me. Maybe you can convince her," he said, making to stand up. "I'm sure your actions will speak louder than words."

CHAPTER 88:
AAIDA 1991

Khaled Damour was my soulmate. He was also my first cousin. He was my soulmate, nonetheless. Of this, I was 100% sure.

We met when I was 17 and he was 20. Once I completed high school and my parent's divorce was finalised, my mother took me to meet our extended family in Lebanon. It was a beautiful thing, to go from having no blood relations in one country (although I could've counted my mother's friends as family, as they were quite literally an extension of her), to a village full of aunts and uncles and cousins. I even had one living grandparent! The experience had been immersive, meeting and greeting each and every member of my family, hoping like crazy I'd be able to remember all their names and how they related to me in the coming days as the visits continued.

The one person's name I couldn't possibly forget was Khaled. From the moment we met, it was as though an invisible magnet was drawing us to one another. He smiled as he introduced himself as Khaled, my aunt Farida's son. For an endless moment, I stood tongue-tied just staring at him, until my mother jabbed me in the side and said *"Wlek, binti, shu sarlek, salme ala ibin khaltek."*

Khaled had merely laughed as I stumbled forward and stuck my hand in his, my my brain shutting down completely and my tongue going numb as I struggled to form the words that needed to be said to introduce myself.

"Ma'alaysh, ekhti," my aunt Farida piped up, hugging me to her fondly. "Khaled's used to this reaction."

"For some reason, girls seem to lose their balance around Khaled," Hassan chuckled and spoke up, his eyes twinkling mischieviously.

I looked at my aunt Farida's husband but said nothing. He and my aunt Farida made a beautiful couple, and I could see that Khaled had inherited the best features of both his parents, cumulating in a soul jarring beauty that left one breathless. At 20, he was tall and muscular, with grey eyes that mesmerised and thick golden brown ringlets that fell loosely across his forehead. Some may have considered him cherubic, but I, having studied and excelled at modern and ancient history, likened him to a modern day Adonis.

Yet it was not only his physical being that made me stumble clumsily in front of him. Khaled possessed a presence unlike any other I had ever come across. When you met him, you automatically wanted to gravitate toward him and be in his orbit.

"Come, Aaida," Khaled said, extending his hand. "I'll introduce you to all your other cousins." And like a lamb unto the slaughter, I left my heart right there where I had been standing the first time I met him and followed Khaled, not knowing that I would never be the same again.

Khaled taught me how to ride a horse.

Khaled taught me how to shoot an arrow.

Khaled taught me how to hunt birds.

Khaled taught me how to look at life with new eyes and cherish every moment and every breath as though it were my last. We were inseparable the whole six weeks we were in Lebanon. He told me all about his life growing up in Dhar Khamra, and I told him all about my life in Australia, my studies and my work and my hopes and my dreams.

"Don't you want to see your father?" Khaled asked me one day, as I lowered my rifle to the side. We had discovered I was naturally gifted at shooting, a hobby my father had been well known for in his youth. He had been the best bird hunter in the whole region, and now I heard stories that he spent his days in Lebanon hunting and also teaching his new family how to do so.

I turned to look over my shoulder at Khaled and threw him a look that clearly told him my father was the last subject I wanted to discuss. But Khaled wasn't fazed. He stood with his hands folded over the butt of his rifle, the muzzle wedged into the earth, using the gun as a crutch as he watched me. Without saying a word, his curious eyes asked me why I didn't want to see him.

"He hasn't come to see me. He hasn't made an effort. Why should I?" I shrugged.

"Because he's still your father. And now you have siblings you've never met."

I turned away from him and lifted my rifle, aiming at the sky, shooting off several shots in rapid succession as a school of pigeons flew overhead in the near distance. The heavy thump of birds falling out of the sky and hitting the ground reverberated through the field, and I could hear a steady stream of shouts from across the meadow as other hunters commended the excellent shots which had downed the passing birds. I set my rifle down and turned to face Khaled.

"A father is not he who merely planted the seed that created you," I told him. "A father is one who nurtures and protects his child, loving and spending time with them the way a father is meant to. He did none of those things."

"He's still your father," Khaled reiterated, and I could see stormy clouds brewing in his grey eyes as he frowned at me.

"Not every father is like yours, Khaled. You will never understand what I mean because you didn't have to go your whole life waiting for your father to come home."

When it came time for us to leave and go back home to Australia, Khaled held me close and lay his chin on my head as the pain of our impending separation loomed upon us. He whispered into my hair that he would be waiting for me to come back, that the thought of me being so far away was strangling his heart and choking his soul, the pain inside him overwhelming. I knew exactly how he felt because I felt the same way. Even though we had done nothing more than spend every waking hour together, at times holding hands or sharing a friendly nudge, it was unavoidable that we had fallen deeply in love with each other. Khaled was the man I wanted to spend the rest of my life with. He was the one whose soul intertwined with my own. I never would have thought, considered even, that I would go to my native motherland and fall so madly in love with someone, let alone my own cousin. For at the end of the day, that's what it came down to. He was my cousin, and love him or not, nothing could change that fact.

I would have married him in a heartbeat, if only he wasn't my cousin. If only what had come to pass hadn't.

When year after year passed and I did not return to Lebanon, for fear of what would happen between Khaled and I, the void in both our lives grew and a wedge was placed between our divided hearts that ensured the roads we travelled were two different highways. 6 years after that first trip to Lebanon, and realising that I would never be back, Khaled broke my heart and married his other cousin Soraya.

And that was when I realised…I broke his heart first.

CHAPTER 89: AAIDA & FARIDA 2016

"You mustn't take things to heart," Aunt Farida warned me, hugging my shoulder.

After so many years, she was still so beautiful, her dark eyes piercing me with her smile. She had an inner strength and wisdom that one could not help but respect and appreciate.

"I've tried to avoid this situation for so long," I reminded her. "I don't know what more I can do."

"I don't want you to think you're not welcome here," Farida started. "This is your home, and it always will be. No matter what may happen. Soraya has insecurities that she needs to overcome. Neither you nor Khaled have done anything wrong, and she needs to understand that your friendship is just that – friendship. It's not fair of her to ask either of you to back away from one another."

"I feel like she hates me," I started.

Farida shook her head and tsked. "She doesn't hate you. She envies you. She envies what you are to Khaled. That's neither yours nor Khaled's fault. One can't help the way one feels, the important thing is that neither of you acts on your feelings. And you haven't. You never will. That's what's important."

"Did I make a mistake coming here, Aunty?"

"Oh shush, my darling," she said, hugging me to her again. "We're all so glad to have you and Aujene here again. Just like old times," she smiled. "Now, go wash your face and join us in the family room for tea. *Yallah*, I'm waiting for you. I don't want to waste one precious moment with you; before we know it, you'll be gone again."

CHAPTER 90: AAIDA & FARIDA & AUJENE 2016

"But you never really told me," I started. "You all start then stop, and I'm in my forties and still waiting for this story to be told!" I squealed, exasperated. We all sat huddled around the heater, drinking endless cups of tea and cracking open nuts. We had covered every topic under the sun except the one we always touched on but no-one ever elaborated on.

My grandmother sat laughing at us, her giggle that of a young girl as her face turned this way and that whenever someone piped up and said something, trying to follow the conversation by voice alone.

My mother and aunt Farida sat side by side on the couch, their arms entwined so tightly one could mistake them for Siamese twins. It was late into the night and everyone else had already either turned in or gone home after we had enjoyed a hearty family dinner and caught up on everything from Abu Jamal's donkey to the next wedding expected to take place in the village.

"*Yallah*, tell me!" I screeched, falling to my side as I laughed hard at a parting comment from my aunt Shamaila as she bid us good night and left the room.

Uncle Hassan poked his head into the room and laughed when he saw the mess we had made and heard our laughter echoing against the walls.

"*Shu ya rohi*," he said, looking at my aunt Farida. I watched the interaction as she turned to her husband, her eyes dancing with warmth and love as she stared at him. They still looked at one another like newlyweds would.

"*Ma'alaysh* Hassan, can we stay here tonight?" she asked. "I haven't had my fill yet." And at that, we all burst into uproarious laughter again and Hassan watched us with amusement, happy that his wife was in such high spirits.

"We'll sleep here tonight," he announced. "I'm sure your mother would like that."

My grandmother nodded quickly and smiled, saying "Yes,yes" over and over until the matter was settled.

"So now will you tell me?" I asked, as we all settled back down again.

My mother and aunt Farida looked at each other knowingly, then turned to their mother simultaneously and asked her if she thought they should tell me. Of course, over the years, I had heard bits and pieces here and there, but I'd never heard the story in its entirety, and most certainly, I'd never heard it from my own family. But it was a subject I was curious about and couldn't wait to hear.

"Are you sure you want to know?" my aunt Farida asked. "because once you know, you can't un-hear the ugly truth if you don't like it."

"Of course I do! Why are so many girls in this village named Farida?"

My mother and aunt looked at one another again and smiled. And within that smile, I could see so many secrets, and endless stories just waiting to be told. It was my aunt Farida that cleared her throat and spoke up.

"It was said, in our village, Tul Ghosn, about a hundred years ago, there lived a woman with mesmerising dark eyes and black hair like the blackest night. She went by the name of Farida. She was a beautiful, stalwart girl whom men lusted after and women envied. The young girls of the village all idolised her, accepting the wayfarer into their village after she broke from a Syrian Bedouin tribe and exiled herself in Lebanon."

THE END

Translations:
In order to better understand the text, especially for those from non-Arabic speaking backgrounds, the following words which appear in the book have been translated for your convenience. They are listed here in order of appearance. Please note phrases are translated as per the context in which they appear; use of these words/phrases have been italicised throughout the book.

Khafiyehs: *a wide cotton scarf providing protection from the elements. It is usually wrapped about the head with flowing sides that can be folded over the lower face to protect against dust and sand*

Maghreb: *sunset*
Istifhfar: *repentance*
Allah: *the arabic name for God*
Dua: *supplications*
Shaikh: *clan leader /Shaikhna: respectful term for "our leader"*
Shu badhu?: *what does he want*
Fellaheen: *farmers*
Na'am: *yes*
Hasbi Allah was ne-emal wakeel: *sufficient for us is Allah and he is the best disposer of affairs*
Shu helwe: *how beautiful she is*
Metl el le3bi: *she's like a doll*
Ayran: *a smooth salty drink derived from goat yoghurt*
Sabah el kheir: *good morning*
Kif el 3arous: *how is the bride?*
Haseeri: *a wide straw mat laid on the floor, usually for eating*
Em el banaat: *mother of the girls*
Ya: *oh*
Akkkh ya ekhti: *oh, dear sister*
Amirna: *our prince*
Ahwi: *Lebanese coffee*
Shu, ya ebni, la wayn rayeh?: *Where are you going, my son?*
Emi: *mother*
Ya ebni,3ayb. 3ayb alaykon tutlaou hayk kum yawm ba3ed el3res: *My son, it's wrong. Wrong to leave the house only a few days after your wedding*
Mashi, emi: *it's ok, mother*
Bas, ya ebni: *but, son*
Rouki, emi: *relax, mother*
Abadoi: *strong hero*
Yallah: *come on*

Shu ya 3arees?: how's the groom?

Elmara bi rebe3 akl: a woman has a 1/4 of a brain

Waynik?: where are you?

Tayeb: ok

Eid: the celebration after a month of fasting and observing one's faith

Asr: Afternoon

Mart 3ami: mother in law

Ma'alaysh, bikoun et3khar bil shegel: It's ok, he would have been held up at work

La3: no

Kettayfeh: a wild green vegetable that is cooked with fried onions

Ma fi daei: there's no need

All yerhamou: May Allah have mercy on him

Tabal: ceremonial drums

Zalghouta/Zalagheet: celebratory ululations

Binti: daughter

Rahma: mercy

Shu sarlek, ya mama?: what happened to you, mother

Meen?: who is it?

Ana: me

Subhan Allah: all praise be to God

La Illaha Illa Allah: All prais is due to Allah alone

Layki ya binti: look, my daughter

Rej3et: returned

Baba: father

Siffra: a spread of food

Naseeb: destiny, fate

Barzi: a traditional throne that newlyweds sit on during the marriage ceremony

Shu ya arous?: How is the bride?

Ma lakayti gayr hal hemra elhamra?: did you not find another shade of lipstick other than this red?

Ajbak ya Samer? Martak labsa lawn el sharameet: How do you like that, Samer? Your wife is wearing the whore's colour

Ma'alaysh, emi: that's ok, mother

Layysh?: why?
Khalo: uncle
Layki, khalo hawn: look, uncle is here
Ya haserti!: Oh my dear!
Ghorba: the foreign land
Yemista: a traditional Greek recipe of stuffed peppers and toma-
toes
Koussa meshi: a popular Lebanese dish of stuffed zucchini
Kheir, shu fi?: Ok, what's up?
Haq is Haq: a right is a right
Ya akhi: dear brother
Allah ykhaleek: May God protect you
Wallah,Wallah: I swear, I swear
Na'am ya ebni: of course, my son
Absar: who knows?
Hal sawt mou ghareeb alayi: this sound is no stranger to me
Kifek, tayta?: how are you, grandmother?
Jibtelek hdiya: I brought you a gift
Binti: my daughter
Wlek, shu jaabek?: What brought you?
Dhar: courtyard
Wahashteeni, ya khalti: I missed you, my dear niece
Wlek binti, shu sarlek, salme ala ibin khaltek: My daughter, what
happened to you, greet your cousin
Ma'alaysh, ekhti: It's ok, my sister
Shu, ya rohi: What's up, my darling?

Made in the USA
Middletown, DE
28 April 2022

64910650R00208